The Robin Hood of Podlasie

# The Robin Hood of Podlasie

## Józef Korycki's Private War with Communism

Marek M. Kaminski and Ernest Szum

PIASA BOOKS
New York

English translation copyright © 2021 by PIASA Books

Originally published by Oficyna Naukowa Warszawa as *Janosik Podlaski: Józefa Koryckiego prywatna wojna z komunizmem.*

Copyright © 2019 by Marek M. Kaminski and Ernest Szum

Published by PIASA Books

The Polish Institute of Arts and Sciences of America
208 E. 30th Street
New York, NY 10016

http://www.piasa.org/pb.html

All Rights Reserved

ISBN 978-0-940962-11-8

Library of Congress Control Number: 2021937459

Printed in the United States of America

Only the truth is interesting.
  —Józef Mackiewicz


Go upright among those who are on their knees
Among those with their backs turned and those toppled
in the dust
  —Zbigniew Herbert

# CONTENTS

# PROLOGUE

The guards picked me up from the caged walk yard. They threw me a plastic bag with my pen, notebook, and letters, items apparently useless to my cellmates who were left behind in Białołęka Jail and were tasked with packing my sack. My sweater, toothpaste, socks, and other precious assets weren't included in the bag. "You'll get them later." Never did. I realized that they were taking me to the Rakowiecka Jail downtown, to the prison hospital. Rakowiecka, which was a deadly name for Polish Home Army fighters in the 1940s and 1950s, over five weeks at Białołęka had become my dreamed-of fairyland. It hosted a prison hospital serving several local prisons. I was faking illness, based on an earlier pancreatic tumor, with the quiet support of a handful of initiated physicians. The goal was to get early release due to a critical health condition. Wardens do not like inmates dying inside. Every death ruins the statistics.

The dark green prison van was full of inmates in transfer. I was standing next to an agitated man, taller than me, who had been arrested a few hours earlier. The militiaman handcuffed his right hand and asked for my wrist. I gave him my left hand, but he brushed it aside and put the handcuff on my right one. "This is not America, handcuffs are scarce," he said with a short burst of laughter, "Now escape with your right hands 'cuffed!" True, it was impossible to run. We—the dangerous criminals—were the only ones handcuffed. Or maybe I was just an anchor to hinder my mate's potential escape.

Grey houses, dirty cars, sad people were flashing past the tiny window. The excitement of the arrest was still amping up my Siamese cuff-twin. He turned his square, sweaty face to me. Outside, it was late April, but inside our van, it was a Florida summer. Emotionally gesticulating with his left hand, he described how the militia caught him red-handed in a Praga robbery, how he was running for his life on Ząbkowska Street, how they were yelling and shooting, and how he was shooting back. "And then I killed the f*cking dog!" he said triumphantly. I didn't understand—there was no dog in his scrappy story. "What dog?" I asked. He was puzzled by my confusion. I later learned that "dog" was one of the names for a militiaman in prison argot.

And later still, I realized that it was possible that he hadn't killed anybody, but he was just working on a good story that would help him with his prison entry. Oftentimes, there turned out to be a "later" in prison, a secret meaning unfolded from superficially simple acts, or a mystery that turned into the obvious. Or vice versa.

The four-meter-tall grey gate of Rakowiecka Jail opened to let the van in. The handcuffs were removed. The guards pointed to a building fifty meters farther away. An old man, maybe in his eighties, couldn't leave the van and was struggling with his sack. I lent him a hand and offered to carry his belongings for him. Immediately, there were a few surprised looks around—*grypsmen* do not extend their hand to anybody before they learn if he is also a *grypsman*. He walked slowly. An inmate laughed and said to me, "Do not bother with the old fraud, they arrest him for a night and then kick him out of prison the next day." But the old man was nice and empathic, and chatted in a friendly way. I needed a friendly, relaxed conversation. "A student? I thought so. Not from Warsaw?" "From Tomaszów." "Your parents must despair? I see, physicians." I left him and his sack in the building's hall and entered the fingerprinting room for those entering for the first time. They took my fingerprints using green ink, the color they had that day, and I wiped my fingers on the walls, adding to a rainbow of fingerprint marks left by past generations of Rakowiecka inmates.

The next day, the old man was released from jail, rode a bus to my hometown, Tomaszów, and searched my parents out in the local hospital. He conned them for a few zlotys to "organize a Solidarity lawyer" for their "brave son."

It was quite late when I entered the hospital cell in the Internal Medicine Ward of Rakowiecka Jail. A loaf of bread for dinner and a big spoon of marmalade was waiting for me. The prison bakery was quite good. A huge luxurious cell! Perhaps twenty square meters and with only five beds. In Białołęka, there were nine inmates per cell in an area of 13.5 square meters.

I met my two cellmates. The heavily tattooed "Skull" was a fine thief, formerly a chess master, a quick-witted joker. "Student?" He was

pleased. "You play chess? We will kill the time with chess!" Later—
again, there was another revealing "later"—I learned during the weekly
baths that the only place on Skull's body that was free of tattoos was his
left buttock. "Can you touch your nose with your tongue?" asked Skull.
I couldn't. "You want to bet that I can?" Sure, no way he could do that.
Skull removed his dentures and effortlessly performed his trick.

The other inmate laughed. This was Skull's usual welcoming con. For
the rookies. The muscular "Boxer" was a less refined, but street-smart
and friendly robber, a card cheater, who was formerly, well, a boxer. The
third inmate was napping. "Korycki. 'Janosik.' Paralyzed," Boxer nod-
ded in the direction of his bed. I only vaguely remembered this nickname, but Boxer lost interest in further explanations.

I took one of the empty beds that was farther from the door—fantas-
tic, one level only!—and unpacked the scant remainders of my Białołęka
possessions. Thank God! My treasured 100 zloty bill, my ticket to buying "stuff" on the prison black market, had survived slipped inside a
letter. I started dreaming about having so much free time now and so
much space and air that I could write down all the incredible stories,
the argot vocabulary, the norms, and the prison exam's question-and-
answer routines, the logistics of a rape attempt that I had experienced at
Białołęka, all this incredible material that I wanted to preserve not only
in my memory but also on paper. From my first days in prison, I had
planned to write my M.A. thesis in sociology on prison behavior. Much
later, I wrote the thesis, a book, and several articles describing and analyzing prison subculture.

The cell doors opened, which was unusual at such a late time, and
a guard tossed into the cell our fifth and final cellmate. Quite a big
man, he was dirty, naked, crazily embracing his sack. And completely
drunk, saliva splattering from his mouth, confused. With light nudges,
the guard directed him toward his bed, the closest one to the door, the
worst one in the cell, and ordered him to go to sleep. The drunk fell
asleep at once.

Then, at night, a scream woke me up. The naked drunk was scratching
the walls, "Mama! Mama! Help me, they will kill me, Mama!" Boxer and
Skull woke up too, and started questioning him, with a dose of irritation
but also residual sympathy, "Who? The communists? They are killing us
all, the f*cking bastards, go to sleep, you drunk." "No, the white mice!
They are killing me, the white mice, they are everywhere."

Boxer jumped out of his bed. Communists could be forgiven, delir-
ium couldn't. He slightly bent his knees, lowered his body, and quickly

started punching the drunk. Boom! A strong blow. Then a series of fast strokes. He was hitting the drunk's back. "To bed, let the good thieves sleep!" Skull watched with approval, ready to help if needed. Boxer got tired, took a break, and the drunk started crawling to his bed mumbling incomprehensibly. In shock, I was trying to gather my thoughts; fear of what would happen if I did something to help the drunk was mixed with an urge to intervene. Boxer started another round.

"Leave him alone, Boxer," a faint voice was heard. I focused my eyes. Janosik slightly raised his body but he was unable to sit up. His voice was gentle. "He will sleep now." Boxer immediately stopped. He was not annoyed; he had just been told what to do by somebody who knew better. The same Boxer, so confident in his powers that he bragged to me how he would manipulate four cellmates to be his servants. One against four, no problem for him. "Give me your Wałęsa, Kuroń, Jaruzelski, Kiszczak, and they will be fetching my shoes in the morning with their teeth and bringing them to my bed." In one breath, he had listed the names of top communist and Solidarity leaders.

"Leave him alone, Boxer." Janosik didn't need to repeat his words. Boxer returned to his bed and smiled to me. He was a soldier who listened to his general. The drunk climbed back to his bed and fell asleep. In the following days, his shoulders turned green and purple. The guard asked a resigned "Awright, so what happened?" knowing that the answer would be "I fell out of bed, chief." The drunk didn't even have to lie. He didn't remember what had happened.

In the morning, I moved my stool to Janosik's bed, sat on it, and introduced myself with, "I am for Solidarity." This denoted in prison argot an "anticommunist political prisoner." Janosik was delighted. He had the serious, wise, lean face of a Roman senator, with a head of scant, thinning greyish hair. He started asking inquisitive questions about politics, the Soviets, and the anticommunist underground. After a week or so, he started telling his own stories. Out of all prison mysteries, puzzles, and surprises, Józef "Janosik" Korycki turned out to be most enigmatic. The nearly a month that I spent in that cell was filled with chess defeats, a gradual transfer of my belongings via poker to Boxer, and long conversations with Janosik.

—MAREK KAMINSKI

# The Robin Hood of Podlasie

# Introduction

In the early 1980s, Józef Korycki (1934–1986) was designated as "Public Enemy No. 1" by the People's Republic of Poland (PRL)—the communist Polish state.[1] At the same time, the locals in the Podlasie region of Poland affectionately called him Janosik Podlaski, giving him the name of a Robin Hood–like figure of the Slavic world.

The original Janosik (Slovak: Juraj Jánošík) was an eighteenth-century Slovak folk hero and outlaw operating in the Tatra Mountains. Legend has it that he led a group of bandits of who stole from the rich and distributed the loot among the poor. Born in 1688, Juraj Jánošík grew up in the village of Terchová near Žilina. He worked with his band of thieves, including mostly Slovak and Polish companions, on the Hungarian-Polish border and attacked mainly merchants, priests, postal deliverymen, and other wealthy people. In 1713, Jánošík was arrested in the house of a friend who had been hiding him, and was sentenced to death by hanging on a hook by the left rib (Sroka 2004; Holland and Adamik 2009).

The protagonist of close to a dozen movies and numerous books, Janosik became a household name in Poland, Slovakia, and Czechia, and was a frequent reference in popular culture. In Poland in the early twentieth century, he became very popular among artistic bohemians and was long considered a noble Polish bandit operating on the Polish side of the Tatra Mountains. In Poland, his name was given to a redistributive tax called "janosikowe," the most popular social GPS app and its derivatives Yanosik, and countless cafes, stores, bars, bed-and-breakfasts, restaurants, or parks—often called "U Janosika" (At Janosik's). Enjoying a similar popularity in Czechia and Slovakia, Janosik even appeared on a Slovak 500-koruna bill (in 1944) and a 2-koruna coin (in 1947). Despite some differences in legitimacy and modus operandi between Janosik and the famous outlaw of Sherwood Forest, "Robin Hood" seems to be a rough equivalent of Janosik in English-language culture. We have thus used "Robin Hood" in the book's title as a metaphor that is justified by both folk heroes' similarities and that conveys our book's content to the international reader. In the text, however, we have retained the name "Janosik."

Our anticommunist Janosik, Korycki, robbed state-owned grocery stores and freight trains full of crude Soviet and Soviet-licensed

0.1. *Janosik* (created est. 1917). Wood
engraving by Władysław Skoczylas
(1883–1934). *Source*: Museum Żup Kra-
kowskich in Wieliczka. License: PD-Art,
PD-old-100.

products, stole "Bolshevik money" from village mayors, and gave away
a cornucopia of goods to poor Polish peasants, including television
sets, carpets, and small appliances. He also spent some of the money
he took on tractors, which he gave to villagers. He escalated his actions
in 1980 and 1981 during the time of the "Solidarity Carnival," when,
for the first time, the Polish communist authorities agreed to register
an independent, self-governing trade union, "Solidarity." In the 1980s,
the communist state organized massive manhunts—with close to one
thousand troops and militiamen, as well as personnel carrier vehicles,
commandos, dogs, and helicopters—to find Korycki. When he was finally surrounded, on May 14, 1982, he shouted, "Long live Poland!" and
shot himself in the head with a Soviet Nagant revolver. Miraculously, he
survived and, partially paralyzed, spent the next four years in Rakowiecka Jail. This is where Marek Kaminski met him in 1985. At the time,
Kaminski was an undergraduate student in charge of an underground
publishing house in Poland. When the secret police stopped one of the
publisher's drivers, Kaminski was arrested and spent five months in jail
as a political prisoner. The "Methods and Sources" section of this chapter describes how Korycki shared his life story with Kaminski.

Korycki was called Janosik, and he was loved by many locals of the Podlasie region of Poland, who looked up to him as an anticommunist hero. In fact, both the locals and militiamen who hunted him called him Janosik. Except for the most vicious communist propaganda pieces, which attributed all types of vices and crimes to Korycki, we found not a single reliable account that questioned his redistributive actions. Korycki fits all three categories of Eric Hobsbawm's (1969) concept of "social bandits": he redistributed goods and sought justice; he was a resistance fighter; and, to some extent, he avenged communist violence. When he was arrested, he became one of the most unusual and hard-to-classify political prisoners of modern times since his criminal and political actions were so closely intertwined.[2]

This book tells Korycki's incredible life story using standard biographical methods, focusing attention on a thematic sequence of events and the milestones of his life in connection to historical events.[3] Korycki's life is inevitably connected with the political history of Poland and opposition to communism. During late communism, some of the activities of the Polish political opposition—such as blowing up the auditorium of the Pedagogical University in Opole by brothers Ryszard and Jerzy Kowalczyk in 1971, the expropriations carried out by the Ruch organization at the turn of the seventies, or various spontaneous actions of workers during martial law—could be classified as criminal. However, most frequently, the opposition's "lawbreaking" was limited to claiming rights to certain freedoms by "natural law" or "human rights" arguments or participating in one of the many manifestations of the "shadow economy," such as using state-owned publishing facilities to print up underground publications (called working in the "entryway"— meaning "the entryway to the communist system").[4]

Our primary goal is to tell the story of an extraordinary man whose life was entrapped by communism. Our motivation is personal. We want to provide an honest account of a man whose life and reputation were demolished by communist propaganda. Regrettably, most of the post-communist Polish media have mechanically repeated the accusations by the communist propaganda and secret police. We would also like to raise more universal questions about the limits of resistance in authoritarian states with low social legitimacy. Additionally, in the first section of the conclusion, "On Rebels and Bandits," we analyze the similarities between Korycki's modus operandi and those of so-called ideological bandits. The "Prologue" and "Epilogue," which open and close the book, include Marek Kaminski's more personal recollections of his encounter with Korycki and the people from his section of Podlasie.

## METHODS AND SOURCES

While searching out information, the authors have dealt with substantial problems in the reconstruction of the basic facts of Józef Korycki's life. Despite having a high profile locally, and despite being hunted by hundreds of communist militia and Special Forces troops, Korycki left behind few reliable sources of information. This is a typical problem with the life stories of lesser-known persons. In Korycki's case, communist censorship additionally strictly limited media information about him, providing only propaganda pieces that presented him as a common and dangerous bandit.

It can be said without exaggeration that this book came about only by sheer coincidence. As a college student in the 1980s, one of this book's authors, Marek Kaminski, ran an anticommunist publishing house in then-communist Poland. In 1985, Kaminski was arrested. It was while he was imprisoned in Rakowiecka Jail that he met and befriended Józef Korycki. Rakowiecka Jail, also called Mokotów Jail, was built in 1902–4 in what was then Tsarist Russia. During various phases of communism, it functioned either fully or partially as a political prison. Kaminski wrote down long stories of Korycki's adventures and imprisonments and then smuggled the notes out of prison.

Due to the passage of time, many sources of information dried up. The full material for this book was collected in 2018 and 2019, over thirty-two years after Korycki's death, when he would have been eighty-four or eighty-five years old. When he died, he had been in jail for four years. This means that there were relatively few people to reach out to who knew him well. Both his only son and the last partner in his criminal actions had died young. There is no record of him in the archives of the Instytut Pamięci Narodowej (Institute of National Remembrance, IPN).[5] The director of the Museum of Cursed Soldiers and Political Prisoners of the Polish People's Republic—which exists in the former Rakowiecka Jail—could not find any information about Korycki. Attempts to reach various people and institutions, including Korycki's former wife; the daughter of his life partner, Krystyna Oksiejuk; the head of the Surgery Ward in Rakowiecka Jail; and fellow inmates, were also unsuccessful. It turned out that many people connected to Korycki were either dead, did not remember much, did not want to talk about the past, or could not be located. Nevertheless, the authors did manage to reach several people who agreed to share information, including close family members and other people who had known Korycki quite well. In particular, the narrative of his life partner, Krystyna Oksiejuk, proved to be extremely valuable. We haven't talked to former members of the Milicja Obywatelska (Citizen's Militia, MO),[6] nor to former members of the riot police, the Zmotoryzowane Odwody Milicji Obywatelskiej (Motorized Reserves of the Citizens' Militia, ZOMO).[7] This was the only point of view that had already been documented well, and numerous existing written and spoken discussions and interviews about Korycki exhaust everything the former functionaries could tell us about their nemesis. Many of those functionaries, including the most important, Colonel Jan Płócienniczak, died several years ago. Moreover, former secret service or militia members routinely deny interviews unless they firmly believe that the authors or journalists would represent their point of view.

This book is based on a Polish edition (Kaminski and Szum 2019) that was substantially modified due to the post-publication emergence of new sources. The most important accounts, that is, Kaminski's prison report and the interviews with Krystyna Oksiejuk and Barbara Korycka, were made available with comments in Kaminski and Szum 2020. A more detailed description of all sources is found below.

### Korycki's Prison Conversations with Marek Kaminski

All information obtained directly from Korycki comes from conversations that he held in 1985 with Marek Kaminski in Warsaw's Rakowiecka Jail. In 1982, Kaminski, then an undergraduate student of mathematics and sociology at Warsaw University, founded an underground publishing house associated with the then-illegal trade union called Solidarity. Kaminski directed the work of this publishing house, which used the names of STOP and Książnica Literacka, for seven years, producing thirty-five books with a total circulation of about one hundred thousand copies (see fig. 0.2). In addition to books, the organization published a few issues of the underground journal *Gazeta Niecodzienna*, and also cooperated with the underground weekly *Tygodnik Mazowsze*, various publishing houses that included Officyna Liberałów and NOWa, the Adam Smith Institute (later, the Adam Smith Center), and other like-minded organizations as well as underground student movements from all over Poland.

Kaminski was arrested on March 12, 1985, a day after communist traffic militia personnel stopped a driver carrying STOP's books. The driver divulged the information they demanded, leading to Kaminski's arrest the next day. After a short stay in "holes" at two militia stations

0.2. Five out of approximately thirty-five books published by underground publishing houses STOP and Książnica Literacka between 1982 and 1989. Photo: Robert Kępczyński.

and thirty-one days in the Białołęka Jail, Kaminski was transferred to the Rakowiecka Jail, from which he was released nearly five months later, on August 9, 1985. Immediately after his arrest, Kaminski decided to conduct a comprehensive study of prison subculture, and he devoted all his abundant time and meager resources to this endeavor. During his imprisonment at the Rakowiecka Jail, Kaminski spent twenty-four days, between April 15 and May 9, 1985, with the partially paralyzed Korycki in a six-person cell in the prison hospital's Internal Medicine Ward. It did not take them long to become friends. Between May 16 and July 26, the two were in the Surgery Ward of the prison hospital, in different— sometimes adjacent—cells, and communicated through intermediaries and secret messages.[8] The most interesting conversations took place in the Internal Medicine Ward when the other inmates went out for their daily walks.

In 1985, the jail's inmates spent most of their time in overcrowded cells. Few worked inside or outside the jail. There was seldom an opportunity to leave one's cell, but these rare occasions included a prisoner's weekly bath, an appointment with a doctor, a trip to participate in his trial, an interrogation, or a very rare visit to the "freedom" hospital for specialist testing or examination. The lucky ones could meet with their family or their lawyer during occasional visits at a table or by using a phone connection behind a bulletproof glass window. The only routine opportunity to leave one's cell was for a daily walk, lasting half an hour for those in regular cells and one hour for the few in hospital cells, although this time was usually cut by five or ten minutes by the guards. This exercise was limited to plodding around a small "walk yard" made of concrete. Nevertheless, almost all prisoners waited eagerly for the opportunity to leave their tiny cells. Some hapless inmates—like Korycki, who was partially paralyzed due to a bullet in his head—were immobile and had no chance to leave their cells. Since the walk was not mandatory, inmates occasionally embraced the opportunity to be alone, or nearly so, in their temporarily empty cells, which also allowed time for the few who remained behind to discuss their secret plans freely. The inmates staying inside could master their plans for swallowing metal objects or faking a suicide, discuss cell secrets, and plot fantastical escapes, which, alas, almost never came to fruition.

One of the inmates who took advantage of this time was Kaminski, a prisoner whose cellmates gave him the moniker "the Student." Kaminski skipped many daily walks in order to have unrestricted conversations with Korycki. An additional incentive for Kaminski to remain behind in his cell was the fact that, according to inmates, the guards and nurses kept records of who went out for these walks; actively walking inmates—"walkers"—were considered healthier or recovering. Thus, skipping the walk helped the Student to substantiate his false claim of being seriously sick, a claim that was supported with the knowing help of physicians from a specialist clinic in the outside "freedom" world and, later, Dr. Possart, head of the Surgical Ward at Rakowiecka Jail. This one hour per day allowed the Student to spend time with Korycki and to record his story.

Initial conversations, conducted in the presence of other prisoners, were quite perfunctory. Korycki limited himself to stating commonly known facts or describing situations unrelated to his case. After about a week, Korycki gained greater confidence and trust in the Student. Since all of the other inmates in the cell were walkers, during their walks Korycki and the Student stayed behind in the cell alone. All of their more authentic and confidential talks, of which there were approximately ten, were held exclusively during the other prisoners' walking time and included stories about earlier arrests, paramilitary organizations that Korycki had founded, unrealized plans, and dramatic details of his final arrest and subsequent imprisonment. During one of these conversations, Korycki revealed why he refused to consent to surgery to remove the bullet from his head.

There was also some information Korycki chose not to discuss, and the Student did not press him. Thus, we do not know enough about his closest underground associates or about the process that he used to recruit them. One has to remember that these conversations with the Student took place in April and May of 1985, just a few weeks after Mikhail Gorbachev had seized power in the Soviet Union and when communism was still seemingly far from its ultimate decay. Korycki surely felt that sharing this sensitive information could jeopardize those who trusted him. Additionally, and quite understandably, information about the identities of the beneficiaries of his redistribution was also quite sensitive. For his part, the Student likewise did not share with Korycki—or anybody else in- or outside prison—his procedures for building underground publishing cells, or information on their geographic distribution, production potential, the overall distribution network, or the identities of the members of his organization.

The pace of most conversations was unhurried, and there was no pressure on Korycki to start his story. Korycki often initiated the conversations, speaking slowly and with effort. A substantial part of every conversation was also spent on the Student's stories about Solidarity's underground publishing enterprise. Korycki was an eager and gracious listener, and after listening, he was clearly uplifted and more willing to share his own experiences. Sometimes Korycki started off by describing his adventures rather quickly and readily answered questions, while at other times, he spent the entire session just listening and asking his own questions. The Student often had a feeling that Korycki was treating him like a son; in fact, the Student was actually born the same year as Korycki's son, Sławomir. Regrettably, the Student realized soon after having left the Internal Medicine Ward that he should have asked many more questions.

The Student transcribed most of the information he learned while still in prison or shortly after his release (see fig. 0.3). The resulting manuscript is referenced in this book as Kaminski (1985b).[9]

Unfortunately, a few handwritten pages of Korycki's account were once discovered by the Student's cellmates and destroyed, and the inmates roughed him up for "spying." Usually, the other prisoners' attitude toward the Student's note taking was ambivalent, and he tried to hide this activity from them. On one more occasion the inmates were also eager to beat up their "spying" cellmate. However, after explanations were provided, the prisoners reversed their attitude and began enthusiastically cooperating with the Student "to provide testimony of communist brutality." The Student promised to immortalize his fellow inmates—in an obviously flattering way—in the book.

Another source of information was Kaminski's prison journal, which he managed to periodically smuggle out of the prison in a piecemeal fashion. Chunks of the journal were dispatched through channels that included his cellmates' contacts, family meetings, and one cooperative guard, who agreed to help Kaminski because his best friend had fallen in love with Kaminski's sister. This information was sent in the form of *grypses*, or secret messages, in five or six separate batches. In this book, the journal references appear as "Kaminski 1985a," along with the date of the entry, and often report Kaminski's thoughts and observations. There was only one time that a secret message was intercepted by the

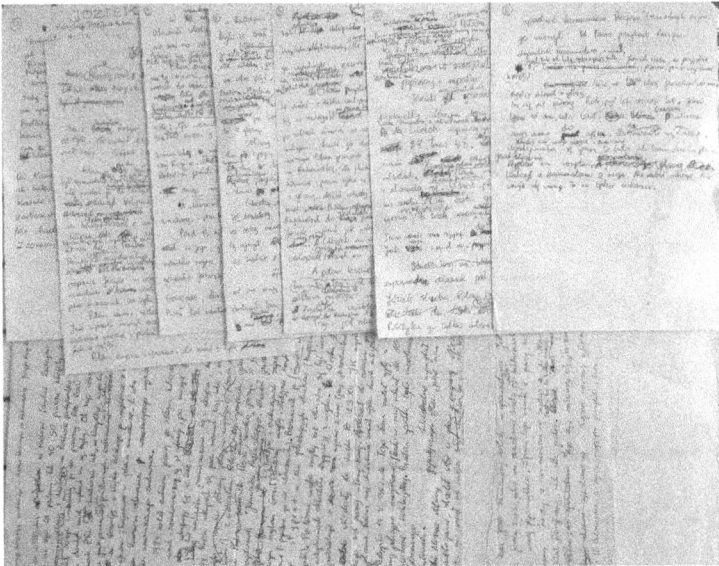

0.3. A few pages of the notes of Marek Kaminski (a.k.a the "Student"), with conversations with Korycki referenced in this book as Kaminski 1985b. *Source*: Archive of Marek Kaminski.

guards and destroyed. Since the Student was at that time at the prison hospital, the hospital rules prevented the guards from punishing him. There was also some less sensitive material describing ordinary aspects of prison life, such as what they were fed, the provisions available in the prison store, parcels mailed to inmates, the daily schedule, and information about clothing and uniforms. This material was mailed out as ordinary letters. All such letters were delivered intact with the word "Censored" stamped on the envelopes.[10]

A useful source of information about Kaminski's prison experiences were this book's authors' emailed conversations. Kaminski's (2004a) book included a three-page concise description of Korycki's adventures and became a major source of information about his life. Before deciding to write a book together on Korycki's life, Ernest Szum had asked Kaminski several questions via email, the answers to which were to be used in an article Szum was writing on Korycki. After discovering that Kaminski had an abundance of unknown facts and unpublished documents about Korycki in his personal archives, Szum convinced Kaminski to co-author a book. Those initial emails are referenced in this book as "Kaminski 2018," along with a number corresponding to each email.

Finally, the authors here sometimes refer to Kaminski's direct and unrecorded experience as a "participating observer."[11] Kaminski's attention was, to a considerable extent, focused on Korycki: his behavior, the treatment he received from prison staff, and his relationships with other cellmates. We have utilized this information sporadically in this book, but without making any formal reference to it.

## Interviews with Korycki's Friends, Family, and Acquaintances

Beyond the sources of information described above, other important resources for material were the interviews conducted with Korycki's family members and acquaintances. These interviews were semi-open; in other words, a minimal number of questions were asked, and the interviewees were free to provide their broad recollections of Korycki.

The most important of these interviews were those conducted by Ernest Szum with Krystyna Oksiejuk on April 23, 2018, and May 9, 2018, at her home in Misie, as well as several telephone conversations Szum had with Oksiejuk. Oksiejuk's thoughts and remembrances mainly concerned the last period of Korycki's activity, the years 1979 to 1982, but she also provided some information on his formal education, his family, and his personality. Oksiejuk's account was extremely valuable to this research because she was Korycki's life partner and confidante from December 1979 until his death in 1986. Initially, she hid him in her kitchen. Later, she gave him one of the two rooms in her house, and when he was in hiding outside the house, brought food to him in the forest. During this long period, she was the person closest to him. She thus was intimately familiar with his activities, views, and emotional states at that time.

It is worth noting that when Oksiejuk presented her account, she was devoid of negative emotions in relation to the communist system or its functionaries. In the course of the conversations, she only used the pejorative term *komuszysko* (commie) once, while talking about the militia invading her privacy during a search of her house without a search warrant. Throughout all of the various conversations, she always tried to communicate her knowledge—of facts, specific events, and people—and to refrain from offering her own opinions or value judgments.

It was thirty-two years after his death that Oksiejuk decided to talk about Korycki for the first time. The passage of those long years erased many of the less significant details from her memory, but the most important issues remained vibrant, in addition to a clear outline of the story in general terms. Earlier, despite many attempts by interested journalists to acquire information from her, she never agreed to talk about Korycki. Thus, her participation in this book provided original, factual material to the narrative. Oksiejuk's decision to speak with the authors was due to her former contact with Kaminski, with whom she exchanged letters about Korycki in 1986. Kaminski gained her confidence with an Easter postcard that Korycki had given him, specifically to prove to her that he was in touch with Korycki (see fig. 3.7 in Chapter 3). In 2018, she stated:

> God, it has been so many years. I did not talk to anyone about it. Józek always said to put it out of my mind and not talk to anyone about him. Even if his friends came forward; [he said] that they would come. He said that there would be various attempts and [that I should] remain quiet. He always warned me not to talk to strangers. He did not want me to get in trouble afterward. And I did not want to talk to anyone about it until now, and I have not talked to anyone in all these years.

In addition to Oksiejuk, Barbara Korycka, Korycki's sister-in-law, the wife of his favorite brother, Władysław, and the last surviving member of that generation of his family, granted us an extremely valuable interview. Barbara and Władysław were very close to Józef, and they visited him many times while he was in prison. In the 1980s, Barbara lived close to Józef's mother, Janina, and when Korycki was initially brought home from prison, he stayed in Barbara's apartment. Her recollections allowed us to reconstruct Józef's family history, and also provided his family's perspective on his last imprisonment. Prior to granting the interview to Szum, Ms. Korycka had refused to talk to journalists due to her conviction that they were out to disseminate sensationalist slander about her brother-in-law.

She agreed to our request for an interview after receiving the Polish edition of our book. In responding, she said, "Perhaps I will be able to convey some [useful] information about Józef. Since for years, lies about him multiplied, I care about restoring the truth. I knew Józef very well. He was a talented, intelligent, and wise man" (Korycka 2020). In her testimony, she described how she and Korycki's wife, Wanda, had spent time writing to the local media to correct their mistakes. In addition to the interview, Ms. Korycka gave us her permission to use seventeen family photos, provided that they would only be used for the English version or the second Polish edition of our book, and would not be used by journalists.

Other important sources of information were provided by conversations carried out between Szum and Korycki's more distant family members, acquaintances, or those who interacted with him in an official capacity. Dorota Boreczek, Korycki's niece—the daughter of his brother, Jan—shared with us her memories of her uncle from when she was a child. It was also Ms. Boreczek who convinced her aunt, Barbara Korycka, to grant us an interview. A retired gamekeeper in the Brzozowica forestry service, Franciszek Trochimiak, described how Korycki's group had attacked his lodge and had stolen his shotgun. In addition, the brother of Korycki's last associate, Waldemar Kaliński, gave us several detailed testimonials about his personal encounters with Korycki, as well as information about his brother's activities and joint hiding with Korycki. A retired forester, Waldemar Czajka, offered plenty of anecdotes about Korycki and described two manhunts that took place on the territory of the forest that he administered, including the final raid in which Czajka was forced to participate. We also received feedback from several people who knew Korycki casually, had heard about him from close family members, served time that overlapped with his in prison, or possessed photos of him. Many of those people, including

Korycki's family, had refused to talk about Korycki earlier because they deeply distrusted the media's lack of objectivity. Convincing them of our sincere pursuit was only possible because of Kaminski's personal relationship with Korycki while the two were in prison and the publication of the Polish edition of this book, which opened many previously closed doors. The authors' conversations with these various witnesses allowed us to reconstruct Korycki's family life; verify descriptions of various important events independently of Korycki's stories, such as some of the robberies; and assess Korycki's level of support among the Podlasie population.

## Militia and Police

The third major area of information was communist militia documents and reports and, secondarily, police/militia sources. However, here it is always important to keep in mind that communist authorities often used militia documents as tools of misinformation and propaganda.

The militia sources consist of memoirs of militiamen who participated in actions against Korycki and include numerous long and detailed statements made for the 2005 documentary film *Janosik z Podlasia*. When a specific person is speaking, we refer to this source as (Bodasiński and Osipowski 2005, person speaking, time in the movie); when we refer to the film's general narration, the format is (Bodasiński and Osipowski 2005, time in the movie).

There are also memoirs and other documents of militia superiors to whom the militiamen reported or provided information for propaganda purposes. The most important of these accounts was offered by an *esbek* (Security Service agent),[12] Inspector Sławoj Kopka, who published his article in the flagship militia magazine *W Służbie Narodu* (*In the Service of the Nation*),[13] as well as information from the functionaries who formed the so-called Special Force for Tracking Down and Capturing Korycki, using the code name "Operation Jackal"; here, the leading account is by a militia colonel and chief propagandist, Jan Płócienniczak.

The sources the authors used as accounts of the police/militia were primarily articles in various police journals, which were published after the "militia" force was rebranded as the "police," which occurred on April 6, 1990. The most prominent is the article of Przemysław Kacak, published in the monthly *Policja 997* (*Police 997*). Generally, the articles typically include references to militia sources, but the content is often distorted by secondary interpretations of the information, as well as biased narration.

In one important case—that of the former militiaman Wojciech Raczuk—the authors used his public statements about Korycki in the documentary *Janosik z Podlasia*, newspaper articles, and online media. We also used a biographical note in the arrest warrant of Józef Korycki, issued by the MO between 1980 and 1982 (the exact date of publication is unclear; we assumed that the most likely year is 1981).

In many of the militiamen's statements, one could identify the psychological mechanism of rationalization, which allows people to maintain their self-esteem despite acting contrary to their declared beliefs. Korycki was called an "ordinary bandit," and the work of the militia was discussed in terms of defending the citizenry against banditry. However, in some descriptions of the former militiamen, Korycki received a surprisingly flattering portrayal: selfless, honest, and ideologically motivated by ideas.

In addition to the bias described above, another problem with these accounts was that this group was often motivated by wishes for promotions or occasional awards from the communist authorities. An additional difficulty with understanding many militia accounts was that some contained serious problems with logic and the clear formulation of thoughts, as well as the proper use of legal nomenclature, for instance, confusing "sentencing" with "execution." We discuss various problems of this nature in the sections later in the book, and, where possible, try to preserve the flavor of this peculiar, often amusing, militia-speak in our translation. Because of all such issues, the authors had more limited confidence in the militia and police/militia sources, as well as in those originating from other communist apparatchiks.

While the quality of some sources is questionable, we considered all available descriptions of facts related to Korycki's life and activities derived from both direct and indirect sources. This is especially important when we discuss Korycki's arrest, which occurred on May 14, 1982. There were several inconsistent versions describing the final dramatic moment right before his capture.

Other Sources

Journalistic articles about Korycki, which have been published for about thirty years in popular magazines, the daily press, and via electronic media, are mostly unreliable. Usually, they are devoid of new facts and repeatedly reproduce the content of Inspector Sławoj Kopka's 1982 article in a completely unquestioning way. Additionally, in the last fifteen years or so, the mass media has started including references to the 2005 film *Janosik z Podlasia* and Kaminski's 2006 book *Gry więzienne* (which is a Polish edition of his 2004 book, *Games Prisoners Play*).

The production of Korycki's content in mass media accounts has now reached a massive scale. Many of these texts include the products of the authors' overheated imaginations, and even offer creative "quotes" from alleged statements made by Korycki and others.[14] These texts typically also provide no references to the sources of their revelations to verify information they contain. There are exceptions, such as Przemysław Kacak's (2011) work, which references some sources; however, it is done inconsistently, thereby producing methodologically faulty results. We critically evaluate the journalistic accounts in the section "Bandit in Communist Propaganda, Janosik in Folk Sentiment."

We also find controversial sources of unclear value in press articles published in the local weekly *Word of Podlasie*, whose journalists in 1982 reported extensively on Korycki's activities and his capture. This journal's articles were based on factual information provided by the militia but then interspersed with elements obviously based on communist propaganda. Frequently, the authors weave into their articles the term "local population" and their hatred and fear of Korycki in order to substantiate and authenticate the populace's alleged contempt for the man. Some articles are signed only by the initials "ch" or "jch," which we were unable to decode. Because *Word of Podlasie* was an official newspaper of the Polska Zjednoczona Partia Robotnicza (Polish United Worker's Party, PZPR),[15] all materials had to agree with the communist party's line. We analyzed all the issues of *Word of Podlasie* published in 1982 with articles on Korycki and found clear indications of bias. Nevertheless, certain factual information that was ideologically neutral, for example, the dates of his releases from prison, seems to be trustworthy.

The book contains descriptions of the norms of prison subculture of *grypsowanie*, prison argot, self-injury, simulation, communication methods, and other aspects of inmate life. This material puts the final prison period of Korycki's life into its proper context. It is based mostly on Kaminski's (2004a) book, *Games Prisoners Play*, as well as a few other works that looked at the subculture of *grypsowanie* and inmates' strategic interactions. *Games Prisoners Play* is also the source of the drawings by Mirosław Andrzejewski that illustrate prison subculture. In the current work, we also reproduce two secret messages by Andrzejewski, who spent sixteen months in prison in the 1980s as a political prisoner, mainly in Siedlce Prison.

Korycki's life partner, Krystyna Oksiejuk, inherited some documents after Korycki's death that included his diary, in addition to some notes and other personal papers. Unfortunately, probably because of the fear that they would be discovered by the communist secret police, no such documents have survived the passage of time. As Oksiejuk (2018a) states,

> Sadly, no souvenirs of Józek have survived. There were once photos, they were even signed, but where are they now, I do not know. ... And there were letters too. Back then, I always kept these letters hidden somewhere, in case of police. There was also Józek's diary, where he described various things. He once described Christmas Eve, as he sat alone in his room. That year, I went with Agnieszka to my mother, brother, and sister-in-law. It was very sad and touching.

In addition to the above sources, we also utilized phone conversations, written accounts or emails that we exchanged with various inmates, historians and other persons whose experience was deemed relevant to Korycki's story. Finally, we used some material from our earlier articles, books, and other documents. These are Kaminski (2003, 2004a, 2004b, 2006), Kaminski and Gibbons (1994), Kaminski and Szum (2019, 2020), and Szum (2012a, 2012b, 2013, 2014, 2018, 2019).

# Rebels of Podlasie

## March 25, 1934–October 1979

> If a law is unjust, a man is not only right to disobey it, he
> is obligated to do so.
> —Various versions of this sentiment are attributed to Mahatma
> Gandhi, Thomas Jefferson, Martin Luther King, and others

"May you live in interesting times!" This English version of an alleged
Chinese curse, and a resigned aphorism in communist Poland, could
have been Józef Korycki's life motto. Korycki's childhood coincided
with the last years of Polish independence and the Second World War,
his early youth with the establishment and hardening of socialism in
the PRL, and his adulthood with socialism's slow disintegration. He
ended his life in prison in tragic circumstances, helpless and partially
paralyzed. Before this, for decades, Korycki rebelled, organized armed
groups, and tried to live a free life outside the system he hated. This was
not just an ephemeral youth rebellion "against the evil world," but a mature attitude, which eventually was accompanied by increasingly wider
resistance to communism in Polish society. With the information that
we have gathered, in this chapter, we describe the insurgent tradition of
his picturesque homeland of Podlasie; reconstruct Korycki's activities
before he became "Public Enemy No. 1," which occurred during his last
campaign in 1979–82; and describe the differing perceptions of Korycki
by the communist Security Service and the local population.

## TRADITIONS OF REBELLION IN PODLASIE

Korycki is from Podlasie, a land of deep forests, impenetrable swamps,
multiple ethnicities, and uncertain governability that is the perfect

setting for rebels, insurgents, forest partisans, and paramilitary guerillas. Korycki's saga is deeply and inseparably connected with the *mała ojczyzna* (little homeland) where he spent his life.

Podlasie is ethnically and culturally diverse: Orthodox Christians, Roman Catholics, and Muslims live there, side by side. Polish customs are interwoven with Belarusian, Ukrainian, and Tatar traditions. Before World War II, important Jewish cultural centers were found in Białystok, in the north, which is the present capital of Podlasie Voivodeship, and Lublin, the city at the southern edges of Podlasie. In some small villages, such as Kruszyniany, Catholic and Orthodox crosses coexist with Muslim mosques. The historical bond that held this ethnic mosaic together was the deep tradition of freedom, tolerance, and respect for individual rights.

## Geography and History

Podlasie is a relatively narrow strip of land stretching from Augustów in the north to Międzyrzec Podlaski in the south. It covers the central and southern part of the present Podlasie Voivodeship, the northern section of Lubelskie, and the eastern edge of Mazowieckie. Historically, the territory of Podlasie was delineated by the cities of Brest, Brańsk, Bielsk, Drohiczyn, Mielnik, Kamieniec, Suraz, and Siemiatycze (Wiśniewski 1977). According to the historian and ethnographer Zygmunt Gloger, the name of the region comes from "Lachy"—an early term for Poles living in this geographical area.

Podlasie contains some of the most beautiful ancient forests on the planet, which provide perfect hideouts for prospective rebels. The Białowieża Forest that crosses the Polish-Belarusian border is the largest primeval forest in Europe, brimming with wildlife, giant oaks, picturesque fallen trees, and decaying moss-covered logs. At the end of World War I, German soldiers killed most of the European bison, moose, deer, wild boar, and other animals residing in the forest, and severely depleted the number of trees. Then, either Soviet marauders or local poachers killed the last bison in 1919, just before the Polish Army assumed control of the area. A small herd of four bison, the largest surviving wild land animals in Europe, was reintroduced in Białowieża in 1929, and from this herd, there are presently around one thousand bison that roam the woodland area. In 1979, the forest was designated a UNESCO World Heritage Site that presently covers approximately 1418.85 km$^2$ (see figs. 1.1–1.4).

1.1. Orthodox church in Grabarka. Photo by Jacek Karczmarz. License: CC BY-SA 3.0.

1.2. The Potocki Palace in Radzyń Podlaski. Photo by Jacek Karczmarz. License: CC BY-SA 3.0.

1.3. Deep forest in Białowieża National Park. Photo by Jacek Karczmarz. License: CC BY-SA 3.0.

1.4. European bison in the Białowieża National Park. Photo by Ernest Szum.

The administrative, political, and ethnic borders of Podlasie have changed many times in its millennial history. Early on, these lands were not clearly associated with any nation and also lacked administrative organization. Starting in the eleventh century, Mazovian princes fought against Lithuanian and Ruthenian rulers, as well as the Teutonic Order, creating a volatile national-cultural-religious melting pot. Colonization by Mazovians and Ruthenians, which occurred simultaneously from the tenth century on, did not settle the political allegiance of these lands. The situation only stabilized with the union of Poland and Lithuania in 1385. In 1569, during the Lublin Union, Podlasie was incorporated into the Kingdom of Poland, and a permanent administration was created based on the legal and political structure of the Polish-Lithuanian state (Tyszkiewicz 1983).

In 1795, after the third partition of what was once Poland, the country ceased to exist on the map of Europe. At that time, Prussia and Austria divided Podlasie along the Bug River, while a few eastern towns found themselves on the Russian side of the partition. In 1807, after Napoleon's victory over the Prussians, the French Army entered Drohiczyn and Bielsko-Biała counties. Many volunteers from Podlasie, coming mainly from the petty nobility, fought in Napoleon's Grande Armée and paid for its defeat with the confiscation of their estates (Maroszek 1992). At that time, most of Podlasie was annexed by Russia, including the Białystok region, and the rest became part of the ephemeral Duchy of Warsaw, and—after Napoleon's final defeat in 1815—the Congress Kingdom of Poland, a puppet state ruled by Russia. Tormented by regular uprisings, it remained the part of the Russian Empire until Poland regained its independence in 1918.

In the words of a Briton, "A perennially unhappy country, fought over, beleaguered, partitioned, rescued and abandoned, Poland teaches her children many virtues, not the least of which is patience" (Monsarrat, in Conrad 1977, vii). And patience was abundant in Podlasie. Over many years, time and again, the Poles from Podlasie relentlessly conspired, formed troops, joined "forest partisans," or fought as lone wolves against revolving enemies. Perhaps because of their own peacefully coexistent diversity of ethnicities and religions and the painful awareness of the near-constant autocratic threat coming from their predatory neighbors, Podlasie produced the most active insurgents, who fiercely worked to defend their precious freedoms. Over the years, during Poland's numerous uprisings, occupations, and wars, strong traditions of

locally backed guerrilla warfare against foreign powers evolved. During each time of trouble, Podlasie's complex geography, the multitude
of small villages owned by impoverished nobles, the numerous ethnic
enclaves, and the overlapping political influences of national and left-
ist forces produced a diverse mosaic of underground organizations.
Korycki's private war was part of this tradition. The dramatic struggles
going back in time to the 1863 January Uprising against Russia, the partisan fight against the Wehrmacht in World War II, and the postwar
guerilla fight against the Polish communist forces backed by the Red
Army are all part of the background of his story.

## Insurgents of the 1863 January Uprising

In 1863, at the time of January Uprising, the Polish-Lithuanian Commonwealth, a former federal state of two nations, remained divided
among the three partitioning powers: Russia, Prussia, and Austria.
While Austria, under its enlightened ruler, Franz Joseph I, was relatively liberal and democratic, both Prussia and Russia were more autocratic and centralized states, and were keen to apply brutally enforced
linguistic and cultural Germanization and Russification, respectively.

This forced depolonization fueled resistance. Among all the Polish
lands, Podlasie was the strongest supporter of insurrection. Here, approximately eight thousand rebellious troops clashed with the Tsarist
army most often, and these fights persisted the longest, up until the last
insurgent unit, commanded by a priest, Stanisław Brzóska, was crushed
in spring 1865.

The years preceding the January Uprising brought a substantial
revival of national and social activity. By 1863, Congress Poland had
been occupied by Russia for over sixty-eight years. Despite prohibitions
against doing so, Polish patriots organized public speeches, demonstrations, and ceremonial services on national anniversaries; crosses in
churches and those by roads were decorated with crowns of thorns and
bows in the Polish national colors; youth gathered in churches and sang
patriotic songs. Those who collaborated with the Tsarist regime were
stigmatized (Skowronek 1990, 302–3; Ramotowska 1971, 317; Kosztyła
1985).

In 1861, Tsar Alexander II introduced reforms in the Russian Empire, granting peasants personal and religious freedom and many
civil rights. However, this reform did not cover Congress Poland,
which caused peasant protests on the "Polish" side of the Bug River.

Within three months, the peasant rebellions encompassed 124 estates in Grodno province. In response, the Russian Army liberally imposed punishment by flogging and suppressed the resistance (Halicz 1955; Kieniewicz 2009, 158). Russian soldiers were cruel pacifiers (Biłgorajski 1956; Kieniewicz 1953, 151). For instance, in their crackdown on the village of Bagny, twenty-five men were castrated (Wincenty Krzysztofik, as quoted in Ryżewski 2013). With the outbreak of the January Uprising in 1863, the "peasant question" lost its place of prominence.

Due to its geographic location and terrain, Podlasie was among the most important areas of insurgent operations. The Russian Army transported men and provisions between the Russian Empire and Congress Poland, using the critical St. Petersburg–Warsaw railroad. The uprising's leaders hoped to sabotage this route early.[1] Destroying the rail route was supposed to disrupt Russian troop logistics (Wojtasik 1995, 28). To prevent this scenario, the Russians deployed about 7,500 soldiers and thirty-two guns in Podlasie (Jasienica 1960, 208–9). In all of Congress Poland, the estimates of the Russian troops ran from almost 100,000 (Jasienica 1960) to exactly 111,245 (Gesket 2013).

In late 1862, a prominent activist of a radical Red underground organization, Władysław Cichorski, arrived in Podlasie from Warsaw. The Tsarist political police quickly focused their interest on him, since they suspected him of an assassination attempt on Aleksander Wielopolski, then the controversial head of the Polish government appointed by the Russian Empire, as well as of the assassination of Warsaw police's chief, Paweł Felkner. The political police searched Cichorski's apartment; the search revealed components for the production of explosives. Cichorski avoided arrest but was forced to leave Warsaw immediately (Szum 2012).

Cichorski quickly gained the trust of the locals. He maintained good relations with everyone, including simple peasants, and pronounced himself a "brother to the people." He hid in peasant huts and described the political situation to his hosts—the residents of Podlasie and Kurpie—but also called for unity and a joint fight by all Poles. When Cichorski received the order to start the uprising, he gathered approximately 1,800 insurgents, although, among them, they were armed with only sixty firearms, along with scythes and lances (Dobroński 2010, 146). He was appointed a colonel.

Two other military commanders played important roles in the uprising in Podlasie: Colonel Walenty Lewandowski and Roman Rogiński (Kieniewicz 1983, 1989, 429–30; Rostworowski and Tyrowicz 1972,

211–13). In December 1862, Lewandowski was ordered to return from emigration, and on January 5, 1863, he was appointed to be colonel and military chief of the Podlasie Voivodeship. After taking his oath, he went to Podlasie with Rogiński, who briefed him on preparations for the uprising. On January 7, both commanders arrived in Biała Podlaska. Lewandowski quickly realized that the few thousand conspirators were poorly armed and had little money at their disposal (Janowski 1923, 35; Mencel 1963, 76; Tomczyk 1963, 28; Rogiński 1898, 1966, 9–70).

As an experienced revolutionary, Lewandowski understood the potentially dire consequences of the poor state of his soldiers' armament. He thus started looking to acquire arms (Mencel 1963, 76; Janowski 1923, 35; Tomczyk 1963, 28). He quickly subordinated Podlasie's civil organization (Deskur 1966, 148) and then appointed new county military chiefs, ordered the rearmament of the conspirators, and started intensive military exercises (Śladkowski 1973, 3).

Rogiński, another prominent leader of the Uprising, as a mere twenty-two-year-old, commanded over one thousand soldiers and officers. As county commissioner, Rogiński oversaw Podlasie's civilian administration. He announced the decisions of the provisional government, formed new troops, assigned commanders, and appointed local civil authorities (Kieniewicz 1989, 429–30). Confident and assertive, Rogiński was also impulsive. In one "frenzy of madness," he killed Ivan Cherkasov, an unarmed Tsarist official, by first using a dagger and then finishing him off with a "shot in the skull from behind" (Kieniewicz 1983, 52–53; Rogiński 1898, 59).). He later explained: "I was twenty-one and hungry for enemy blood" (Rogiński 1898, 59). His subordinates were terrified of him (Góra 1965, 378).

## Partisans of World War II

In 1918, after 123 years of being partitioned by Russia, Prussia, and Austria, Poland regained its long-awaited independence. The First World War ended with what, for the Poles, seemed like a miracle. The descendant states of all three partitioning empires lost the war and their state apparatuses temporarily disintegrated. Poland thus recovered its independence on the symbolic day of November 11, 1918, which is when World War I formally ended. It seemed that the dire misfortune of being located between Germany and Russia had been overcome. However, only twenty years later, the specter of the German-Russian alliance hung over Poland and other Central European countries once again,

1.5. A battle. 1863 drawing by Artur Grottger (1837–1867). No 4 in the series of nine pictures *Polonia* depicting scenes from the January Uprising. *Source*: Országos Magyar Szépművészeti Muzeum, Budapest. License: PD-Art, PD-old-100

this time in the form of the Molotov-Ribbentrop Pact between Nazi Germany and the Soviet Union. The secret protocol of the Pact divided several countries of Central Europe, including Poland, between Germany and the Soviet Union.

Shortly after Poland's defeat in the 1939 German Blitzkrieg, Podlasie was once again divided, with the Germans getting the southern portion containing Biała Podlaska, and the Soviets taking the north, including Białystok. The years of the Second World War brought with it another painful revival: the villages that in 1863–64 had supported insurgents again became bases for the "forest people"—partisans hiding in Podlasie's forests. The partisans, who upheld the tradition of Poland's armed insurgent service, were recruited mostly from the Podlasian gentry (Lewandowska 1982, 25).

Most of the initial underground resistance quickly consolidated as the Home Army (in Polish, the Armia Krajowa, AK). Its territorial structure reflected the prewar administrative division of Poland (Sikora 2005, 94–95, 117; Piskunowicz 1990, 547; Kopiński 1998, 7). What fundamentally animated the AK was the idea of a countrywide uprising that, at a favorable moment, would liberate Poland with Polish forces. In early 1940, a so-called Plan A was developed to implement this idea. At that time, the first units were formed of the Gwardia Ludowa (People's Guard, GL), the military arm of the communist Polska Partia Robotnicza (Polish Workers' Party, PPR).[2] Until the early postwar years, the Українська повстанська армія (Ukrainian Insurgent Army, UPA) also operated in southern Podlasie, where they observed a ceasefire with the Polish underground (Piskunowicz 1990, 551).

One spectacular action of the Podlasie underground was stealing a German V2 rocket that was meant to be part of the Nazis' "Wunderwaffe." This advanced weapon was the world's first long-range guided ballistic missile, and was used to bomb London, Antwerp, and other cities of the Allies. On May 20, 1944, a rocket launched from a nearby German base fell near Klimczyce in Podlasie. Local peasants were used to seeing "flying torpedoes" that were exploding somewhere in the forest, but this time, the rocket did not explode when it hit the ground. Home Army Intelligence, with the help of locals, quickly masked the live bomb in the rushes of the Bug River. As a result, the Wehrmacht soldiers could not find it. A few days later, two carts drawn by six horses stealthily transported the bomb to a nearby village. After its disassembly, it was moved to the AK's munitions laboratory in Warsaw, where full documentation was prepared. The documentation and the most important parts of the rocket were later sent to London using a special plane (Chociej 2012).

By mid-1943, it had become clear that German occupation of Poland would be ended by the Red Army. A new countrywide uprising plan, code named "Operation Tempest," was conceived as a demonstration of political and military resolve. The underground Government Delegate would act as the host on Polish lands, liberated entirely by AK troops. Podlasie was to be one of the first regions to implement Operation Tempest.

Starting in mid-1944, partisan activities in southern Podlasie intensified in expectation of Operation Tempest. The Lublin Region Headquarters assigned a special role to the Inspectorate of Radzyń Podlaski because the main retreat routes of German troops stationed in the east intersected its territory. For this reason, beginning in May 1944, the region had been fully mobilized. Locally, Operation Tempest lasted from July 21 to 26, 1944, and it was the last stage of the Home Army's war activity in Podlasie. Yet, despite the courage of the Home Army's soldiers, the operation suffered a defeat (Piskunowicz 1990, 551; Kopiński 1998, 21–23).

The Soviets betrayed their Polish allies, who had initiated the anti-German uprising. Because of this, immediately after Operation Tempest, the Home Army's underground network in Podlasie was dissolved after mass arrests were made by the militia, the USSR's Народный комиссариат внутренних дел (People's Commissariat for Internal Affairs, NKVD)[3] (Charczuk 2006), and the emerging Urząd Bezpieczeństwa (Security Office, UB, PUBP).[4] The report of the PUBP, compiled in Radzyń Podlaski on November 30, 1944, detailed, "Due to our actions carried jointly with the NKVD, any plans of the hostile organization AK were neutralized" (IPN Lublin Archive, as quoted in Dąbrowski 2008, 316). Starting in July 1944, the Soviets destroyed the same Home Army units with whom they had liberated the cities of eastern Poland only a few days earlier. By January 1945, thirty thousand partisans were arrested all over Poland, of which sixteen thousand were sent deep into the Soviet Union (Kopiński 1998, 206). Among those remaining in the underground, discipline weakened and banditry appeared.

Postwar Unbroken Soldiers

After another devastating German-Russian war fought on Polish soil, this time Poland was claimed by the Soviets. The brutal German "black death" was gradually replaced by the milder "red plague" of Soviet occupation. During this time, part of southern Podlasie was incorporated into the Soviet Union.

The Soviet Red Army's pushing of German troops out of Podlasie aroused both hope and anxiety in Poland. Announced in July 1944, the manifesto of the Polski Komitet Wyzwolenia Narodowego (Polish Committee of National Liberation, PKWN) and the deceitful actions of the "liberators" against the Polish underground state quickly dispelled any illusions. It became clear that the Soviets and their Polish puppets, *poputchiks*, and other "useful idiots" were about to take over the country.

After a period of despair, once the front moved west to Germany, in 1945, the underground network in Podlasie rebuilt its structure and morale. The units that were active during Operation Tempest were restored, and from March to October 1945, these units reclaimed almost the entire area of the Radzyń Inspectorate. The descendants of the dissolved Home Army created new conspiracy organizations that included, among others, the group Wolność i Niezawisłość (Freedom and Independence, WiN). The communists consistently called all such organizations "bands," implying their illegal and criminal status (Malinowski 1998, 74–82; Piotrowski 2004, 217–19; Dąbrowski 2008, 312, 314–15).

In the early postwar years, resistance in the area of Radzyń was strong. In 1945, the local UB noted that "bands" had carried out sixty-five robberies, including twenty-five at MO stations, as well as thirty "acts of terror" against Soviet soldiers. A report stated that a "total of 128 people were murdered as a result of gang activity" (Dąbrowski 2008, 317–19). Further, there were massive desertions from the communist military service, including 420 Polish soldiers and six militiamen. The subsequent year was similar (Dąbrowski 2008).

The countryside of Podlasie was actively anticommunist. Between 1945 and 1946, many peasants successfully boycotted the obligatory in-kind payments of provisions: grain, potatoes, and milk. A common belief was that this food would go to the USSR. A UB report from the Białystok Voivodeship stated that there were "no provisions coming from some villages. They do not recognize the government"; the substantial scale of this boycott forced the government to lift quotas in 1946 (Górski 2009, 112).

In 1946, the partisans dominated in parts of Podlasie, successfully fighting the expeditions of the UB and the Korpus Bezpieczeństwa Wewnętrznego (Internal Security Corps, KBW). They captured prisons in Białystok, Lublin, Zamość, Radom, and Kielce and released the political prisoners. They also took over entire small towns, including Radomsko, Hrubieszów, and Puławy, robbed trains and banks, dismantled MO posts, and ousted the most hated new local administrators.

In Radzyń, New Year's Day, 1947, was greeted with underground attacks on UB, MO, and KBW facilities of "up to two hundred people led by 'Jastrząb' and 'Kłos,' [who] attacked the Security Office in Radzyń" (Piotrowski 2004, 221). However, this was the swan song of the anticommunist underground. By 1948, the opposition in Podlasie—as well as in the rest of the country—was almost completely pacified, and most of the armed opposition units had ceased operations (Smolarek 2005).

The communist war with the underground brought mass pacifications of the villages, widespread torture, and public executions. Between 1945 and 1948 alone, the fighting had claimed the lives of 8,700 partisans, nearly 9,000 UB, MO, ORMO, KBW, and Polish Army officers and soldiers, and 1,000 Soviet soldiers and NKVD officers. The balance of wartime deaths included about 2,500 sentenced executions, at least 10,000 executions without a sentence, 10,000 deaths in prison "due to natural causes," and the capture of over 100,000 political prisoners (Górski 2009, 115–16). Just in Radzyń, there were 1,790 people who were arrested and went through the cells of the PUBP in the years 1944–54 (Dąbrowski 2008, 311). One of them was Korycki.

The communist strategy of alternating ruthless repression and periodic amnesties yielded results. The number of armed partisans active throughout Poland dropped from one hundred thousand in 1945 to only one thousand in 1949. Numerous arrests caused a decrease in morale and general apathy among the partisans. About fifty thousand of them benefited from the 1947 amnesty, where they hoped to return to a normal life. In 1949 and 1950, Radzyń's PUBP recorded only the activity of "individual former members of the illegal organization WiN-NSZ" (Piotrowski 2004, 226). The anticommunist underground had lost (Dąbrowski 2008, 320–21). Society appeared both intimidated and resigned.

However, in 1950, a second wave of conspiracy started emerging. An underground youth organization called Wolność-Równość-Niezawisłość (Freedom-Equality-Independence, WRN) was founded in Radzyń Podlaski by Jerzy ("Grom") Boguty. Up to seventeen members of WRN were arrested in August of that year. Other organizations followed: the Walka Młodych Bojowników (Struggle of Young Warriors, WMB), a group headed by Józef Korycki; the Związek Ewolucjonistów Wolności (Union of Freedom Evolutionists, ZEW), and the Wolna Idea Polski (Free Idea of Poland, WIP). In the year 1952, the UB attributed eleven robberies to these various groups, including one that attacked a Soviet train. In reality, however, the groups mainly focused on propaganda—editing and distributing anticommunist leaflets, sabotaging communist countryside initiatives, and blocking the formation of production cooperatives (Piotrowski 2004, 224–25; Dąbrowski 2008, 320–22).

Peasants, threatened by forced collectivization, began to organize. The years 1950–52 signified the revival of peasant self-defense and the strengthening of the partisans. In some Podlasie villages, all of the men had been imprisoned by that time. In response, the communist government was forced to make concessions and alleviate the policy in rural communities. This yielded results, and the countryside ceased to be a center of resistance (Górski 2009).

A few groups remaining in the underground continued to fight until the amnesty of April 1956. Their activity in Podlasie effectively ended in October 1956, with the onset of the post-Stalinist "thaw." Between 1957 and 1959, the UB did not record any "hostile activity" in the Radzyń area, or even a single arrest (Piotrowski 2004, 226).

Józef Franczak, nicknamed "Lalek" (Dolly) due to his impeccable appearance and boyish looks, is considered the last "unbroken" partisan of the Polish anticommunist underground. Franczak had volunteered to join the prewar Polish Army and was then forcibly conscripted in August 1944 to serve in the communist Polish Second Army. In January 1945, while stationed in Podlasie, Franczak witnessed the communists murder Home Army soldiers in Kąkolewnica and Uroczysko Baran. He deserted and went into hiding for over eighteen years. Ultimately, he was shot and killed on October 21, 1963, in a raid about one hundred kilometers south of Radzyń Podlaski by thirty-five ZOMO officers under the command of two Służba Bezpieczeństwa (Security Service, SB) officers. The communist prosecutor ordered the decapitation of his dead body (Wieliczka-Szarek 2013).

Postwar guerrilla warfare had no chance to exert a decisive influence on the fate of the country. From the very start of the armed anticommunist resistance in 1946, the combined forces of the MO, ORMO, UB, KBW, and other troops fighting against the underground numbered about 270,000 soldiers and militia, supported by an additional 200,000 Soviet soldiers. The communists manipulated the recruits, who were often called up in western Poland, but then sent to serve in the east and south. The newcomers were told that the partisans were fascists and German collaborators. The regime's military advantage was overwhelming.

## FAMILY: CALL OF FREEDOM

According to official data, Józef, son of Zygmunt and Janina, was born on March 25, 1934, in Radzyń Podlaski, Poland. Radzyń, a small town of about 16,500 inhabitants located within the Lublin Province, is the seat of the county at the heart of Podlasie. Józef came from a poor, working-class family with patriotic traditions. His family name suggests roots in an impoverished branch of the nobility. His family home was located at 27 November Seventh Street (now 27 November Eleventh Street). He grew up there with his father, Zygmunt (born 1897), and mother, Janina (née Celińska, born 1910), along with four brothers: Stanisław (born

1931); Henryk (born 1936); Jan (born 1940); and Władysław (born 1952) (Korycka 2020).

During his childhood and early youth, Józef did not have any problems in school. On the contrary, both in adolescence and, later, in adulthood, he distinguished himself by his cleverness, vast general knowledge, sociability, and charisma. He always cared about his appearance and made sure he was well-groomed. Others perceived him as an enlightened, talented, and, by some accounts, brilliant man with a strong but well-balanced personality and no signs of social maladjustment. Considered tall (over 180 cm), he was strong, muscular, and physically fit. His appearance engendered respect, which was enhanced by a sense of his calmness, firmness, and confidence. His niece described him as a tall, elegant, and smiling man with a long black leather coat and a black hat (Boreczek 2019). In high school, his academic results were slightly above average, but he excelled in sports. He completed his formal education with a high school diploma with honors. Raised in a patriotic spirit, he wanted to study history in college and applied to a university in Lublin but was rejected because of his father's wartime participation in the Home Army.[5]

Józef's father, Zygmunt, had been born out of wedlock with the last name Kot. When Zygmunt met his father as an adult, he changed his last name to that of his father, "Korycki." After World War II, Zygmunt worked as a paramedic. He died in March 1976, when Józef was not yet in hiding and could still attend the funeral.

Józef's mother, Janina, a resourceful person, was a stay-at-home mom who focused on bringing up her five boys. She was unhappy that her beloved son Józef chose such a difficult path in life (Boreczek 2020), and she blamed Zygmunt because he "always was involved in 'such things' [i.e., being a partisan] and now his son [was] doing the same, and she has to tremble in worry about him" (Korycka 2020). Barbara Korycka, Korycki's sister-in-law, believed that it was Józef's mother's right to lament his son's risky choices, but Barbara and the rest of the family were supportive of Józef. Janina saw him only infrequently, but when they met, they had nice, honest conversations. She would repeat, "Child, give up. If you left everything, you could start a new life," but Korycki was already too involved (Korycka 2020) (see Fig. 1.6–1.9).

In fact, it was Korycki's father, a veteran of the Home Army struggle for independence, who imbued young Korycki with his own dislike of communism, which, in time, turned into feelings of contempt and hostility toward the system. Korycki later told a fellow inmate about one

1.6. Józef's mother Janina and father Zygmunt Korycki with their son Władysław, around 1960. *Source*: Archive of Barbara Korycka. Photo of the original by Ernest Szum.

1.7. Zygmunt Korycki (right) and other workers of the Radzyń clinic, around 1960. *Source*: Archive of Barbara Korycka. Photo of the original by Ernest Szum.

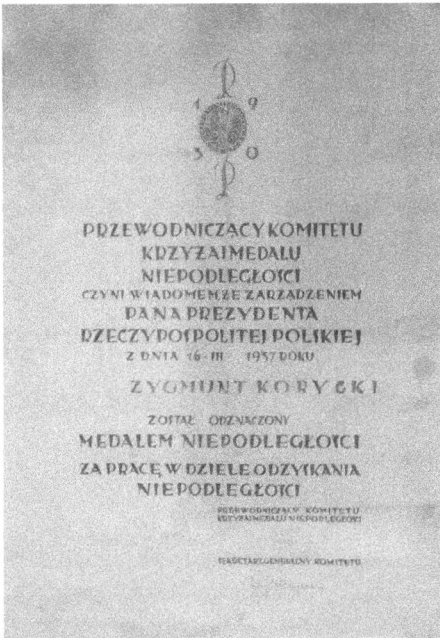

PRZEWODNICZĄCY KOMITETU
KRZYŻA I MEDALU
NIEPODLEGŁOŚCI
CZYNI WIADOMEM ŻE ZARZĄDZENIEM
PANA PREZYDENTA
RZECZYPOSPOLITEJ POLSKIEJ
Z DNIA 16 · III   1937 ROKU

ZYGMUNT KORYCKI

ZOSTAŁ  ODZNACZONY
MEDALEM NIEPODLEGŁOŚCI
ZA PRACĘ W DZIELE ODZYSKANIA
NIEPODLEGŁOŚCI

1.8. In 1937, Zygmunt Korycki obtained the Medal of Independence "in recognition of his work for restoring Polish independence." Recipients of the medal, and after their death their dependents, were entitled to numerous privileges including eligibility for a state pension. *Source*: Archive of Barbara Korycka. Photo of the original by Ernest Szum.

1.9. Józef Korycki (in the middle) at his father's funeral in 1976. He was not hiding at that time and could safely attend the funeral. *Source*: Archive of Barbara Korycka. Photo of the original by Ernest Szum.

of his earliest memories: "He [Korycki] saw a communist for the first time … in 1939. After September 17th, when the Russians entered Poland, the communists in Radzyń grew bold. He remembered a scene: a Polish officer on a motorcycle takes the red flag off the post in the city square. A communist who hung it runs up, screams that it is the end of bourgeois Poland. And this officer shoots him in the head, without dismounting. War. There is no mercy for traitors" (Kaminski 1985b). Years later, Korycki spoke emotionally about how strong an impression this incident made on him. Also, "he [Korycki] remembered Russians. They destroyed everything. He remembered Germans too. Actually, Austrians. Several of them were stationed in the town. His mother washed their shirts and socks. They helped, handed out rationed candy to children. When the order came to march on Russia, they cried. They did not want to die for Hitler. They left pictures. Of wives, children" (Kaminski 1985b).

Józef's relationships with his brothers were very close. Władysław was his favorite, despite being eighteen years younger. Władek always respected Józef, boasted about being his brother, and talked about him with pride. He considered him to be a great man. Władek and Józef even worked together for a while in the forest industry. When Józek was incarcerated, initially in Chełm, and later, at the Rakowiecka Jail, Władysław and his wife, Barbara, visited him regularly. After leaving prison around 1960, Józef lived with his brother Henryk, and there he met Henryk's sister-in-law, Wanda Kurek, the older sister of Henryk's wife, Irena. Soon, the two Korycki brothers were married to the two Kurek sisters (Korycka 2020) (see Fig. 1.10–1.12).

Korycki's civil marriage with Wanda, a worker in a fruit and vegetable processing plant, was short and unhappy. After their son, Sławomir, was born, Wanda was not able to take care of their child properly, possibly because of postpartum depression. When Sławomir was three weeks old, a desperate Korycki wrapped him in a sheepskin coat and brought his son to his mother. His parents took care of their grandson, supported by Irena, Korycki's sister-in-law. Eventually, Sławomir was returned to his mother when he grew older (Korycka 2020).

The marriage ended on a sour note. Once Korycki's mother, anxious that she had not heard from Józef for a long time, went to his home and discovered that he was lying in a cold room with a high fever. Józef's wife and sister-in-law told the older woman that they had been afraid that Józef had pneumonia and so they would not go near him. Józef's father called the emergency services at Biała Podlaska Hospital and got

1.10. From right, Józef Korycki, an unidentified man, brother Stanisław, an unidentified man, and brothers Henryk and Jan, around 1970. *Source*: Archive of Barbara Korycka. Photo of the original by Ernest Szum.

1.11. From bottom right clockwise: Józef's youngest brother Władysław, his wife Barbara with their newborn son Witek, an unidentified woman, and Józef's son and Barbara and Władysław's godson, Sławomir, around 1979. Barbara Korycka helped the authors to reconstruct her family story and offered access to her family photographs. *Source*: Archive of Barbara Korycka. Photo of the original by Ernest Szum.

1.12. Józef Korycki (right) and his brother Henryk, around 1972. *Source*: Archive of Barbara Korycka. Photo of the original by Ernest Szum.

him seen by medical personnel there. In fact, he was diagnosed with pneumonia. After he was discharged from the hospital a few weeks later, Józef refused to return home to his wife. Instead, he moved in with a nurse, a woman named Stanisława, who had taken care of him at the hospital. A "very attractive woman," she was deeply in love with Józef and established some ties with his family (Korycka 2020).

Józef visited his son on a regular basis, and while he did not pay formal alimony, he provided sufficient funding until Sławomir's adulthood. He would visit his son in the evenings, and they would have long conversations. Józef's son was very fond of his father, always enjoying his visits and talking about them with the family. As an adult, Sławomir unsuccessfully and desperately tried to emigrate to Sweden in 1983. He then started binge drinking and died young (Oksiejuk 2018a; Korycka 2020).

One can learn more about Korycki's spiritual and family life from accounts given by him and his relatives, which are quoted in more detail later in this book. The description of his capture in 1982 is a testament to his religiousness and patriotism. Immediately before his arrest, he attempted suicide; but right beforehand, he made the sign of the cross and then shouted, "Long live Poland!" before shooting himself in the head. As is discussed later, he survived. In the last years of his activity, he was in a relationship with a hairdresser from the village of Misie, a woman named Krystyna Oksiejuk; Korycki and Oksiejuk considered getting married in a church but finally decided not to since they were both worried that the ceremony would blow her cover as Józef's secret helper.

From his early youth, Korycki fought his private war against communism in the name of freedom. His anticommunist activity was apparently motivated by an extreme idea of "freedom," understood as the highest value worthy of fighting and suffering for (Bodasiński and Osipowski 2015, Dudziak, 7'14"). In order to pursue this idea, he resorted not only to violent but also to nonviolent methods, including educating the locals by editing and disseminating anticommunist leaflets—sometimes personally nailing them to the door of a church in Radzyń Podlaski—as well as writing letters of protest (see fig. 1.13).

Due to his modus operandi, Korycki was nicknamed by the people of Podlasie—and later by the national media—Janosik from Podlasie or Janosik Podlaski: he stole goods and money from communist stores, freight trains, and local authorities, and distributed the loot among the poor local peasants. He shared the view of many Poles that "communism is illegal." He rebelled against the PRL regime, convinced that he

1.13. The Holy Trinity Church in Radzyń Podlaski. Korycki nailed his various political manifestos to the doors of this church. On August 28, 1986, his funeral mass took place here. Photo by Jacek Karczmarz. License: CC BY-SA 3.0.

was fighting against a government and state established by a foreign power, one that had no legitimacy. Indeed, no fully democratic elections to the Sejm—formally the main center of legislative power—were held in the entire history of the PRL.

## THE RISE AND FALL OF THE PRL

Korycki's adult life spanned almost perfectly the years of the PRL, the puppet state created by the Soviets for Poles after the end of World War II. The PRL, its institutions and functionaries, were Korycki's enemy. The aim of the German occupiers during World War II was the biological elimination of the elites of the *Untermensch* Polish nation, the extermination of all Jews, and the retention of only unskilled labor, with infamous limits on students of a maximum of four grades of education and the ability to count up to 400. The aim of the Soviet occupiers was the ideological enslavement of Poland by slaughtering the Polish elites and compelling the rest to be obedient communists.

The communist takeover in 1944–48 brought profound political, economic, and social changes. Real power fell quickly into the hands of the communist PPR, supported by the powerful Ministry of Public Safety and the Soviet Red Army troops stationed in Poland, which, in the years 1944–47, numbered from two hundred thousand to three million soldiers. Despite somewhat naïvely imposing on Stalin in Yalta a commitment to hold democratic elections, Americans and Britons soon lost interest in the peripheral countries of Central Europe, which they had already begun to call "Eastern Europe." The first secretary of the Central Committee of the PPR, Władysław ("Wiesław") Gomułka, confident in the support of Soviet bayonets, declared ominously and infamously: "We shall not give back the power once obtained" (Gomułka 1945). Indeed, the communists "won" all elections. The 1946 referendum and then the 1947 parliamentary election were falsified with the help of the Soviet NKVD. The communists, using the so-called salami tactic, eliminated their opponents one-by-one: they started with the neutralization of the underground partisans, then the elimination of Stanisław Mikołajczyk's opposition centrist party, the Polskie Stronnictwo Ludowe (Polish People's Party, PSL), followed by the absorption of the socialist Polska Partia Socjalistyczna (Polish Socialist Party, PPS) by the PPR, and the creation of the Polska Zjednoczona Partia Robotnicza (Polish United Workers' Party, PZPR). Finally, even Gomułka

1.14. The auditorium of WSP in Opole on October 6, 1971 after it was blown up by brothers Ryszard and Jerzy Kowalczyk. *Source*: Archiwum Główne Uniwersytetu Opolskiego. Author unknown. Permission: Polish copyright law of 1994 (public domain).

was sidetracked and arrested for "right-wing nationalist deviation." His replacements, who were more subservient Soviet puppets, went ahead with "agricultural reform" and the nationalization of private enterprises.[6] Similar shifts toward orthodoxy took place in other "people's democracies" (Paczkowski 2003, 25–45; Dudek and Zblewski 2008, 10–70; Eisler 1992, 12–32).

The removal of Gomułka from power in 1948 heralded the intensification of repression and the beginning of Stalinism. Crude socialist realism began to reign in the arts, literature, and cinema. In September 1953, Primate Stefan Wyszyński was imprisoned for three years, as he was seen as the most important spiritual leader of Poland. The army was subjected to purges and further sovietization, and attempts to collectivize agriculture were launched. It was not until the death of Stalin, on March 5, 1953, that a slow liberalization process began in the Soviet Union, eventually filtering down also to the satellite states. The thaw culminated on February 25, 1956, when a secret speech by Nikita Khrushchev about Stalinist crimes came to light. The first large wave of strikes occurred in the PRL in June 1956, and on October 21 of that year, Gomułka returned to power (Paczkowski 2003, 46–58; Dudek and Zblewski 2008, 74–154; Eisler 1992, 33–78).

The breakthrough of 1956 and the triumphant return of Gomułka symbolically separates the repressive Stalinist era from a period of less aggressive "real socialism," which, while abandoning plans for a profound social revolution, kept in place the planned economy. The perception of the Soviet system in many countries—from being considered as a highly successful alternative to capitalism to being synonymous with the practical failure of half-baked theories—changed more gradually. Among the important successes of Soviet propaganda were the production of atomic and hydrogen bombs shortly after the Americans, as well as the 1957 launch of Sputnik 1, the first satellite put into space. Moreover, Soviet athletes routinely won most medals in the Summer and Winter Olympics, while other Eastern Bloc countries occupied many of the top ten places throughout these competitions. However, these successes were not translated into a standard of living that could rival the West. With the fall of Stalinism, the communist regimes began to lose their position in cold war competitions and quality-of-life measurements. While Yuri Gagarin still became the first man in space in 1961, the American astronaut Neil Armstrong won the race to the moon in 1969.

In comparison to Western Europe, the PRL began to fall into decline, along with the rest of the Eastern Bloc. Between 1965 and 1990, life expectancy stabilized in the PRL at approximately seventy years, while in West Germany and the United States, despite starting at about the same level, life expectancy systematically increased to reach about seventy-five years. The distance separating the Polish economy from the free market economies of Western Europe also gradually increased. While in 1950 Poland's gross domestic product (GDP) per capita was 102 percent that of Spain's, by 1970 it had fallen to 72 percent; in 1990, after the fall of the communism, it constituted only about 43–45 percent of Spain's GDP at purchasing power parity.[7] The press gained more freedom than it had under Stalinism, but the media still parroted party propaganda. Prospective college students with "inappropriate" family backgrounds were no longer blacklisted, but most students, no matter what their major, had to take a course in the "political economy of socialism," using Oskar Lange's fat textbook. Running your own small business was possible, but the options to do so were quite limited.

Generations of Poles grew up with the belief that "nothing can be done" because "the Russkies would not allow it." The opposition element, shattered and atomized in the years of Stalinism, did not integrate into more permanent structures, but instead, limited itself to more-or-less isolated resistance acts. These acts included "The Letter of 34," written by prominent Polish intellectuals in 1964; the self-immolation of Ryszard Siwiec in 1968; activities of the Ruch (Movement) organization in the late sixties and early seventies; blowing up the auditorium of the Pedagogical University in Opole by two brothers, Ryszard and Jerzy Kowalczyk, in 1971 (see Fig. 1.15); and spontaneous eruptions of unorganized strikes in 1956, 1968, and 1970 (Dudek and Zblewski 2008, 158–220; Eisler 1992, 87–114).

"Our little stabilization"—Tadeusz Różewicz's ironic subtitle to his play *The Witnesses*, which referred to Gomułka's policy of so-called real socialism—meant economic and social stagnation. Reluctantly resigned to the unavoidable view that they would live under communism forever, Poles protected their mental health by telling endless jokes: "What is the difference between democracy and socialist democracy? The same as between a chair and an electric chair." They also quoted delightful *bon mots* of Comrade Wiesław: "Before the war, the Polish peasant had nothing, now he has twice as much," and "In 1945, Poland stood on the edge of the abyss. ... Since then, we have taken a huge leap forward!" It was not until 1976 that the opposition consolidated, and the disintegration of the system gained momentum.

## YOU ANARCHIST!

Korycki started his anticommunist activity early. In a conversation with the Student—recalling that "the Student" was Kaminski's prison nickname—Korycki reminisced:

I came across the Security Service for the first time when I was seventeen. It was called UB then. Boys from "Wilk" ["Wolf," referring probably to Lieutenant Józef Brückner] and "Szary" ["Grey," probably Cadet Józef Chojnacki] were still active in the woods. I was walking with a friend along the edge of the road when a military off-road vehicle cut us off. I did not wait for them to get out. I had a concealed gun and could not allow them to search me. Back then, everyone in Podlasie carried one. I fired all the rounds at them and jumped blindly in the brush. I never saw my friend again. (Kaminski 1985b)

Korycki almost certainly remained unidentified during this first violent rendezvous with the UB. Had he been identified, his punishment would have been severe and could have even led to his death, since armed encounters with the UB were serious offenses.

In 1952, when he was still a high school student, Korycki began to appear on the UB's operational radar. He was seen as an ideological and political enemy and a potential "bandit." One of the Security Service files in Radzyń describes the youth group that Korycki founded in June 1952 under the code name acronym WMB, standing for Walka Młodych Bojowników (The Struggle of the Young Warriors). The Security Service referred to groups of this type as "terrorist-robbery bands."

Today, there is little information about the WMB, but according to the reporting officer, Korycki was only able to recruit three people to his group because the UB soon detected it. An illegal organization, it allegedly planned to publish and distribute anticommunist leaflets, and also to acquire weapons by attacking MO and UB officers. The Security Service files on the WMB were closed with a note stating that members of the group were not tried because of their young age and that only preventive talks were held with them, their parents, and their school headmaster (Dąbrowski 2008, 322). It is possible, however, that young Korycki was also in touch with another local organization, the ZEW, described in the "Postwar Unbroken Soldiers" section, which had tried to unscrew the rails near Międzyrzec Podlaski and had made an unsuccessful attempt to derail the international Moscow–Berlin express train. At the very least, the latter deed probably inspired Korycki to contemplate a similar action in 1982, after General Jaruzelski had introduced martial law.

It is unclear how Korycki's—likely anonymous—encounter with the UB described earlier might be linked to the WMB activity in which he was specifically identified. We strongly suspect that the UB never connected the two events, as apart from the punishment he would have received for the shooting incident, Korycki would have also been much more severely punished for organizing an anticommunist group.

In the PRL, ending one's formal education with high school resulted in an automatic mandatory two-year conscription. College graduates were subject to shorter service. Since Korycki was denied admission to college, in the autumn of 1953, the nineteen-year-old Korycki was drafted into the Polish People's Army. Unsurprisingly, he did not feel comfortable in the ranks of the Communist Army and was not a model soldier (see fig. 1.15).

1.15. Józef Korycki in the army in 1953 or 1954. *Source*: Archive of Barbara Korycka. Photo of the original by Ernest Szum.

Possibly because of his attitude, in 1954, Korycki was sent to a penal company working in a mine (Kaminski 1985b). From the account of another inmate, Zdzisław Celebrak, who was transferred from a Wrocław prison to one of the Silesian mines, we know the situation in the penal mines at the time. Celebrak—like Korycki, a captive miner—recalled:

We were re-uniformed, we got equipment: a helmet, a carbide lamp, they made us look like first-class miners. … We went down with the miners. The foreman tells us to pull the props forward. … It takes us the whole day to pull one. I got a job pressing the conveyor button, I fell asleep, [and] the coal buried me. (Stwora 1993, 25–26)

Korycki worked hard in the mine. However, his foreman was intent on applying corporal punishment. Once, down in the mine, the fore-man slapped a soldier who happened to be Korycki's friend. In a surge of anger, Korycki pushed the foreman into the elevator, closed the door, and sent him upstairs. For this act, he had to report to the commander in charge of the mine—a Soviet colonel—who scornfully screamed in his face, "You anarchist!" Korycki lost his temper. He grabbed the colo-nel's gun, took the Soviet at gunpoint, and led him outside the gate. There, he let the colonel free, which likely saved him from an abduction charge. Apparently, the humiliated Soviet covered up the incident.

Once outside the gate, Korycki decided to escape. Interestingly, one of the mine guards joined him. They walked only at night and slept in the fields or in the woods during the day. Korycki wrote and mailed a letter to Poland's minister of national defense, wanting the ministry to know what had really taken place. Meanwhile, Korycki's desertion attracted the curiosity of not only the Wojskowa Służba Wewnętrzna (Military Internal Service, WSW) but also the UB and the MO, all of which sought his capture. Finally, both deserters came forward. They were taken to Wrocław. At the trial, Korycki bluntly blurted out and spoke about the humiliation of a fellow man and the insult to the uni-form of a Polish soldier, as well as about his own behavior as a sincere expression of outrage. This was the first time that Korycki's pronounce-ments caught the attention of the newspapers (Kaminski 1985b).

Since Korycki's escape from the army occurred during the so-called "thaw" after Stalin's death, he got a relatively short sentence. The UB locked him in a dark, solitary-confinement cell. After serving six months, he was released under an amnesty. As he was leaving, he said, "the light made him narrow his eyes. But it was not bright out-side. It was evening, streetlights were on, and it was snowing. The world seemed like a fairy tale."[8] Korycki was still a healthy young man at the time and had a strong mind, so he recovered in due time. He owed his relatively short prison sentence to the political situation, which brought a broad amnesty for many. Celebrak, another deserter from the mine, who escaped under less dramatic circumstances, was only sentenced to three months in prison (Stwora 1993, 27–28).

Korycki was a free man again, but can one truly speak of freedom in post-Stalinist Poland? In any event, his half-freedom did not last long.

After serving that first sentence, he was quickly sent back to prison and served time for petty theft, burglary, and illegal possession of weapons. In 1965, together with local Roma, he burglarized the family crypt of the Korwin-Szlubowski family, former landowners from the Radzyń Podlaski area (Zawada 2011, 144–45; see fig. 1.16). For this crime, he was sentenced to two years. He did not serve this sentence in full, however. After serving a year and a half, he managed to escape from the prison in Czarne because he worked outside the prison walls in a local sawmill (Kaliński 2018).

After the escape, Korycki hid in unpopulated areas, rarely venturing into surrounding villages. During one of his rare "trips," he managed to obtain firearms and ammunition. Korycki was able to survive in extreme conditions. He foraged in the woods near Włodawa, where, in the vicinity of Adampol, he constructed a dugout that served as his main shelter for a time. After a while, Korycki allegedly voluntarily reported back to prison to finish his sentence, but he was quickly released due to another amnesty (jch 1982).

During his time in hiding, Korycki received both material help and emotional support from the surrounding villages (Zajączkowska 2012), where "he would [flirt] with local [village] girls, eat, drink, and disappear" (Kaminski 2004a). He no longer kept in touch with his wife. In the PRL at that time, an inmate's wife had the right to dissolve the marriage unilaterally, and this is probably how his marriage formally ended. However, during the winter months, he sometimes lived with single women—both unmarried women and widows. Yet, with one exception, which we discuss in much greater detail later, Korycki did not engage in any lasting emotional relationships with any of these women.

The next stage in Korycki's life was his stay in Biała Podlaska. After being released from prison in 1969 under the amnesty program, and after serving part of another sentence with Jacek Kuroń in 1970–71, in the summer of 1971, Korycki settled in a rented room and took up a job in Biała Podlaska. There, he was employed as a clerk by the Zakład Komunikacji Miejskiej (Municipal Transportation Company, ZKM). After three weeks of work, Korycki took advantage of having access to company money and embezzled a considerable amount. Using these funds, he organized a new underground group. From among the people he met in Biała Podlaska, Korycki chose several convicts whom he considered capable of undertaking not only anticommunist but also criminal activities with him. He used the money he had embezzled from the ZKM to arm the group, and they swore an oath of loyalty and secrecy to

1.16. The crypt of the Korwin-Szlubowski family burglarized by Korycki and associates in 1965. Photo by Jacek Karczmarz. License: CC BY-SA 3.0.

their leader. However, while preparing for a series of planned jobs, one of these men sold out Korycki to the militia. The group ceased to exist, and in October 1971, Korycki was sentenced to four years' imprisonment by the verdict of the County Court in Biała Podlaska (jch 1982).

After his release from this incarceration, Korycki returned to business as usual, which he considered to be undermining the communist social order. Disguised in the uniform of a militia captain, Korycki inspected the financial documents in one of the Podlasie health centers and imposed a fine on the manager for detected "irregularities." Then he proceeded to direct traffic and collect ticketed fines from drivers with dysfunctional cars, all, of course, without providing receipts (jch 1982).

After Korycki was released once again from another prison sentence, Captain Romuald Dudziak, the head of the Criminal Department of the MO Provincial Headquarters in Siedlce, stated that the militia attempted to create a legal workplace for Korycki. For this reason, he was employed in the forest inspectorate as a money courier, delivering pay to forest workers in various forester units. Korycki took this job and, contrary to what some would likely have expected from a man in and out of prison, he did not try to steal any money. It was, after all, the private money of the workers with no connection to the communists, so he fulfilled his duties honestly. A month or two later, however, he decided to quit because he felt restricted. Dudziak recalled that Korycki "had to be a free man, as he called it," and "he had to move not where he was told to go, but where he wanted to go, and [to not do] what someone told him [to do], but what he thought right and necessary" (Bodasiński and Osipowski 2015, Dudziak, 7'14").

After he left the job, in January 1977, Korycki and one of his local friends broke into a liquor store in Janów Podlaski, where they took both alcohol and cash. In March of that year, he was active in the vicinity of Łuków. In Aleksandrów, he broke into a grocery store, where he was "caught red-handed" by two militia officers. He tried to run away, shooting, but without success, and thus, he was caught and arrested yet again (jch 1982, 14).

He was again given a short sentence, ending with parole, and therefore Korycki was soon back out on the street, but, once again, not for long. He was imprisoned again in June 1978, this time receiving a three-year sentence, which ultimately ended with another—the last— conditional release in October 1979 (jch 1982). There are two differing accounts describing this last arrest. A militiaman, Jan Skrzypiec, and his militia colleague, Romuald Dudziak, recalled the first one in two slightly different versions; the second one was given by Skrzypiec alone. One of these narratives seems to relate to this event, and it is possible that the other one was referencing a previous arrest.

According to the first account, Skrzypiec received a report from Łuków about an attack and a shoot-out involving Korycki. The incident took place at the residence of Władysław Jeż, the president of the Powiatowy Związek Gminnych Spółdzielni (County Association of Municipal Cooperatives, PZGS). Pompously, Skrzypiec stated, "I arrived with my people in battle formation." Once on site, militia officers found Korycki, who had fired four shots into the ceiling of the room with an illegal weapon. The militia took his gun away and detained him at the local militia station. It turned out that their detainee had a sentence—as Skrzypiec put it, "conditional or suspended"—so, on that account, he was arrested and transported back to prison (Bodasiński and Osipowski 2015, Skrzypiec, 3'35").

Romuald Dudziak, presenting a slightly different version of these events, stated that Korycki had committed many crimes in the area. During an attempt to break into the shop of Agricultural Cooperative, militia on patrol startled him, and as he tried to use his weapon, his gun jammed (Bodasiński and Osipowski 2015, Dudziak, 3'58"). The

investigation led to Korycki's arrest, and then his conviction, incorpo-
rating the assault on Władysław Jeż as well (Bodasiński and Osipowski
2015, Skrzypiec, 4'08").

In the second, separate account, the story begins with two militia
officers, Skrzypiec and Kamiński, receiving a tip that Korycki was at his
residence. They went there to arrest him for weapons possession. The
initiator of the action was Captain Kamiński. When Skrzypiec knocked
and announced the arrival of the militia, the host opened the door with
a pistol in his hand. The militiamen also had their weapons drawn and
ready. Skrzypiec later stated, "if only he had moved, I would have shot
him." For a moment, there was a psychological duel, but Korycki did
not behave aggressively. Ordered by Kamiński to lay down his gun, Korycki did so. He was then taken to the militia station and placed into
custody (Bodasiński and Osipowski 2015, Skrzypiec, 10'45"). No matter
which version of the events is correct—this report may have described
Korycki's last arrest in 1978 or one of his earlier captures—Korycki was
convicted and sentenced in court, but, as mentioned above, he was released early again, in October 1979 (Bodasiński and Osipowski 2015,
12'36").

That same autumn, when Korycki got out of prison after his final
conditional release, he took one more look at what we called "communist freedom"—at the poverty of the villages of Podlasie—and decided
to return to the forest (Kaminski 1985b). Contrary to the official propaganda, social inequalities in the villages of Podlasie were significant. The
lives of the poorest residents were miserable. Korycki felt that "it can't
be that way any longer." He couldn't stand the "communist normalcy":

> Sometimes, he took a motorcycle and rode through town in
> broad daylight. Or he would walk into a restaurant in big style
> and buy vodka for everyone. He had a grand gesture. He liked
> to live large. Once he met a militia patrol. They pretended not to
> recognize him. And his hand was already wandering under his
> jacket. Only, he did not carry anything on him this time. (Ka-
> minski 1985b)

Such conduct meant that "the communists were afraid of him and the
people respected him" (Kaminski 1985b). The overall negative emotions felt by Korycki reflected the mood of almost all of Polish society.
These feelings were bound to explode, which they finally did during the
"Solidarity Carnival" in 1980.

## BANDIT IN COMMUNIST PROPAGANDA, JANOSIK IN FOLK SENTIMENT

For Polish communists and their propaganda, Korycki was a common bandit. The communist leadership recognized that he exposed the flimsy legitimacy of their power and reinforced society's drive for freedom. Korycki's activity quickly became a painful stain on the sugary-sweet propaganda image painted by the Communist Party. However, directing fire at a dangerous dissident is hardly specific to communists. All government-run mass media in autocracies create distorted images of enemies and demonize the state's foes.

Television, magazines, and newspapers, all under communist control, worked hard to create a negative image of Korycki. In the mass media, his name was always prefaced by epithets such as "bandit," "murderer," "felon," or "dangerous criminal." Even many years after his death, locals recalled how the media tried to scare them, saying that "Korycki would come and attack them in their own homes."[9] Thus, while Korycki received a lot of emotional and material support from local people, some people echoed the official propaganda's enmity. This hostility was not only directed toward him, but also at Korycki's family members, who were subject to hostile comments and avoided talking about him when children were listening (Boreczek 2019). His sister-in-law, when she was introduced to new people, heard many times, "Korycka, from those bandits?" His brother, Władysław, despite stellar academic credentials, was denied employment as a professional soldier due to the bad reputation of his brother (Korycka 2020).

Among the media, local newspapers especially ran intensive "black campaigns" against Korycki. They repeatedly and with no factual basis suggested that he was coercing help through acts of intimidation (see jch 1982; ch 1982; Borkowski 1982). For example, a newspaper article about Korycki, published in the official communist newspaper, *Word of Podlasie*, in Biała Podlaska, concluded with the statement: "despite the intensive activities of the MO, this currently most dangerous criminal—not only in the Voivodeship but also in the country—remains at large. How much longer? It also depends on the help that the public can lend to authorities" (jch 1982) (see fig. 1.17).

Former militiamen and the regime's journalists portray Korycki and his activities in a negative light. Colonel Płócienniczak, chief militia propagandist and later police journalist, was especially active in denigrating him, setting the direction for other communist propagandists

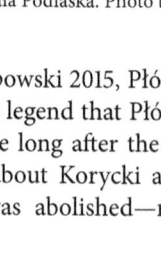

1.17. Newspaper clippings from the communist press in Podlasie (1982). *Source*: Miejska Biblioteka Publiczna in Biała Podlaska. Photo by Ernest Szum.

(Bodasiński and Osipowski 2015, Płócienniczak, *passim*). Surprisingly, it turned out that the legend that Płócienniczak constructed remained the most popular one long after the fall of communism. Most of the columnists writing about Korycki after 1989—when the communist media censorship was abolished—merely repeated the communist propaganda narrative with minor, commercially catchy, modifications. For example, an investigative journalist, Piotr Pytlakowski, who reproduced content from earlier press publications, wrote a typical sample story in this spirit: "At the beginning of the 1980s, during martial law, Józef Korycki's gang prowled the vicinity of Międzyrzec Podlaski. They were guilty of dozens of armed robberies and several killings. Legends about the robber's trail circulated in the villages" (Pytlakowski 2006, 47). This text does not uncover any new information, and it also contains glaring factual errors, since, during Poland's period of martial law, Korycki remained in hiding and did not commit any assaults, much less murders. Moreover, Korycki's group, described by Pytlakowski as "a gang," no longer existed.

Kazimierz Kunicki and Tomasz Ławecki (2017) published a more objective and relatively reliable outline of Korycki's activities, although the authors' account drew from secondary sources. These authors refrained from using epithets like "murderer" or "bandit" in relation to Korycki.

Journalists writing about Korycki often justified their copying of communist stories by arguing that they were "creatively interpreting" those stories. They demonized his actions and ignored popular accounts that depicted the man as an anticommunist patriot. They presented Korycki as an ordinary criminal who did not deserve any respect and barely mentioned his fight for freedom.

In spite of the efforts undertaken by the communists to win over the people who were helping Korycki, they were unsuccessful. In many minds in Podlasie, Korycki functioned as both a hero and a benefactor. He stole from the rich and powerful—the communist state—and gave to the poor and oppressed—the rural inhabitants of Podlasie. There are numerous reports of cases when he neither accepted any private property of village mayors nor stole the private salaries of workers despite having easy access to the money.

In the area where he operated, the local perception was unmistakably positive. Even though he was sometimes forced to cooperate with the militia and Special Forces in their pursuit of Korycki, a forest ranger who knew him painted a flattering image of the man:

It was not that he was some thug, a dangerous man, or that he attacked people. He was mild-tempered and had really good relationships with people, and that's why they were willing to help him. People liked that he fought against the authorities, against

communists. And for us, for bystanders, he was not a threat. He
had such a quirk that he liked weapons, explosives, it thrilled
him, but for the locals he was not dangerous. And on the other
hand, whenever he stole something, for example, a TV from a
freight wagon at a railway station, he gave it away to someone
poor. (Czajka 2018)

Further, Korycki's life partner confirmed, "he had nothing. He stole the
communist stuff and the tax money from village mayors. He always
quickly gave everything away" (Oksiejuk 2018a).

Korycki had many loyal supporters who participated in the risk-
taking and offered him long- or short-term shelter. One of his hosts,
Mr. Kuczyński, did not betray him until the end when the militia was
searching his house looking for the rebel (Bodasiński and Osipowski
2015, Raczuk, 15'05"). Korycki also received a lot of help from former
Home Army partisans and liaison officers (as well as their children),
who felt they were contributing to the fight against communism in this
way (Kaliński 2018). Korycki had no problem obtaining any weapons he
needed since the former partisans provided them generously, including
one attempt to give him a working T-34 tank. Indeed, the villagers and
partisans liked and respected him. Stories abound about Korycki boldly
entering a tavern in Witoroż, where he drank, joked, and then disappeared. When the militia arrived to try to capture him, nobody helped
them; in fact, the customers made subtle fun of the militia by providing
disparate characterizations of the culprit's appearance (Kaliński 2018;
jch 1982, 10).

After Korycki's arrest in 1982 and his death in 1986, his legend
survived. In fact, some did not believe he had died. A neighbor once
asked Józef's sister-in-law, "Mrs. Korycka, is that true that you buried an empty coffin? And he got out and is still out there, fighting as a
partisan?" (Korycka 2020). Mrs. Korycka then added, "For me, he was
a wonderful man. I remember him with the highest respect." Later, a
young resident of Podlasie wrote in a 2012 blog post under the pseudonym dodek777, "I come from Podlasie, born 1976, so when I grew up,
Korycki was only a legend, but I remember that we played [imperson-
ated] 'Korycki' in our backyards." There is also a story from Korycki's
niece, who recalled how a traffic policeman stopped her shortly after
the fall of communism. When she presented her driver's license with
her maiden name "Korycka," the policeman, clearly a recent militiaman, became interested. When he learned that Józef was her uncle, he

sighed and commented, "He was a super fellow." She believed that even before the end of communism, many militiamen did not want to catch her uncle (Boreczek 2020).

After his death, Korycki's legend helped his son to get employment at a local business. Franciszek Stadnicki employed Sławomir Korycki—sadly, then an alcoholic—exclusively due to his respect for Korycki (Korycka 2020). A local historian wrote to Korycki's life partner that, thanks to Korycki's courage and her help, Korycki had become a symbol of the fight against communism in Podlasie, and later, in all of Poland. The historian stated that she was teaching children about his patriotism and his fight for an independent Poland.[10] As recently as 2019, during a lengthy meet-the-author gathering in Radzyń Podlaski, the audience of approximately fifty participants who were attending spoke of Korycki fondly as their local anticommunist hero. There were no dissenting voices.[11]

For their part, communist journalists, while painting Korycki's legend in exclusively dark colors, from time to time let facts slip about his ideological motivation that were inconsistent with their propaganda. For example, newspaper reports describing one of his first robberies, that of a village mayor in Hołowno, acknowledged that he refused to accept the mayor's private money and was clearly only interested in the communist money (Borkowski 1982; jch 1982; Zajączkowska 2012).

Both interestingly and surprisingly, some militiamen and Special Forces officers who dealt with him frequently have spoken about Korycki positively and respectfully but only after the fall of communism when the state's propaganda gags no longer silenced them. Their accounts, perhaps accidentally, both corroborated Korycki's Janosik legend and contradicted the earlier communist propaganda. Militiamen who were most involved in his hunt and capture have admitted, somewhat reluctantly, that "he was considered a little bit of a local hero since he did not steal from the poor" (Bodasiński and Osipowski 2015, Płócienniczak, 0'40"). Further, "Generally, he was considered Janosik, that he saved the poor. … There was an opinion about him that to refer to Janosik movies they more or less considered him. Well, he did not hurt anybody" (Bodasiński and Osipowski 2015, Skrzypiec, 8'57"; the formulation of sentences approximates the original language). There is also a statement from a Special Forces member who was involved in the manhunt who confirmed that Korycki stole state property to distribute it among the poor: "This is why he had such  …  strong social support. The problem was that his activity was illegal. … Locals loved him and hid him from us" (Schwertner and Baczyński 2019). Indeed, the 2005 movie about Korycki, *Janosik z Podlasia*, based exclusively on the accounts of former militiamen and accepting their version of events, ended with the acknowledgment: "Until today, the residents of Podlasie talk about their Janosik. Some recall him with contempt, others with fondness."

The question of whether Korycki was a "partisan" or a "bandit" continues to come up. We need to remember that initially only Korycki's adversaries—communist apparatchiks and Security Service officers—told his story. Long after the fall of communism, others mechanically repeated this legend created for propaganda reasons, and it has become deeply embedded in collective memory. A more objective account of this rebellious man is worthy of an honest retelling.

# Public Enemy

## October 1979–May 14, 1982

> Everyone who rebels should be shot.
> —Lev Davidovich Bronstein, aka Leon Trotsky

The last phase of Korycki's activity took place during the acceleration of the collapse of socialism in the late seventies and early eighties. From a romantic rebel and robber who was not a real threat to the communist system, Korycki became the communists' "Public Enemy No. 1." At one point, a special team coordinated the search for Korycki. In addition to the militia and the army, this team sent helicopters and armored personnel carriers to fight him. Meanwhile, his activities began to be a serious image problem for the communists. Not only was he acting against the "people's" authorities—often ridiculing communist organizations and officers—but he was also receiving popular support from the Podlasie community. Firm action and loud laughter at the authorities were powerful weapons in undermining the legitimacy of communist rule.

### CONSUMER AND CREDIT CRISIS OF THE LATE GIEREK PERIOD

The "opening to the West" by Edward Gierek in the early 1970s created consumption fever. State credit drawn from Western banks financed this excessive consumption, and this cycle soon turned out to be unsustainable. On June 24, 1976, the government of Premier Piotr Jaroszewicz made a veiled announcement about drastic price increases for many necessities, especially sugar. The message sparked a wave of strikes in Ursus, Radom, and nearly a hundred other places. The authorities quickly pacified the strikers. Radom's "fitness trails," which involved chasing detainees through a row of militiamen who beat them with batons, became symbols of militia brutality.

Both the attempts to raise prices and the strikes were strong predictors of what appeared to be an imminent overheating of the economy and the country's problems with paying off foreign loans. Poland's GDP, calculated according to purchasing power parity, decreased by about 20 percent between 1978 and 1982 (World Economics n.d.; IMF 2018). The regime had given society the chance to taste the delights of Western consumption and now deprived it of them. Social frustration grew.

As the economy deteriorated, centers of social and political resistance to communism emerged. There were two catalysts to that process: The first was the strikes of June 1976. The second was the changes to the PRL's Constitution announced by the communists—referred to colloquially as the "alliance and control"—which were constitutional amendments requiring official alliance with the Soviet Union and the establishment of a formal leadership role for PZPR, the communist party. In 1976, the Komitet Obrony Robotników (Workers' Defense Committee, KOR) was established, and in 1977, the Ruch Obrony Praw Człowieka i Obywatela (Movement for Defense of Human and Civic Rights, ROPCiO) was founded. After the first underground publishing house, the Nieocenzurowana (later: Niezależna) Oficyna Wydawnicza (Independent Publishing House, NOWa), was founded in 1977, others followed. This soon created a powerful decentralized structure of underground media consisting of over one hundred underground publishing houses, hundreds of magazines, underground cinemas and theaters, and, later, Radio Solidarity. In 1978, the Wolne Związki Zawodowe (Free Trade Unions, WZZ) were established in Silesia and the Baltic seacoast region—precursors to the independent trade union called Solidarity.

In the face of growing political ferment throughout the country, an extraordinary event occurred in the late seventies at the Vatican. On October 16, 1978, the College of Cardinals elected Karol Wojtyła, Archbishop of Kraków, as pope; he took the name John Paul II. John Paul's visit to Poland in June 1979 contributed to the radicalization of the mood with a simple message, "Do not be afraid." At that time, the pope, referencing Bible verses, spoke these famous words: "I am calling. I—the son of the Polish soil, and I—John Paul II, the Pope. I am calling from the depths of this Millennium. ... I am calling with you all: Let Thy Spirit descend! Let Thy Spirit descend and renew the face of the land. *This land!*" (Wehikuł czasu 2013). These words not only electrified millions of Poles, but also prepared them spiritually for the upcoming political changes.

Meat and sausage price increases, which went into effect on July 1, 1980, lit the fuse. On that day, the first strikes broke out and quickly spread across Poland, reaching a scale that prevented easy pacification. After attempts to extinguish the strikes or to manipulate strikers failed, on August 31, a government delegation signed the "August Agreements" in Gdańsk with the Międzyzakładowy Komitet Strajkowy (Inter-factory Strike Committee, MKS), the main committee leading the strikes. Among the twenty-one more or less important postulates, the first one turned out to be the most significant; this was the demand to have free trade unions independent of the PZPR. Thus, the independent trade union Solidarity was registered on September 17 (Paczkowski 2003, 108–13; Dudek and Zblewski 2008, 272–304; Eisler 1992, 115–66).

In 1980, several strike committees, including the largest one, the MKS in Gdańsk, joined forces to become the Solidarity free trade union. It declared its purpose to be the protection of workers' rights. Over time, the various strike committees developed into the local founding committees of Solidarity. Later, up until 1989, Solidarity gradually evolved into a social movement and became the most important center of opposition against communism. In addition to Solidarity, in 1980 and 1981, other related organizations were created, such as Solidarność Chłopska (Farmers' Solidarity, SCh) and the Niezależne Zrzeszenie Studentów (Independent Student Union, NZS) (Friszke 2011).

Amid the economic downturn, lengthening queues, and disappointed social expectations, and also the diminishing fear of repression, Korycki attempted his last contest with communism in 1979. The time of this last activity coincided with the birth of Solidarity, and with the joyful breath of freedom that ended with the imposition of martial law on December 13, 1981. Throughout this era, Poles had increasingly begun to reject the very idea of socialism and rebel against not only its "distortions" but also the very nature of the system.

## ON JANOSIK'S TRAIL

In his last battle with communism, Korycki's activity achieved an increasingly higher profile. Due to his "extremism," the communist authorities declared him a dangerous criminal. Consequently, state media called him a bandit, a terrorist, and a public enemy to the country. The regime's functionaries also tried to weaken his social base and to paint him as an enemy of the "the working people of towns and villages" (see, e.g., Paluch 1981). Still, although he was considered an enemy of the communist state, most locals did not perceive Korycki as their enemy. For many people of Podlasie, Korycki was symbolic of the broad disapproval and civil resistance they felt toward the hated authority imposed on them by a foreign power.

One day, something unbelievable happened: a delegation of peasants offered Korycki a Soviet T-34 tank, which lay hidden in a barn (see fig. 2.1). However, although the tank was technically sound, Korycki did not accept the gift due to the tank's lack of ammunition. It is clear that he did not think about using the tank for any type of more aggressive action.

Some later questioned this anecdote, and others characterized it as part of Korycki's exaggerated mythologization. However, Korycki laughed while recalling the anecdote and clearly relived the whole situation, stating that, to paraphrase Korycki, he "regretted a little bit that he had been unable to accept the gift." The Student considered the story credible, given the psychological circumstances in which Korycki told it to him (Kaminski 2004a, 176; Kaminski 2018, email 3).

Korycki had some personal disagreements with PRL officials from whom he stole "communist money" on his expropriation expeditions. But these were quite exceptional situations, because, according to the previously cited Skrzypiec, "he was generally regarded as Janosik" (Bodasiński and Osipowski 2015, Skrzypiec, 8'58"), and even the chief propagandist Płócienniczak admitted that Korycki "was considered a hero" (Bodasiński and Osipowski 2015, Płócienniczak, 0'35"). Another prominent militiaman, Dudziak, stated that the inhabitants of Podlasie, thought of Korycki as a "good uncle" because "when he broke into a store and seized food, everyone profited" (Bodasiński and Osipowski 2015, Dudziak, 8'36").

It is no wonder, then, that various state officials, such as village mayors and employees of the state institutions that he robbed, were hostile to him. If he knew that someone was a communist, he would confront that person, "You son of a bitch, whom are you serving? Poland or Russia?" He would often ridicule and intimidate these people by ordering them to resign from office within one day. Such humiliating treatment was bound to make enemies. According to Korycki, he never had to repeat his instructions twice, since the village mayors always obediently accepted his orders (Kaminski 1985b).[1]

2.1. A famous Soviet World War II T-34 tank erected as a Red Army monument close to the border with Belarus. Presently, it is a tourist attraction with the memorial plate removed. In the 1980s, local peasants chopped off the cannon of the tank and rewelded it so that it faced the Soviet Union. After World War II, many defunct T-34s littered the Soviet Bloc as so-called Monuments of Victory. An identical tank in working condition was offered to Korycki. Photo by Ernest Szum.

Korycki left the prison in Chełm on October 5, 1979. The warden of the penitentiary unit had again applied for his conditional early release. The application to the Chełm Voivodeship Court highlighted the prisoner's exemplary behavior throughout his entire period of imprisonment, as well as his diligent community service, his paid work (which he used to pay child support), and his interest in family matters. During his parole hearing, Korycki declared before the penitentiary judge that he would take up a job after his release, adding, "And I am honest at work" (Zajączkowska 2012). However, Korycki probably understood this declaration differently than the judge did.

After leaving prison, Korycki once again ignored the obligations imposed on him by the court. He did not contact the probation officer in Radzyń Podlaski appointed to supervise him, nor did he take up a job. He also ignored his formal duty to provide child support, but he did secretly pass money to his family without disclosing this fact to the authorities because the funds had come from criminal activities (Zajączkowska 2012).

After each stay in prison, Korycki became better organized. Thus, after leaving prison in 1979, he was immediately ready for action. He was well acquainted with the area where he worked and familiar with the local residents. He also chose not to work alone any longer; he always had at least a few friends around him who formed a well-organized group (Bodasiński and Osipowski 2015, Dudziak 2005, 5'02"; Bodasiński and Osipowski 2015, Skrzypiec 2005, 9'30"). Unsurprisingly, the communist authorities and the militia routinely referred to them as a "band." At this stage of his activity, Korycki was receiving help and shelter in the small village of Misie from Krystyna Oksiejuk, with whom he later became involved romantically, maintaining the relationship until his death (Oksiejuk 2018a).

The authors of this volume interviewed Oksiejuk in 2018 when she was eighty-four years old, and although time had blurred some of her memories, she still remembered well those associated with Korycki, discussing them with strong emotions:

> I met Józek at the end of 1979. At that time, I lived in Misie with my ten-year-old daughter, Agnieszka. My mother, brother Jan, and sister-in-law Krystyna lived in the house next door. There were several outbuildings around our neighboring houses. And one day, I saw Józek in the barn. … He said he had been hiding there for several days and watched us to see if he could trust us. He also said that he did not eat anything during these days, but he did not ask for anything. I brought him food and said he could stay. I took pity on him. (Oksiejuk 2018a)

In total, Korycki hid in Misie for two and a half years. At first, he stayed in the barn on the Oksiejuk farm, and then, in Oksiejuk's home. Initially, she hid him in a kitchen that was equipped with a lock, and later gave him the smaller of two rooms (Oksiejuk 2018a). Oksiejuk recalled,

> There were two rooms in my house: one larger [about 5 meters by 8 meters], the other, smaller [about 3 meters by 6 meters], and a kitchen. I decided that Józek would move in with us. Agnieszka and I took the larger room. I was a hairdresser at the time, seeing male and female customers at home. Nobody suspected me

of anything because many people came to see me. There were not as many hairdressers at the time as there are now, so people came to me from all over the area. I had a lot of work and earned good money. I could feed Józek, who lived with us now at home. He occupied this small room, and my daughter and I were in the larger one. (Oksiejuk 2018a; see figs. 2.2–2.5).

Oksiejuk's hairdressing work meant that there were always strangers in her home, which gave her an alibi but also posed a threat to both Korycki and her. She described their solution to this problem in the following way:

In his room, there was a bed, a table, and a chair. He sat there quietly listening to the radio. In winter, he made himself a hideout. The floor was made of wooden planks, so Józek lifted a few boards, dug out the sand that was underneath, and made a hole there. It was the length and width of his body and he could barely fit in there lying down. Many people were coming to my house to have their hair cut and styled. All the time, Józek was in the next room, and he had to hide in the hole in the floor. He lay there for a long time, but it was safer. Only Agnieszka and I knew about this hideout. (Oksiejuk 2018a) (see fig. 2.6).

Oksiejuk continued her narrative in a voice full of emotion: "He always had a gun next to him, a pistol [actually, a Nagant revolver] and a rifle—this Kalashnikov [actually, a PPSz submachine gun colloquially called a "Pepesha"]. He told me that if the militia ever came and found him there, I should get down on the floor. Or if they suddenly came [into the] house when he was there. I believed that in such a situation, he would not be taken alive and [that they] would shoot" (Oksiejuk 2018a). Even though Oksiejuk realized the seriousness of the situation, she agreed to place herself in harm's way. Yet she also tried not to focus on anything negative; instead, she enjoyed what was good: "On Sundays, we were together longer, because usually no one came to see me," she recalled with nostalgia. "Józek would even play Ping-Pong with Agnieszka; they came to like each other" (Oksiejuk 2018a).

During this period, Oksiejuk was the one person closest to Korycki. She fed and sustained him. They talked a lot and got to know each other better: "He gained confidence in me, and I began to trust in him. He was gentle, kind, friendly. We came to like each other quickly. He

2.2. Krystyna Oksiejuk, Józef Korycki's life partner in the years 1979–86 (2018). Photo by Ernest Szum.

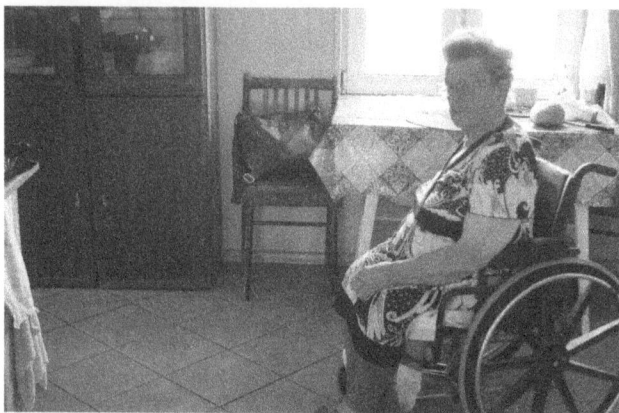

2.3. Krystyna Oksiejuk in the kitchen. Initially, the kitchen was the place where Korycki was hiding and living (2018). Photo by Ernest Szum.

2.4. Misie 107, Oksiejuk's house (2018). Photo by Ernest Szum.

2.5. Backyard of Oksiejuk's house. Before he revealed himself to Oksiejuk, Korycki hid in a barn that was located near the trees (2018). Photo by Ernest Szum.

2.6. The small room in Oksiejuk's house with a hideout beneath the floor dug by Korycki (2018). Photo by Ernest Szum

would talk about his different adventures, these court trials and all that" (Oksiejuk 2018a). Over time, their increasingly emotional relationship turned into love. As Oksiejuk remembered sentimentally, "Józek and I got to know each other very well and we fell in love. We were very close. Józek suggested going to church and talking to the priest and secretly getting a church wedding. But somehow I was scared and we did not do it" (Oksiejuk 2018a). Still, the lack of a formal marriage certificate did not prevent them from forming a close relationship.

However, their deepening relationship intensified Korycki's anxiety about the fate of the woman and her daughter in the case of his arrest. As Oksiejuk remembered it, "Later, he did not want to be there because he was afraid for me. My mother said that my brother and sister-in-law were very unhappy that he was there. He was afraid that if they informed on him, I would be in trouble as well because I was hiding him." Korycki, concerned, told her: "You know what punishment you are facing for harboring me? Five years, and you have a child." (Oksiejuk 2018b). Indeed, in the eighties, if the authoritieshad found out that Oksiejuk had been hiding Korycki and providing him help, she would certainly have been imprisoned for years. Such an act, according to PRL's Penal Code, was punishable by up to five years in prison, and as an associate of a "dangerous bandit," she would have very likely received a long sentence.

Only a few weeks after his parole in October 1979, Korycki became the leader of a new group, this one composed of young and less experienced people, all captivated by the ideas he instilled in their minds. The group financed its activities and supported themselves by burglaries and robberies (jch 1982). Repeating the common claims of the communist propaganda, the author of a local newspaper hiding under the pseudonym "jch" wrote that Korycki forced the cooperation of his group members by applying "physical and psychological pressure"; however, there is no actual proof of this whatsoever.

Korycki's new group consisted of former prison associates and local friends:

- Twenty-four-year-old Mirosław Kaliński, from Brzozowica Duża, who also had a criminal past and was wanted by the militia with an arrest warrant issued;
- Adam Adamowicz, also from Brzozowica Duża;
- Józef Oponowicz, from Misie;
- Ryszard Nużyński "Smędziak," from Dębowica;

- Ryszard Raczyński, from Paszenki; and
- Marian N.—Korycki's prison friend, with an unknown last
  name, who came from Janów Lubelski (Oksiejuk 2018b;
  Trochimiak 2018; Kaliński 2018).

The activity of Korycki's group revolved around Międzyrzec Podlaski. Under Korycki's command, the "band" carried out several dozen
robberies with weapons, mainly at the homes of tax-collecting village
mayors in Podlasie villages and at communist co-ops. One of their
first attacks occurred at approximately 8 p.m. on November 14, 1979,
in the village of Hołowno. Three masked men—one of them was Marian N.—armed with guns and led by Korycki, burst into the home of
the village mayor, Józef Bliźniuk. They demanded that he hand over
the "communist money"—the land tax money paid by the farmers.
This time, Korycki and his partners stole 70,000 zlotys in cash, as well
as sugar rationing vouchers and various official questionnaires. When
Bliźniuk wanted to hand Korycki his personal money, Korycki replied,
"I don't want yours, I only take the communist property" (Borkowski
1982; jch 1982; Zajączkowska 2012). In fact, Korycki now repeated
this declaration, "I take only communist property," routinely during
robberies.

   In 1980, in addition to heads of communist co-ops and tax-collecting village mayors, Korycki and his men also frequently robbed state
stores, warehouses, and state gas stations. Oksiejuk recalled, "Józek ate
at my place all the time because he had nothing. Sometimes, when he
broke into a GS [Gminna Spółdzielnia "Samopomoc Chłopska"] store,[2]
he had some food leftovers, sometimes vodka. He stole the communist
stuff and the tax money from village mayors. He always quickly gave everything away" (Oksiejuk 2018a). Korycki redistributed the loot, which
included not only groceries but also carpets, washing machines, and
color TVs called "Rubins," which were produced under a Soviet license.
The goods went to poor local villagers.

   Oksiejuk also mentioned, "He liked to have a drink. But it did not
change him. He behaved normally; he did not go crazy like some people. He never insulted anyone. Maybe it was some consolation, some
joy, because what kind of life did he have? He was hiding all his life, he
was being spied on" (Oksiejuk 2018a). Others also reported that Korycki was a restrained drinker. As Korycka discussed, "He never got
drunk in his life. Absolutely. He could do that many times, but always—
one glass, and he said, 'Thank you very much. Enough for me, but you

can do whatever you want.' He was such a smart and resourceful man" (Korycka 2020).

The Podlasie residents repaid their benefactor by sheltering him and his companions and providing information about militia ambushes. The local villagers provided Korycki with support and assistance despite the government's threat that they could spend many years in prison for helping him. Ignoring these severe warnings, they equipped Korycki and his men with weapons and ammunition, which they had hidden from the time of the Second World War (Kaminski 2004a; Kaminski 1985b). Korycki always had a gun with him, often a Soviet PPSz ("Pepesha") machine gun, with the butt cut short so that it would fit under a jacket, and several magazines of ammunition. Waldemar Kaliński once accidentally met Korycki in a farm field and saw that he had a popular Polish World War II pistol, a Vis, with him (Kaliński 2018; Paluch 1981, 13).

When he needed weapons, Korycki often used the friendly help of Mikołaj J.—an amateur gunsmith from Biała Podlaska who had been convicted three times for the illegal possession of firearms. Korycki hired Mikołaj J. to replace damaged parts, repair weapons, and adapt them to his needs. The gunsmith also supplied Korycki with fresh ammunition. Korycki was able to stay in touch with him thanks to Mirosława, the daughter of a friend, a World War II female courier. Mirosława was a nearly twenty-year-old girl who lived with her mother in Kożanówka and studied at a high school in Biała Podlaska. Sometimes on her way to school, she would take Korycki's weapon to the gunsmith, and then pick it up, occasionally with extra ammo, and return it to him. She also occasionally supplied Korycki with food cooked by her mother, and, when necessary, also temporarily hid him, for which he repaid her with financial and material support, which came, of course, from his robberies (Kaliński 2018).

Korycki also eagerly obtained hunting weapons with which he equipped his group. Usually these guns came from thefts. A gamekeeper from forestry in Brzozowica, Franciszek Trochimiak, remembered one such robbery well:

> They came to me in the forester's lodge in the evening, in October 1980. I had a shotgun, a new one, which I got from the management in Lublin. And Korycki knew about it because he was working for a short time in the Radzyń Forest District. I opened the door and someone is aiming at me with a gun. He was wearing

a mask, but I recognized him. He was Korycki's man—Nużyński from Dębowica, they called him "Ględziak." Korycki was further away in the yard, a few of them were there, four or five; he did not come up because he knew I would recognize him right away. Nużyński aimed at me with the pistol and said, "On the ground!" I saw that it was a real weapon, so I stepped back and lay down because there was no way out. And he said to me, "Where is the gun, where is the shotgun?" He took the shotgun with the ammo, the ammo belt, and left. I called the militia from the railway station because there were no phones in the village yet. The militia later picked them [Korycki's group] up at Oponowicz's place in Misie. (Trochimiak 2018)

On another occasion, on the night of either May 14 or 15, 1980, in the village of Żeszczynka, Korycki and his partners again expropriated tax money in a high-profile robbery that was widely publicized. This time, they visited the village mayor, Grzegorz Lewczuk, who lived with his family on the outskirts of the village. After cutting the home's telephone cord, they used a crowbar to open a basement window and entered. From there, they climbed the ladder to the apartment. They did it so quietly that the household did not wake up. Korycki had to poke the mayor with a weapon to awaken him. When the shocked man opened his eyes, Korycki put a gun to his head and quickly demanded, "Give me the Bolshevik money or I will shoot you!" (Borkowski 1982, 1, 10; jch 1982, 14; Zajączkowska 2012; Wasiluk 2014, 8). The terrified mayor tried to buy time despite the threat. He claimed that there was no money because he had just deposited it with the village office cashier. In fact, the day before, the mayor had deposited nearly seventy thousand zlotys in land tax money collected from peasants in the office in Sosnówka. Nevertheless, Korycki easily found a kitchen table drawer that had cash in the amount of sixteen thousand zlotys, which had also come from tax collections (Paluch 1981).[3] With the money in hand, the burglars left the house and headed toward the nearby forest. It turned out that the mayor's daughter had more courage than the mayor himself. She was not afraid of the big men with stockings on their heads and firearms in their hands. Disregarding the thieves' earlier threats, she chased after them. When they quickly realized that she was following them, they fired a few times in the air as a warning. Only then did the mayor's daughter give up and return home (Borkowski 1982, 1, 10).

2.7 Korycki's arsenal. (Top) Soviet PPSh-41 "Pepesha" submachine gun with a drum magazine (1942 version), Korycki's primary weapon. (Middle) Soviet Nagant revolver M1894. This or a similar model was used by Korycki to shoot himself in the head. (Bottom) Polish prewar semi-automatic pistol Vis a.k.a. Radom (Pistolet wz. 35 Vis) designed in 1935, popular in the Polish Army and Warsaw Uprising in 1944, and also used by German paratroopers near the end of the war. Waldemar Kaliński saw Korycki carry the Vis pistol. Korycki acquired his weapons from former Home Army partisans, local peasants, and a local gunsmith, Mikołaj J.; sometimes he stole them, e.g., from a Soviet colonel or local ranger Franciszek Trochimiak. *Sources*: (top) Lposka; (middle) Mascamon; (bottom) Photo by Askild Antonsen. Licenses: License: CC BY-SA 3.0, 3.0 LU, and 2.0.

Korycki's group made a series of successful assaults and burglaries, still always robbing only the property of the communist state. Korycki and Mirosław Kaliński always took part in these attacks, sometimes accompanied by other partners (Paluch 1981; jch 1982). According to Paluch (1981), the list of successful actions was long:

*   A break-in to a liquor store in Łomazy: according to different sources, either 23,000 or 5,000 zlotys in cash, as well as several bottles of alcohol, including vodka and champagne, cigarettes, and groceries;
*   A break-in to the Farmer's Club in Huszcza through a broken window: a "Rubin" color TV, several hundred zlotys; chocolates, cigarettes, and tights valued at six and a half thousand zlotys;
*   A burglary of the Post Office in Horodyszcz;
*   Several restaurant break-ins in Jabłoń and Rossosz;
*   A burglary of a general store in Polubicze: 2,790 zlotys, as well as alcohol, cigarettes, and razor blades valued at fifteen thousand zlotys;
*   A robbery of a department store in Mokre: 31,600 zlotys, chocolate, raisins, coffee, cigarettes, and razor blades;
*   An attack on the CPN (Centrala Produktów Naftowych) petrol station in Komarówka. Initially, their goal had been the tavern in Komarówka, but it turned out that it was adjacent to the MO station, so they changed their plans.

As a point of comparison, the average monthly salary in Poland in 1981 was 7,689 zlotys, corresponding to somewhere between $20 and $30 in 1981 black market prices, or about $100–$150 at the official exchange rate (Baczyński 1984).

With time, other members of Korycki's team became more active while Korycki himself kept a low profile, and sometimes even appeared only as an "accompanying person" (Bodasiński and Osipowski 2015, Dudziak, 6'41"). Nonetheless, during the attacks, both his authoritative bearing and his legendary status were sufficient to assure the cooperation of robbed officials and potential witnesses.

The militia persistently hunted Korycki, for parole violations as well as on arrest warrants for crimes in which he was a suspect. Over time, the militia dedicated more and more people and resources to his capture (Bodasiński and Osipowski 2015, Dudziak, 9'47"), collaborating with foresters, railwaymen, and the local state administration—primarily village mayors—in their efforts to capture him. Poland's mass media consistently reported on the hunt for Korycki's whereabouts (Bodasiński and Osipowski 2015, 10'35").

Later in 1980, Korycki's group focused on freight trains. They usually robbed trains at marshaling stations, where trains stopped to rearrange, add, or switch out railcars. Because these were often relatively short stops, the Railway Protection Guard did not usually guard the railcars there.

One especially dramatic attack occurred on the night of October 10 or 11, 1980, at the Łuków marshaling yard. A few people took part in the action. Wojciech Dąbrowski, a twenty-year-old man, was nearby, riding with some railwaymen who were accompanying his father as they carried cement and other building materials. When Korycki and his people broke into one of the railcars, Dąbrowski surprised the thieves with a shout: "Militia! Freeze!" In response, the robbers, convinced that they were dealing with a real militia ambush, opened fire. One of the bullets hit the young man's forehead, instantly killing him. The regime held Korycki personally responsible for this death; however, there was no evidence that he was the one who had fired the tragic shot. According to the militia, the piece of "evidence" proving that Korycki had killed Dąbrowski was a beret found at the crime scene, which was determined to belong to Korycki. In fact, the beret only proved that Korycki was present at the crime scene, not that he had fired the fatal bullet. The militia failed to apprehend any other robbers for this attempted heist, and Korycki, when arrested a year and a half later, neither confessed to the attack nor gave up any of his accomplices.

The communist authorities placed this tragedy at the center of their propagandistic efforts against Korycki. In the communist party-controlled weekly *Word of Podlasie*, published in Biała Podlaska, the author falsely claimed, "There is undeniable evidence that in October this year, using automatic weapons, Korycki murdered an escort of a train that was carrying cement" (jch 1982).

Korycki later recounted this event to his partner, Krystyna Oksiejuk, who remembered his story in the following way:

Once, Józek and his colleagues attacked a train. They robbed railcars. There was a shooting at that time. A young boy shouted: "Militia! Freeze!" and they started shooting. One of them hit the boy and they killed him. But Józek—as he told me—did not know which of them hit him. He thought it was the militia and fired, but not to kill, but to get away. He told me that "everyone has someone who cries after him," and he just "protected himself as much as he could." (Oksiejuk 2018a)

## PUBLIC ENEMY NO. 1

From the time of the Łuków train robbery and the death of the young man, on October 10, 1980, the militia started pursuing Korycki with great ferocity and by using all available means. They branded Korycki as a killer. The national media regularly reported on the militia's activities as they attempted to seek him out. The media gave Korycki the catchy epithet "Public Enemy No. 1," a term that was applied by the militia propagandists as well (Bodasiński and Osipowski 2015, 10'35"). A more appropriate term would have been "Communist State Enemy No. 1."

The militia were continually checking out locations in hopes of finding Korycki's potential shelter, and the areas of his previous activity were thoroughly searched. Additionally, the authorities launched a large-scale informers' network. Korycki became the most wanted criminal in the country (Bodasiński and Osipowski 2015, 10'35"). However, the enemy himself seemed not to care too much about such attention. Stories are told how, at a tavern in Witoroż, he emerged in the uniform of a militia captain, sat at a table, and ordered vodka for everyone. He also drank "a hundred" (100 ml glass of vodka) and calmly chatted with a friend. After Korycki paid the bill, the innkeeper realized that he had paid with money having serial numbers that were on a militia-provided questionable banknote list. The woman called the militia, but the Biała Podlaska militia squad appeared after Korycki had already left the premises. In typical fashion, none of those present claimed to have known his real identity, and there were major discrepancies in the descriptions of his appearance. Helpless and resigned, the officers gave up their search and only prepared a report containing the testimony of the innkeeper (Kaliński 2018; jch 1982, 10).

The historical record is unclear as to whether the extensive search for Korycki finally yielded the result the militia was looking for, or if they simply got lucky. Regardless, on February 8, 1981, the head of the KWMO in Biała Podlaska, Major Jerzy Wyszkowski, received a tip that Korycki had been seen by neighbors in buildings belonging to the Kuczyński family in Olszewnica Duża. Four militiamen from the

KWMO in Biała Podlaska were immediately ordered to Olszewnica. Two of them—Ensign Wojciech Raczuk and Wiesław Marczuk—conducted reconnaissance on Czesław Kuczyński's property while the other two remained in a car parked alongside a road several hundred meters away. The group reached the property around 10:30 p.m. The farmer, Czesław Kuczyński, claimed that he did not know Korycki and had never seen him. The functionaries checked the house, barn, and other outbuildings and areas, finding no trace of the fugitive. However, the locked summer kitchen intrigued them. When asked by one of the militiamen about the room, Kuczyński replied simply, "He is not there." At their request, he opened the door. While opening it, the farmer suddenly stepped back and then dodged to the side, hiding behind a wall. There, in the room, the militiamen recognized Korycki sitting at a table. When Korycki saw the two militiamen, he reached for the Pepesha lying beside him and immediately fired a series of shots at them, as they quickly sought cover. Then, shooting into the air, Korycki escaped through the window and into the nearby fields (Bodasiński and Osipowski 2015, Raczuk, 16'20"; Kaminski 1985b, 2–3; Borkowski 1982, 10).

For thirteen days, Korycki wandered in the forest. He ate only snow. His body weakened, so he had to tie the Pepesha to his belt and pull it behind him because he was unable to carry it (Kaminski 1985b; Borkowski 1982, 10). Finally, crawling with the last of his strength, completely exhausted, he reached Oksiejuk's house. The woman recalled the situation:

> Once, in winter, he was in Olszewnica and wanted to spend the night there. One farmer hid him in the summer kitchen. But someone must have noticed and reported it to the militia. They came after him, when he was settling down to sleep. They knocked down the door and started yelling, but he already knew that they were coming up and had the rifle ready. He started shooting around and jumped out the window. Somehow, he escaped to the forest. He was barefoot and without a jacket, and it was winter and [there was a] heavy frost. Some way, he came to me later, but he already had frostbitten legs and a fever. He had a bad cold. Luckily, he recovered. He had a strong organism. (Oksiejuk 2018a, 3)

As a result of the shoot-out in Olszewnica, the two militia officers who had confronted him were wounded. Ensign Raczuk was seriously injured and was later awarded the Knight's Cross for courage (łuq 2018). Six of the eighteen bullets fired by Korycki had hit Raczuk, in the neck, chest, and stomach. Later, Raczuk recounted that he "took part in chasing a bandit, who—during the attempt to apprehend him—fired eighteen shots from a machine gun in my direction," and, as a result, "the bullets fired by the bandit destroyed my liver, spine, and diaphragm" (Baczyński and Schwertner 2018).[4] The other militiaman, Marczuk, was hit by two bullets and was only slightly injured (Borkowski 1982, 10). Upon learning about those facts from a newspaper, Korycki decided that he was not guilty of injuring the militiamen. In his view, when he was attacked, he had simply defended himself. His behavior was just a reaction to the actions of the militia, and he stated that "he did not invite them" (Kaminski 1985b).

The prosecutor obviously did not share Korycki's interpretation. Instead, the prosecutor found that Korycki had acted with premeditation and that his intent was to shoot to kill. On behalf of the Polish People's Republic, he charged Korycki with the attempted murder of two MO officers in the act of performing their official duties. Thus, yet another arrest warrant was issued, and as a result, the militia once again intensified their operational activities even further. The militia gave orders to all field agents to find Korycki, and they carried out extensive searches of all potential hideouts. After each sign of Korycki's appearance, the militia organized ambushes in that area (Borkowski 1982, 1, 10, 12).

Years later, Raczuk stated that he had forgiven Korycki for the event in the kitchen and its consequences, which were very serious for him. Commenting on recent Internet texts about Korycki, Raczuk said, "After what I have gone through, I am happy with every hour of my life. I have forgiven Korycki, liars not yet" (red. 2014). At the time of the shoot-out, Raczuk was a low-level functionary of the communist regime, but before formally retiring from the force, he was promoted to the position of MO officer so that he could receive higher benefits. Since October 2017, he has been fighting—not only legally, but in the media as well—to restore the amount of his disability benefits, which was reduced by a special bill in 2015 that limited the amounts of pensions received by former Security Service agents to the level of an average pension. Raczuk stated that they had "served the state and chased bandits so that others could live in peace" (Baczyński and Schwertner 2018). Raczuk also testified about the merits of his service during the time of the PRL: "he had served in the criminal department for years. He had the task of catching bandits, and "did not care about politics," because there was no time even to think about it." In an interview with a journalist of *Wirtualna Polska*, Raczuk said, "Not one moment had I worked for SB, the Security Service. I caught killers, rapists, for which, as you can see, the current government wants to punish me" (Rogaska 2018).[5] To support this assertion, he often referred to the search for Korycki. In the text supporting Raczuk's fight for his full pension, he further presented his motto: "As long as you fight, you are the winner." The journalist who interviewed him also described how, in 1982, Raczuk had participated in the attempt to capture Korycki: "He took part in an ambush on the dangerous criminal Józef Korycki, then called "Janosik" because he sought justice on his own terms. Korycki was mainly employed in robberies and burglaries" (Rogaska 2018). The journalist also reported, "Raczuk caught him on one of the farms." Raczuk added in his own words, "I hesitated too long whether to shoot. I didn't want to have a human life on my conscience, so he drew his weapon first. I got shot six times. I lost a piece of liver; the bullets also damaged my spine."

While Raczuk declared that he forgave Korycki, he never stopped slandering him. At the end of his account, he described Korycki's character, stating, "He was not just an ordinary bandit," and then concluding his account with a sensational statement: "It sometimes happened that he would show up in a house and molest the host's wife. He would take her, put a grenade on the table, and the man could do nothing" (Rogaska 2018). In reality, Korycki was never charged with rape—or multiple rapes, as Raczuk's statement suggests. Certainly, if there had been even the slightest evidence to accuse him of such an act, the militia's and PRL's propaganda would have made sure to have used it long before. Moreover, Korycki never used grenades. In fact, there is no reliable evidence confirming that he ever had a grenade in his possession at all. The only other mention of a grenade is another unsupported statement by a militia officer, Edward Misztal, who stated that Korycki "wore two grenades at his belt" (Jasiak 1989b), which Ambroziewicz (2016) repeated after him. When questioned on this matter, Oksiejuk stated that she had "never seen him with a grenade. I have not heard that he ever had one" (Oksiejuk 2018b). Also, Korycki himself never mentioned grenades in any of the extensive conversations he had with his cellmate, the Student. There was no use for a grenade in his modus operandi of robbing village mayors or trains.

After the shooting in Olszewnica on February 8, 1981, Korycki guessed that someone had informed on him. As Oksiejuk (2018a) recalled, "He knew that someone gave him away in Olszewnica. At that time, there were many arrest warrants for him. He suspected my brother and sister-in-law could now expose him." For a while, Korycki remained at Oksiejuk's home, but after becoming suspicious, he was thinking about arranging another hideout, primarily for her safety.

Following the Olszewnica incident, Korycki became the main enemy of the militia and their most sought-after target. The SB also started an anti-Korycki propaganda campaign to discredit him in the minds of the Podlasie residents, and the nation in general, to prevent him from becoming a symbol of fierce anticommunist resistance. Earlier, when the militia had no formal reasons for arresting Korycki, they would still tail him and sometimes detained him for forty-eight hours "for questioning" (Bodasiński and Osipowski 2015, Dudziak, 9'47").[6]

A forester from Brzozowica found out that Korycki once had a hideout in the forest complex near the Krzna River, close to the village of Przychody. It was a semi-dugout, masked by moss and branches of deciduous and coniferous trees. According to the forester, "[Korycki] stayed there during the day, even lived there; and at night he would wander around visiting trusted people, sometimes carrying out burglaries or robberies" (Czajka 2018). Korycki moved efficiently at night because he knew the area well, but also because he used a compass. Sometimes he would cover distances of up to thirty kilometers. He also remained vigilant regarding whom he could trust. Once, on the edge of the forest, he met a man, Waldemar Kaliński, who Korycki knew was the brother of one of his associates, Mirosław, yet he questioned him nonetheless. Kaliński said that he asked him, "What are you doing here, why, etc.," and all the time, he had a weapon at the ready (Kaliński 2018).

The shooting in Olszewnica brought a search team to Mirosław Kaliński's home. The day following the shooting, a district officer appeared at the Kaliński family home, along with two other MO officers. Mirosław Kaliński was not at home. Still, the militiamen thoroughly searched the house and its outbuildings. Because of the events at Olszewnica, however, the men were afraid to enter individual rooms, so they sent one of Kaliński's brothers forward. The Kalińskis did not store any weapons or ammunition there, so the militia found nothing. The militia also did not find the hideout under the floor, which Kaliński had built in his room on the model of Korycki's earlier dugout at Oksiejuk's house. Even if Korycki had been in the apartment and had used the hideout, he probably would have not have been discovered (Kaliński 2018).

The militiamen did not know that their chances of finding Korycki in the Kaliński house were slim. Only once—much earlier—had Korycki paid Mirosław Kaliński a rare, but short, visit. Waldemar Kaliński remembered the visit well:

> My brother brought him once for dinner. It was such a short conversation because Korycki was in a hurry. He was so afraid of staying here long. He did not want to expose us, because he was wanted at the time [there were three arrest warrants issued for Korycki and thousands of leaflets with his image were distributed (jch 1982, 10)]. I noticed that although he was living in the woods, he was clean, tidy, elegantly shaved and dressed. He presented well. He was also a man of intelligence, polished, familiar with everything, who could express himself and had something to say. He made the impression of a man fighting for a better world, pursuing a goal—the overthrow of communism. He spoke about freedom, about an independent Poland, that he would like to meet people who, like him, would be ready to fight for it and sacrifice everything for this fight. (Kaliński 2018)

Meanwhile, in early 1982, the militia mobilized even greater forces against Korycki. One day, Skrzypiec received a telephone call from the Deputy Provincial Commandant of the MO in Siedlce, Tatarczak, who stated that near the border of his district, Korycki had carried out "an attack … on officers who surrounded the apartment" (Bodasiński and Osipowski 2015, Skrzypiec, 16'40"). Skrzypiec organized a commando team and immediately went to the scene. Once again, however, neither the militia officers already operating on-site nor the commandos managed to capture Korycki.

About this same time, the Komenda Główna Milicji Obywatelskiej (Chief Headquarters of Citizen's Militia, KGMO) forensics laboratory in Warsaw provided a forensic report on the shell casings from Korycki's gunshots in Olszewnica. They matched those found at the site of the October 1980 Wojciech Dąbrowski killing at the Łuków Railway Station (Borkowski 1982, 10). This forensic information confirmed that Korycki had fired shots at the railway station, but it did not prove that Korycki was the person who killed Dąbrowski, as several of his companions were also taking shots at the scene, and any one of them, including Korycki, could have been the killer. The shooter who fired the deadly bullet was still unknown.

At the beginning of January 1981, the provincial commander of the militia in Biała Podlaska appointed a special team charged with capturing Korycki. However, this dedicated team was only able to catch a few of Korycki's associates. The capture of Korycki himself was turning out to be a near-impossible task. Therefore, that same month, the commander in chief of the MO in Warsaw appointed a special operational and investigative specgroup (militia jargon for "special group") with one goal: "to catch Korycki" (Bodasiński and Osipowski 2015, Płócienniczak, 17'18"). The deputy director of the Biuro Kryminalne Komendy Głównej MO (Criminal Bureau of the MO General Headquarters, BK KGMO), Colonel Marian Grabowski headed the specgroup, and the team also included various senior inspectors: Colonel Płócienniczak, Major Stanisław Szkodziński, and Inspector Captain Zbigniew Lis. In addition, Lieutenant Colonel Bogusław Zając represented the Department of Internal Affairs, and the heads of criminal departments from the provincial headquarters, Romuald Dudziak, from Siedlce, and Jerzy Wyszkowski, from Biała Podlaska, rounded out the team (Kacak 2011, 41).

In total, the militia created five regional subgroups. For their headquarters, the management of the specgroup chose Łuków, where all future information regarding Korycki would be gathered and disseminated. As Płócienniczak stated, "this way, we acted effectively, and we had some operational contact with Korycki already in probably early May [of 1981]" (Bodasiński and Osipowski 2015, Płócienniczak, 17'36"). The specgroup cooperated extensively with local administrations and security services, forestry and railway services, and with the army. When the group needed help, officers from the BK KGMO in Warsaw supported the local militiamen. The national media reported on news about the progress of their search (Zajączkowska 2012).

The militia prepared numerous ambushes and round-ups in places where they expected Korycki to be. In fact, he actually did appear several times in these places, and almost fell into the militia's traps. Ultimately, however, due to the militia's incompetence and clumsy bureaucratic procedures, they never caught him. The militia evasively explained their lack of success by referring to restrictions placed on them out of concern for public safety (Bodasiński and Osipowski 2015, Dudziak, 18'02").

Waldemar Czajka, then a young forester from Brzozowica Duża, remembers well one such ambush on Korycki. One night in 1982, when the winter was turning to spring, just before dawn, the protracted barking of the dogs at his lodge disturbed him. Czajka figured that the dogs would have quickly scared a wild animal away, so it must be a man lurking in the dark. He thought it might be Korycki, who had been seen in the area the previous day. The forester went out into the yard adjacent to the forest and shouted toward the forest line, "Who's out there?" Nobody responded. However, the dogs were still barking in one direction. Czajka went back into his house and told his wife that perhaps someone had come to rob them. The woman, who was far along in her pregnancy, became very frightened. Therefore, the forester again went out into the yard, stood in an illuminated place, demonstratively loaded cartridges into a shotgun, and warned the invisible intruder, "I have a gun, it's loaded, and I will use it if I have to." Then he fired twice into the air. The dogs fell silent, and it became quiet. There was no reaction from the forest side, so the man went back into his house. Around 5 a.m., he was awakened by unusual mechanical noises. Czajka looked out the window, and at a distance of about fifty meters, he saw an armored personnel carrier, a BTR-60, commonly called a Skot, as well as several dozen people armed with Finnish rifles and other specialized weapons. He decided that they were some type of special forces team—militia or military. Above them, a helicopter hovered in the air. The forester put on his uniform and left his house. He walked over to the group of uniformed men, and after identifying the commander, asked, "What's going on?" The officer didn't reply, and instead, started talking to someone over the radio. Moments later, the helicopter landed in a nearby meadow and several anti-terrorist officers in black uniforms emerged. They were led by Płócienniczak, who immediately asked the forester, "Who's at home?" Czajka replied that his terrified pregnant wife and his tearful three-year-old son. This, however, made no impression on the men. They ordered him to let them inside and then they searched the building from top to bottom.

At one point, one of the officers was heard over the radio, "Attention! Object identified." In response to this signal, all the militiamen present in the house immediately surrounded the forester and pointed their guns at him, shouting, "Don't move!" Czajka recalled, "I had barrels in the abdomen, in the back, the sides." A witness to all of this, his three-year-old son, pleaded with the officers, saying, "Don't kill my daddy." They all ignored him. Soon after, it turned out that the anti-terrorists had detained someone else, in the nearby forest. It was not Korycki, so Czajka was released. Once they finished searching his home, the militiamen left without explanation, and the gathered forces withdrew, leaving just one small guard. It was from the sentinels that Czajka learned the objective of the operation—to detain Korycki (Czajka 2018).

As Czajka found out later, the militia had been searching all the buildings in the neighborhood, and there had been a total of four helicopters patrolling the area from above. There were even machine gun positions around the village, and a full military company had been deployed (Czajka 2018; Borkowski 1982, 12). Clearly, Płócienniczak and his specgroup were expecting to capture Korycki in the forester's house. The tip, which probably triggered the action, was found to be false. At the time, the forester had been fighting vigorously with poachers and wood thieves, which suggests that someone wanted to harm Czajka by accusing him of harboring Korycki.

The Security Service also remained very active in Czajka's neighborhood. He remembers a time when three suspicious-looking men came to his lodge—one of them, not even bothering to conceal a pistol stuck behind his belt—and demanded a tractor. They were aggressive, vulgar, and smelled of alcohol. As it turned out later, they were *esbeks* (Security Service agents), who got bogged down in a nearby forest. They spent time hanging about in the village and sniffing around for information. They chatted up random locals, sometimes buying the locals vodka and drinking with them, just so they could obtain information about Korycki (Czajka 2018). However, no one gave these outsiders any information. Many of the local people were actively helping Korycki: hiding him and leading the militia onto false trails. As stated by Waldemar Kaliński, Korycki "was already considered Janosik, he did not rob people, but took the money that was collected in the villages for the communists. Everywhere he appeared, he not only aroused respect, but also brought some hard-to-describe goodness, gentleness, and calmness. He didn't look like a bandit and didn't act like a criminal. He was an ordinary man" (Kaliński 2018).

Prior to the raid on Czajka's land, the intensive militia actions had already located and detained the majority of Korycki's partners. The Provincial Prosecutor's Office in Biała Podlaska prepared an indictment against twelve persons who had been directly cooperating with or indirectly assisting Korycki. Their trial was to begin in the fall of 1981. However, Korycki, still at large (along with Mirosław Kaliński), was determined to avoid any trials for his associates. Korycki mailed letters to the court, threatening that if the trial of his accomplices began, he would immediately "deal" with the entire panel of judges. He also telephoned the court several times with similar threats. The court's administration took the threats seriously since Korycki was known not to hold back using weapons against officers of the communist state. At the request of the Provincial Court in Biała Podlaska, the Supreme Court decided to transfer the trial to the Provincial Court in Warsaw. The start of court proceedings was set for May 5, 1982. However, the chief justice became severely ill, and so the trial was postponed (Borkowski 1982, 10).

## MARTIAL LAW

On the infamous night of 12–13 December 1981, an even greater war overshadowed Korycki's private war on communism. The communist authorities introduced martial law, called in Polish *stan wojenny*, "state of war," throughout the country, with an unlawfully issued decree. Henryk Jabłoński, the puppet chairman of the Council of State, formally signed the decree (Dziennik Ustaw 1981); however, a nonconstitutional group appointed that same night—the Wojskowa Rada Ocalenia Narodowego (Military Council of National Salvation, WRON)—assumed the real power. WRON comprised twenty senior army officers and generals,[7] headed by Generals Wojciech Jaruzelski and Czesław Kiszczak. According to official WRON documents, its purpose was "to protect the legal order and create conditions for restoring stability in the country." It was established as a response to the "anti-state and subversive activity of anti-socialist forces," who were allegedly preparing a "reactionary coup d'état" (Dudek 2002, 233–35; Paczkowski 2002, 202, 308; Majchrzak 2011, 2016b; see also Magier 2018 on martial law in the Podlasie region).

With good reason, WRON's takeover of power was called a "military coup" and "junta rule." Immediately after December 13, the council and its proxies—military commissioners and various departments' staff who were subordinate to the Ministerstwo Spraw Wewnętrznych (Ministry of the Interior, MSW)—administered personnel changes in the state and party structures. Thus, in 1982, eighty-eight army officers took up top positions in the state administration, and thirty-two in the party apparatus. Among them, there were eleven ministers and deputy ministers, thirteen voivodes and deputy voivodes, and nine secretaries of PZPR Voivodeship Committees (Dudek 2002, 233, 235). In other words, most of state and county-level government became militarized.

The martial law was the culmination of several months of preparation. The Political Bureau of the PZPR had been considering this option since August 29, 1980. The main burden of preparation rested on the Ministerstwo Obrony Narodowej (Ministry of National

Defense, MON) and the MSW. On October 22, 1980, at the General Headquarters of the Polish Army, the team, led by General Florian Siwicki, urgently started developing a plan that they dubbed "W," standing for the word *wojna* (war). Within two weeks, General Jaruzelski reported that the "necessary legal acts regarding martial law" were prepared. In March 1981, further documents were approved, including the "framework plan for the armed forces in the event of martial law" (Majchrzak 2011).

The MSW carried out parallel preparations. All units of the MSW were required to update their own "W" plan and to be ready for action by October 20. Among other components, in this "update" agents drew up lists of persons to be interned and elaborated a plan for the control of communications and the "security" of special facilities, as well as the strengthening of the border. On December 12, 1981, at 11:30 p.m., Operation Azalia (Azalea)—seizing Polish radio and television facilities and blocking telecommunications—was to begin. Immediately following this seizure, Operation Jodła (Fir)—the internment of the people on the lists—was scheduled to start at midnight.[8]

In fact, the army and various forces subordinate to the Ministry of the Interior were already prepared to introduce martial law as early as mid-March 1981. The communists were apprehensive about public reaction and social resistance, particularly mass strikes and protests: they feared angry crowds in the streets that would burn party committee buildings, as had happened in 1970. The communists' dread of this potential social unrest bordered on psychosis. At least some MO officers were told that they should move their families to the countryside or to areas outside of major urban centers. The superiors of the party and the government created self-defense units for party members and their allies "whose life or health may be threatened by hostile elements in case of unfavorable developments" (Majchrzak 2016a, 121). After the implementation of martial law, active party members formed various associations—the Workers' Militia, the Party Guard, and so-called Self-Defense Groups associated with the local committees of the PZPR. In January 1982, these units had about sixty thousand armed persons. Additionally, party activists secured forty-nine thousand weapons and seven million bullets (Majchrzak 2016b).

On December 5, the PZPR's Political Bureau met and finally approved martial law. Jaruzelski—the first secretary of the PZPR—the prime minister, and the minister of national defense were tasked with choosing the time to officially start "W." The Council of State met and formally approved the relevant legal provisions on December 13, 1981, just after midnight, a few hours after martial law had already begun. The order initiating the activities of the MSW units had been forwarded to the Voivodeship commanders of the MO nine hours earlier (Dudek 2002, 233–35; Friszke 2003; Majchrzak 2016b).

Almost immediately after the imposition of martial law, the SB focused its efforts on combating the emerging underground—the so-called hostile element (Majchrzak 2016a, 183). Korycki, aware of the overall situation, quickly reacted to the communist regime's "Polish-Jaruzel War" (see Paczkowski's 2006 book with the same title). At the turn of the New Year 1982, Korycki attempted to reactivate the forest guerilla forces in Podlasie on a large scale, but his attempts eventually collapsed. [9]

Solidarity, which after the imposition of martial law, had become an underground organization, also considered armed resistance as a strategy, although only a small part of the organization supported it, and an even smaller segment went about trying to implement it. Jacek Kuroń, an influential leader of the opposition, considered a variant of armed resistance. In an important text published in March 1982 in the underground newspaper *Tygodnik Mazowsze*, Kuroń went so far as to suggest an armed uprising against the communists but then quickly withdrew this idea (Kuroń 1982, 3). The Student also mentioned the issue of armed resistance:

> In my underground publishing house, I discussed the option of robbing a van carrying confiscated illegal books (*bibuła*) to a mill in Konstancin-Jeziorna on its monthly route. One of my contacts identified the route and timetable. Instead of sweating out tons of printed materials, we could easily recover books stolen by the SB. I did not decide to follow this plan because of the potential "Raskolnikov effect" in a situation of high uncertainty, i.e., a high probability of an accidental tragedy during the robbery. Similar ideas often came back in the conversations of various employees of my publishing house (Kaminski 2018, email 4).

The leaders of Solidarity limited the resistance activity of the underground to the formula of nonviolence. Nevertheless, for the next several years Poland became the arena of frequent massive demonstrations that resulted in small battles with the ZOMO.

Korycki personally distributed anticommunist leaflets, including nailing them to the door of a church in Radzyń Podlaski, and sent a letter to General Wojciech Jaruzelski. He later told the Student that he wrote the letter literally "with his own blood," saying, "General, why did you declare war on Poland?" (Kaminski 1985b). Yet there were also occasions when Korycki again felt that violent acts would be more effective. He considered blowing up the Berlin–Moscow Mitropa express train, which commonly transported Soviet military personnel and their families.[10] Possibly, he got the idea from an earlier unsuccessful attempt to blow up this train by the anticommunist organization ZEW—a group that was active in the early 1950s in his hometown of Radzyń Podlaski—or possibly from the attempts to immobilize this rail route during earlier uprisings and partisan wars. He obtained the right amount of dynamite for this attack, fully planned the logistics of the operation, and even tested how long a flame would travel over spilled gasoline. However, his friends—both those from Solidarity and the Home Army veterans from the "Wilk" unit, to whom he had confided his plans—persuaded him to abandon such an extreme act of terrorism, which could have resulted in numerous civilian casualties (Kaminski 1985b; Kaminski 2004a, 175).

Korycki's strong connections with former Home Army soldiers,[11] as well as with the Solidarity activists, support a political and oppositional interpretation of his activities. Before December 13, 1981, during the period of Solidarity's legal existence, when Korycki wanted to reveal himself, one of the opposition leaders, Zbigniew Bujak, from the Mazowsze region, attempted to negotiate Korycki's case with the communist authorities, but, as Korycki told the Student, "the war broke out and it ended" (Kaminski 1985b).

Now, once again, Korycki waged his own lonely guerrilla war against communism. He seemed to be on something of a warpath leading toward a final clash. However, he also understood that he had no chance to win such a fight. In the end, exhausted, he wanted to give up. Krystyna Oksiejuk described his situation at the time:

It was worst when the martial law came. Józek thought it was over, that the fight for Poland's freedom had already been lost. He had enough. Resigned, he decided to turn himself in. He thought about it and told me: "maybe you can take my weapon to the militia, maybe they will let me go." I was a bit afraid that they would lock me up, but I said I could go. However, he was not entirely sure about this idea either. We decided that we would not do it, because they would ask where I got his weapon, where I knew him from and where he was. And he gave up. We decided not to take the risk that they would lock him or me up. ... Now it is not clear how it was better to proceed, whether to give away the weapons and come out or not. Maybe if he had volunteered, then he would have still been alive. Maybe he would have lived to see freedom. (Oksiejuk 2018a)

After the introduction of martial law, Korycki's activity slowly withered. His adversaries, however, went to other extreme, and strengthened their anti-Korycki forces.

## THE MONTH OF THE "JACKAL"

On April 10, 1982, the desperate militia leadership, pressed by party and state notables, directed the specgroup to carry out a military action called Operation "Szakal" (Jackal), codenamed after the infamous Venezuelan terrorist Ilich Ramírez Sánchez. The media had dubbed Sánchez "The Jackal" when the popular 1971 novel by Frederick Forsyth, *The Day of the Jackal*, was discovered among his belongings. For the next month, enormous resources would be devoted to the goal of the Polish Jackal operation: capturing Korycki. The offensive focused on an in-depth penetration of the towns and forested areas in the vicinities of Łuków, Radzyń Podlaski, and Międzyrzec Podlaski (Zajączkowska 2012; Pietrzak 2013, 53).

After about two weeks of searching, the militia received a tip that Korycki was hiding in a former German bunker in the forest. As part of an undercover operation to capture him, an SB agent sold Korycki a small propane bottle that he needed, but with a concealed radio transmitter. After establishing Korycki's whereabouts based on the locator signal, the militia prepared a broad ambush. The militiamen from the specgroup tactically planned and coordinated the trap. Płócienniczak characterized it as a "giant" operation. Somewhere between four and five hundred ZOMO officers took part in the roundup, working in compact formations, and equipped with a number of BTR-60 armored vehicles and two MI-6 helicopters (see Fig. 2.8). Describing the action, Płócienniczak stated that "everything was like a real war" (Bodasiński and Osipowski 2015, Płócienniczak, 18'32"; Kacak 2011, 40; Borkowski 1982, 10).

2.8. The weaponry used against Korycki in his last battle (From top left, clockwise)
Soviet armored personnel carrier BTR-60 (Skot); Austrian Glock FM 78 assault knife;
Polish submachine gun PM-63 RAK; Soviet AKS-74U rifle; Soviet Dragunov sniper rifle
SVD-63; Heavy Soviet transport helicopter MI-6. *Sources*: Billyhill; Credit: M62; MON
www.wp.mil.pl; Guzbenz; Hokos; Photo by Rob Schleiffert. Licenses: CC BY-SA 3.0, 2.0,
and 4.0.

The "bunker" identified by militia intelligence turned out to be a simple shed. Once the militiamen surrounded it, one of them, an officer named Skrzypiec, who arrived in an armored vehicle as a militia negotiator, spoke through a megaphone. He appealed to Korycki to surrender while also providing safety guarantees (Bodasiński and Osipowski 2015, Skrzypiec, 19'18"). To the amazement of the militia commanders, instead of Korycki, they found in the shed only two of his colleagues, who were drunk. It was later established that Korycki had left the shed at 5:40 a.m.; since the militia's raid began at 6:00 a.m., they had just missed him (Bodasiński and Osipowski 2015, Płócienniczak, 19'33"). After this near miss, the specgroup's commanders speculated that Korycki must have had informants within the militia. However, a more likely explanation is that Korycki was aware of the militia's bureaucratic procedures and was careful to leave his hideout early, before 6:00 a.m. If he had had informants, it seems unlikely that he would have snuck out at the last moment, but rather, would have avoided the ambush entirely.

During the second half of April 1982, ZOMO officers systematically combed the forest in the Łuków–Radzyń Podlaski–Międzyrzec Podlaski triangle area (Pietrzak 2013, 53). In early May, militia agents established Korycki's whereabouts in the Dąbrowica forest. This occurred because his partner, Kaliński, visited a nearby village and was careless and talkative during the visit. However, given the fiasco of the previous attempt at his capture, this time the commanding officer of the Jackal operation did not order the men to take immediate action. Instead, over the next two weeks, Korycki was under surveillance, and an ambush was carefully planned (Zajączkowska 2012; Kaminski 2004a, 176). The militia officers understood that another failure might cost them their careers, so they decided to optimize logistics and gather all available technical resources.

Finally, on the morning of May 14, they made the decision to proceed and start the manhunt. At the time, Korycki was in one of his forest hideout bunkers located near the village of Druchówka, sometimes spelled Druczówka or Drucówka (Oksiejuk 2018a). Druchówka sat about six kilometers from Międzyrzec Podlaski (see fig. 2.9). Mirosław Kaliński was with Korycki, armed with a shotgun. Kaliński had spent three years in hiding with Korycki, hoping for eventual amnesty (Kaliński 2018). Due to their association, the militia had also intensively sought Kaliński.[12] The militia and the supporting army, entering from the side of the village of Misie, surrounded the entire forest area.

2.9. A typical German bunker left in Podlasie forests after World War II. Korycki used several such bunkers as hideouts. Photo by Ernest Szum.

Once again, the militia mobilized enormous forces. Dozens of officers from local MO stations, a dozen or so from the specgroup, and seventy-two so-called commandos from the assault brigade—these were officers from the anti-terrorist ZOMO Special Platoons unit of the Security Department of the Warsaw Metropolitan Command—joined five hundred militiamen, including ZOMO officers, all working in close formation. The commandos had specialized equipment, including a parachuting version of their uniform, jumper helmets, bulletproof vests, PM-63 RAK submachine guns, AKS-74U rifles (a shorter version of an AK-74), Soviet Dragunov sniper rifles SVD-63, American Colt and Smith & Wesson revolvers, and Glock-78 assault knives (Głowacki 2014). Additionally, there were three snipers from WZ KSMO and six tracking dogs with guides tasked to find Korycki's hideout. Once again, the forester Waldemar Czajka, who acted as a guide, was an involuntary participant in the raid. The militia categorically forbade Czajka not only to ask any questions but also to speak on matters other than those related to his role as a guide (Czajka 2018). The militia forces were supported by the army, with several BTR-60 armored vehicles (called *Skots*) and two MI-6 helicopters (Bodasiński and Osipowski 2015, Płócienniczak, 19'10"; Bodasiński and Osipowski 2015,

Dudziak, 20'04"; Kaminski 2004a, 176; Kacak 2011, 42).[13] Thus, it is clear that the scale of the manhunt was massive, and due to the participation of the special units and the army, it was more complicated logistically than ever before.

According to militia sources, they surrounded Korycki's approximate hideout location in the forest with a circle measuring about two kilometers along the radius (Bodasiński and Osipowski 2015, Płócienniczak, 19'10"). Dudziak stated, "The forest complex was surrounded around [*sic.*]" (Bodasiński and Osipowski 2015, Dudziak, 20'4") Korycki found himself trapped and without any way out. Initially, accompanied by Mirosław Kaliński, he appeared at the edge of the forest, but then soon recognized that he was surrounded and retreated to the hideout. The militiamen realized that Korycki had spotted them, so they decided to bring in the helicopters for aerial monitoring. Armored Skots with commandos entered the forest, followed by the militiamen from the specgroup and local units. At that moment, the "combing of the forest began, from below and from above" (Bodasiński and Osipowski 2015, Płócienniczak, 19'10"; see also Bodasiński and Osipowski 2015, Dudziak, 20'04"; Kacak 2011, 42).

The militia called for the fugitives, entrenched in their hideout, and now surrounded, to surrender. The militiamen told Korycki and Kaliński to drop their weapons and come out with their hands raised. Unsurprisingly, they did not comply with this command. Kaliński could not bear the tension and made a desperate attempt to escape. However, after a short run, a river stopped him from going any further (Borkowski 1982, 10). He was captured on the riverbank by the ZOMO, who beat him—as Skrzypiec put it, "the boys spanked him a bit"—and took away his shotgun (Bodasiński and Osipowski 2015, Skrzypiec, 21'21"). The militiamen who transported Kaliński later reported that "after he was detained, he cried, he bawled like a child." Unlike Korycki, who was "well groomed, shaved and clean," Kaliński "was overgrown with dirt, he looked like a savage" (Borkowski 1982, 10).[14]

While Kaliński had made a fast break for it and was apprehended, Korycki remained cool. Firing his guns, he moved in the opposite direction, hoping that the militia had not yet closed the ring. The descriptions of the next events differ significantly, with the discrepancies in the accounts resembling those of the characters of Akira Kurosawa's *Rashomon*.[15] The militia officers and their successors told their versions of events. In a conversation with the Student, Korycki told his own.

## POLISH *RASHOMON*

According to the local militiamen participating in the action, when the noose got tighter around Korycki, and they spotted him, a battle took place. The officers engaged in a shoot-out with Korycki, they soon hit him, and he fell to the ground. Skrzypiec and other militiamen rushed over to him, shouting, tugging at him, and accusing him of pretending to be unconscious (Bodasiński and Osipowski 2015, Dudziak, 21'58"; Bodasiński and Osipowski 2015, Skrzypiec, 22'12"). Skrzypiec, apparently driven by the desire to record a "success" in a movie-like manhunt, wished he could have shot Korycki personally. He recalled, "I, myself, had he not fell, would pump him full of lead" (Bodasiński and Osipowski 2015, Skrzypiec, 21'43"; Kacak 2011, 42). A bloodied Korycki lay motionless with a bullet in his head.

Others at the scene tell the story differently and attributed their success to the special forces rather than militia. Major Edward Misztal, the head of the commandos and one of the founders of the Special Platoons of ZOMO, reported how bravely and professionally he and his men arrested the fugitive (Jasiak 2018a, 2018b):

The action of capturing the dangerous bandit Korycki in the Podlasie region lasted almost two years. … He was hiding in the woods where he had several well-masked bunkers at his disposal. He was extremely clever, he knew the area perfectly, he always walked armed with a Pepesha gun and a pistol, and he wore two grenades at his belt. All in all, it was a very expensive action; many people took part in it, sometimes remaining camouflaged in the woods for weeks. Finally, we got a tip that the bandit was in a certain area of the forest. I was walking a little to the side, my two subordinates on the front right. Korycki stood hidden in a juniper [bush], dressed in a sheepskin coat that harmonized with the surroundings. Our boys walked several meters from that juniper and, as they later admitted, they would never have noticed him. The bandit, however, lost his cool and blasted at them with his Pepesha. Fortunately, he missed. Our trained commando fell to the ground in a flash and fired three shots with a colt revolver. All accurate.

There are certain problematic elements and factual mistakes in Misztal's dramatic account. First, it seems unbelievable that Korycki's

Pepesha would have missed the three militiamen passing nearby. Second, he hid not for two, but for almost three years. The reliability of the remainder of Misztal's version of the events is further undermined by other mistakes or fabrications: He attributes the Łuków killing to Korycki. He states that Korycki injured three militiamen while he was in hiding, but he only injured two. Finally, Misztal falsely claimed, "Korycki, although wounded in the head, hand, and buttock, survived, then his trial took place" (Jasiak 2018b). Korycki, in fact, never had a trial.

For its part, the report of the manhunt in the local communist weekly *Word of Podlasie* attributed the success of Korycki's capture in part to the local militia, and in part to the militiamen from Warsaw:

> After encircling the forest, an assault group transported by a helicopter proceeded to arrest armed criminals. They did not listen to the call to lay down the weapons and raise their hands. Korycki was the first to open fire, while M. Kaliński began to run away. Following the exchange of shots, Korycki was wounded twice, and the second criminal was detained without injury. … At the time of his arrest, Korycki was armed with a Pepesha submachine gun and a Nagant-type pistol. M. Kaliński had a shotgun. Officers from the KG and KS MO in Warsaw and KW MO in Biała Podlaska and Siedlce took part in the search and capture of the criminals. None of the officers was injured (ch 1982, 11).

The newspaper also informed its readers about the fate of the two captured men: "The wounded Korycki was taken to the hospital in Międzyrzec Podlaski, where he is under medical supervision. The second man is held in the detention center in Biała Podlaska." This coverage then concluded with the standard propaganda statement: "Considerable assistance in apprehending and detaining criminals was provided by the residents of nearby towns" (ch 1982, 11). Similar propagandist assurances about the support from the local population appeared in many other press accounts. However, since no specifics about this "residents' assistance" were offered, this part of the relation seems unreliable. The only non-militia and non-military resident who took part in the manhunt as a guide, the forester Czajka, pointed out years later that he had been an involuntary participant, and then went further to say that he considered Korycki to be a normal man, not posing any threat to the local community (Czajka 2018).

The militiamen and commandos had strong incentives for claiming credit for "taking down" Korycki. Capturing him became of the utmost importance for the communist leaders and those in charge of the MO. Because of widely publicized manhunts, "the Jackal's case"—as the media called it—gained substantial significance as propaganda. The success of Korycki's final capture meant not only financial rewards and promotion for the successful functionaries but also possible budget increases for their organizational units.

Aside from the official accounts discussed above, we have another version of that day's events based on information from a direct source—the version Korycki told to the Student. The Student recalls the circumstances of the conversations he held with Korycki in prison as part of his research: "I tried to start conversations without making any suggestions that could distort the accounts. ... The stories that I heard from Józek, I had to press him to tell them—he did not give the impression that he deliberately wanted to exaggerate. He told them only to me. ... to the rest of the cell, he gave publicly known facts" (Kaminski 2018, email 5). Korycki did not seem to care about pushing his side of the events. He probably assumed that his version would not have any chance against the powerful communist state propaganda.

According to his own account, as told to the Student, when the militia surrounded Korycki, he saw the ZOMO riot police passing in front of his hideout, but he did not want to shoot at them. From his hiding spot, he could see their faces well. He saw that they were very young men and thought that, although they had enlisted on their own volition, they had little—if any—awareness of what they were actually doing. He decided that he did not want to have their deaths on his conscience (Kaminski 1985b). Korycki had to choose between the death of several young people and ending his private war on his own terms. Faced with this ethical dilemma, he chose suicide. According to him, he came out of hiding, knelt on the ground, and put the Pepesha down. He then crossed himself, shouted "Long live Poland!" and shot himself in the head with an old 7.62 mm Soviet Nagant revolver.[16] The young ZOMO officers had no similar ethical scruples and wanted to finish off the wounded man, but a Polish Army officer intervened and saved Korycki's life (Kaminski 1985b; Kaminski 2004a, 176).

Korycki's description of events explains why he, an armed fugitive, failed to wound or kill any militiamen in the final shootout. However, two questions remain unanswered although some plausible explanations are possible. First, it is unclear from whom he learned about his dramatic survival after he lost consciousness. Second, in addition to the bullet in his head, he had two other bullets in his right hand and left groin; it is unclear who shot him there and how. After his death, the physician performing the autopsy removed the bullet from Korycki's head during the postmortem, but he declined to identify its origin or return it to the family (Korycka 2020).

The dramatic capture of Korycki stimulated journalistic imaginations and produced a myriad of other accounts. Most do not cite any sources. One example is a 2017 article by Małgorzata Lipczyńska that contradicts Korycki's testimony. The article, under the intriguing title "The True Story of the Polish Janosik," presents an alternative version of Korycki's arrest. The text is devoid of facts from new sources and repeats an exaggerated mishmash of fabrications and previously published accounts of the fate of Korycki by other researchers. Supposedly, Korycki had tried to run away but "quickly fell." Apparently, only one bullet, aimed straight at his head by a militiaman, hit him. Then, the commander of the action personally ran up to Korycki and called him a coward. Later, the "beating of the bandit started." Furthermore, Lipczyńska writes, "He probably would not have survived if not for the intervention of one of the soldiers, who assisted the militia in the action."

The author provides no references and merely mentions as the source for the information an anonymous "ZOMO man." The relation of this "ZOMO man" seems to be actually a compilation of the accounts of two militia officers: Dudziak and Skrzypiec, as given in the 2005 documentary film *Janosik z Podlasia*. The "intervention of one of the soldiers" actually comes from Kaminski's (2006) book, where Korycki's account was first published. Further, Lipczyńska's article makes clear mistakes. For instance, we know that Korycki was hit not by one but by three bullets. The entirety of Lipczyńska's confusingly titled story is packed with distortions, mistaken facts about various people and actions, unfounded overinterpretations, value judgments, and, frequently, mere fantasy, and provides an extreme example of the speculative, sensational, and deceitful storytelling about Korycki, which persisted even after the fall of communism.

Solidarity's underground press also noticed Korycki's capture. On May 14, 1982, the social and political opposition monthly *Głos*, an underground journal published by the KOR community, included a brief message in its monthly calendar of events:

In the woods near the village of Druchówka in eastern Poland [the militia,] using a helicopter, six guides with dogs and seventy specially trained agents, shot and captured Józef K. [later Polska Agencja Prasowa (Polish Press Agency, PAP) would clarify—Korycki], who had been hiding in the forests since 1979. A 1952 deserter from the army, who was imprisoned several times, he took up banditry and specifically Janosik-style thievery—he only stole from the communist state. (Głos 1982)

We also have the slightly different, more personal perspective from Korycki's life partner, who recalled the circumstances of this event in this way:

In spring and summer, when the day was getting longer, he stayed in the forest for a long time. Later, he had a dugout made in the middle of the forest near Druczówka, masked with branches and moss. He sat there and listened to the radio from abroad [Radio Free Europe, which broadcast anticommunist news and stories], he always listened to this radio. At first, he was there alone, and then with a friend from Brzozowica, a young boy, I don't remember his name anymore [Mirosław Kaliński]. Only in the evening, when it was already dark, they would come to the edge of the forest here, near us, about a kilometer from my house, and I would bring them food there. … In the spring of the following year, they caught him. The day before, in Jelnica [a neighboring major village], there were plenty of them. They came by helicopters. They came to Józek in the woods following the radio. Maybe they wouldn't have found him if it wasn't for the radio. When he knew he was trapped, he shouted to them: "Long live Poland!" He came out and shot himself in the head with a pistol. (Oksiejuk 2018a)

Oksiejuk then went on to describe the aftermath of Korycki's detention, which affected her personally:

Later yet, after everything happened, this main commie from Warsaw, the loud one, from television [Płócienniczak], landed here, at my brother and sister-in-law's, in the yard. And they came to me, two more were with him, with those "kałach" [kalashnikov] rifles. They wanted Józek's weapons and things. He ordered the wardrobes to be opened and drawers and everything. They searched the whole house but found nothing. They didn't find Józek's hideout under the floor either. This chief policeman was so … unpleasant. But it was calm enough. I don't know why they came to me then, but now that I think of it, maybe someone informed on me. In addition to me and my daughter Agnieszka, only my mother, my brother, and my sister-in-law knew that Józek was hiding with me. (Oksiejuk 2018a)

In fact, there is some evidence supporting the suspicion that Oksiejuk's brother, Jan, and/or possibly her sister-in-law, Krystyna, had informed on her. Both of them had been unwelcoming to Korycki. Krystyna Oksiejuk's sister-in-law's name was also Krystyna Oksiejuk, since she took her husband's last name when she married him—a fact, as it turned out later, that had some significance. Korycki had previously told his partner about another event, which she reported as follows:

He was once in Pościsze [one of the neighboring villages] and wanted to hide his gun there. In some yard, he found old hives and decided to hide it in one of them. But there, unexpectedly, he came across gold, various precious jewels and wedding rings. Probably someone was hiding loot from thefts. He took them and brought them home, but somehow my sister-in-law, Krystyna, found out and took them away from him. Apparently, he was afraid that she would reveal him if he did not give her the gold. But maybe she exposed him anyway, so that he would not ask for this gold again, because soon the militia appeared in our yard. (Oksiejuk 2018a)

The militiamen, who, for some unknown reason, suddenly appeared at the Oksiejuk estate, then set a trap for Korycki, but they failed to capture him (Oksiejuk 2018a). Apparently, Korycki considered giving up the gold and jewelry as a sort of ransom for his and his loved ones' safety.

Later, this story gained an interesting punch line. Oksiejuk recalled:

When he was already in prison, civilian militia came asking me to give it [the gold and jewelry] back. I didn't have anything and they found nothing. Now that I think of it, it was about my sister-in-law, who also was named like me, her name was Krystyna, and her surname after her husband was also Oksiejuk. They had some information that Krystyna Oksiejuk had the gold, but they came to the wrong one. Instead of looking for her, they found me. And I had nothing. (Oksiejuk 2018a)

This intriguing puzzle is bound to remain unsolved. It is unclear if the visitors to Oksiejuk's home were SB officers, or maybe just criminal police. Based on information from Korycki's case, it seems possible that one of the militia officers had spotted an opportunity and had tried to steal the loot. This wouldn't be an isolated incident. Historians believe that some party members, the Security Services, the militia or military special services, took part in many different types of criminal acts in the PRL, including major crimes. The research shows that the regime's functionaries "sometimes dipped their fingers in the killings related to the attacks on banks and other offenses involving illicit proceeds" (Kunicki and Ławecki 2017, 8). Moreover, "The birth and success of organized crime in the late period of the PRL would be—if not impossible—at least delayed. It would occur on a much smaller scale, were it not for the cooperation of mafia gangsters with Security Service officers and high-ranking people from broadly understood power elites" (Kunicki and Ławecki 2017, 8).

A month after Korycki's arrest, in a lengthy article published in the party organ *Word of Podlasie*, a description of the villages that were "terrorized" by Korycki, and finally "liberated from his tyranny by the militia" was presented: "Józef Korycki captured! The inhabitants of Podlasie received this news with great relief. Since the end of 1979, Podlasie villagers have lived in fear. A resident of Brzozowica says, 'A man would go to sleep not sure if he would not be woken up by the sound of a broken window or shooting. There was great panic in the nation'" (Borkowski 1982, 1). The author then continues in a similar tone, "You are asking how the society took it? Very well. Nobody regrets Korycki. People say—he attacked this guy, he attacked that guy, and he could come for me at night. People were that afraid of him. Children at school are also happy that they finally caught Korycki" (Borkowski 1982, 12).

## CHAPTER 3

# Prisoner

## May 15, 1982–August 21, 1986

> And besides, he was what one would call a good man.
> –Joseph Conrad

The last stage of Korycki's life was prison. Like many rebels before and after him, he lost his fight against the system. However, prison would neither break him nor humiliate him. Behind bars and in the extreme conditions in which he had to live, Korycki remained calm and disciplined. He enjoyed great respect from the other prisoners, who admired his toughness as a robber and respected his anticommunist actions. For many, both in- and outside prison walls, he was an icon of Poland's anticommunist struggle.

## GRYPSMAN SUBCULTURE

Before we begin telling Korycki's prison story, it is first necessary to describe how communist prisons functioned, including the workings of the Rakowiecka Jail, and its most important element, the subculture of grypsmen—inmates of the highest prison caste.[1]

Commonly known as Rakowiecka or Mokotów Jail, the prison in which Korycki spent the last four years of his life was built rapidly during the Tsarist Russian occupation of Poland in 1902–4. It was designed to house eight hundred prisoners. In the worst years of the Stalinist terror period, the complex, located at 37 Rakowiecka Street, functioned mainly as a confinement center for Polish political prisoners, and sometimes as their place of execution. Underground Home Army heroes mingled there with German war criminals. In 2017, the government closed it as a jail, and in 2018, converted it into the

Museum of Cursed Soldiers and Political Prisoners of the PRL, which is open to visitors.

In 1985, the Rakowiecka Jail mainly hosted "temporarily arrested" men awaiting trial for criminal charges, as well as several political prisoners and a small number of women. The authorities sent convicts, that is, those who had already received their sentences, from this prison to other locations, but a small contingent of convicts was also present at Rakowiecka. Those who were "temporarily arrested" wore *freedom*[2] clothes more often than the convicts, but they also were less often permitted to work. The "temporarily arrested" men were subject to stricter isolation, especially if the authorities assumed they had accomplices. They also spent more time than the convicts did in their cells, and their interactions with their cellmates tended to be more intense. Their greater isolation than the convicts' created certain inconveniences, such as cells with multilayered windows that prevented them from looking outside (see fig. 3.1). In fact, the term "temporary arrest" is a misnomer, as such detentions were often arbitrarily long; the prosecution and courts sometimes extended the holding of these men for years. The record holder during the time that the Student was incarcerated was a man who had been "temporarily arrested" for over six years. Korycki, who never faced a trial, was "temporarily arrested" for well over four years.

The division of those who were sentenced convicts and those who were "temporarily arrested" was not sharp, and sometimes the

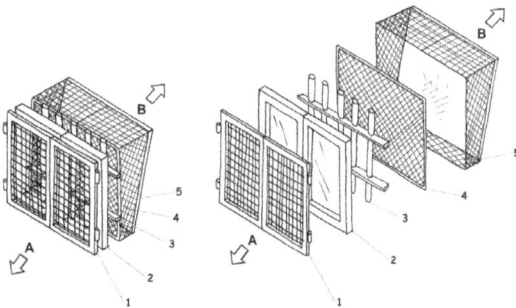

3.1. Layers of a typical prison window around 1985. Arrows indicate the window's orientation: A = inside cell; B = outside cell. Numbers denote the following: 1 = bars inside the cell; 2 = window; 3 = outside bars (*tigerbars*); 4 = metal net; 5 = translucent glass with embedded metal net. This picture was a part of Mirosław Andrzejewski's *gryps* (secret message sent inside prison or from prison to the outside world). *Source*: Kaminski (2004a).

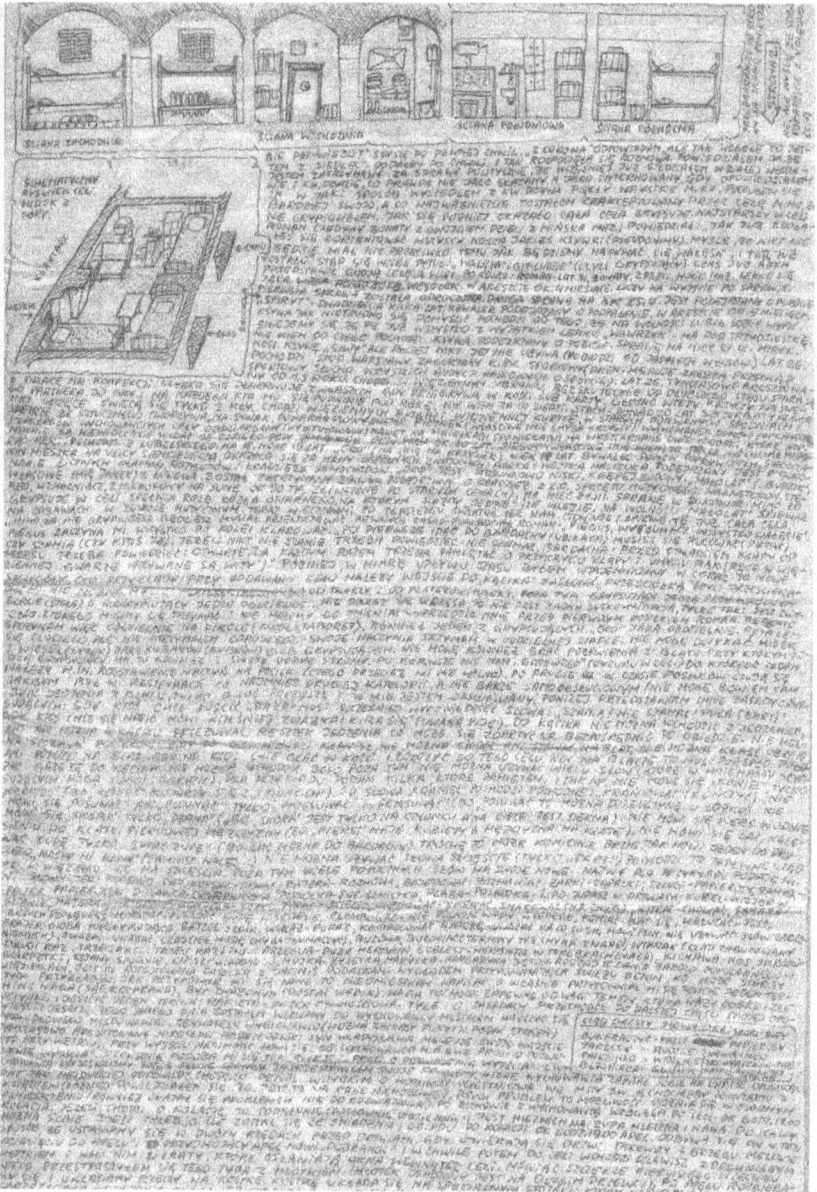

3.2. Mirosław Andrzejewski's *gryps* sent from prison to freedom, containing his drawings showing the inside of a typical prison cell around 1985.

authorities housed both types of prisoners in the same cell. In the prison's hospital in 1985, both categories were treated equally. In a regular cell, there were usually about 1 to 1.5 m$^2$ of area per prisoner (see fig. 3.2). In a hospital cell, this crucial number was much larger—approximately 4 to 5 m$^2$ per prisoner.

In 1980s Poland, the most important element of the prison environment was the *grypsman* subculture, with its complex rules for using the quickly evolving *bajera* (prison argot) and the strict enforcement of rules. For instance, the *grypsmen* considered the old name, *grypsera*, outdated and incorrect by 1985; if somebody used the term, this was proof of language incompetence and could be punished with what was a standard penalty, *mounting the plate*, that is, hitting a fellow prisoner's forehead with an open hand. Similarly, in the sixties and seventies, the word *grypser* denoted inmates from the highest caste, but in the eighties, the term's meaning had changed and represented a non-grypsman impersonating a grypsman; it was also an alternative term for penis. In total, the grypsmen, the highest caste, constituted about 70 to 80 percent of Rakowiecka prisoners. Below the grypsmen in the hierarchy were the *suckers*, and then the lowest caste, the *fags*. An estimated 1 to 2 percent of inmates belonged to the fag caste. In general, a grypsman could steal from a sucker, but the grypsman was not allowed to offend a sucker too much by using profanity, which was reserved only for the fags. A prisoner's assignment to one of the castes took place immediately after that man's arrival *under the cell* (common substitute term for "in the cell," "to the cell," etc.).

Almost anyone could eventually become a grypsman, although there were some exceptions, including militiamen or judicial officers, child molesters, and communists, who were always prohibited. A grypsman had to follow a pentalogy of general rules, called *principles*: *honor, hygiene, solidarity, refusal to cooperate*, and *help*. The specific rules were subject to slight local variations, but all variants imposed a general direction for grypsman behavior. For example, the "refusal to cooperate" rule prohibited voluntary cooperation with the administration, as this could harm other grypsmen.

Moreover, a grypsman also had to be fully aware of the more detailed rules about one's proper conduct in specific prison situations, called *behaviors*, as well as the rules of bajera, including its secret norms and prohibitions. For instance, the behavior called *handshake* regulated with whom the grypsman could exchange handshakes (i.e., only with other grypsmen, with exceptions made for a physician who had saved the grypsman's life and for his family members). The biggest insult was to call a grypsman a "fag," a "rat," a "communist," or any other derivative term, or to compare him to a woman.

Below the grypsmen in the prison hierarchy were the "suckers." Intimidated by the grypsmen, they cleaned the cells and performed other chores. A sucker was never allowed to sit at a table with a grypsman, nor, as mentioned above, to shake his hand. In fact, a sucker was considered to be an actual or potential informant, and therefore was isolated in his cell by the other prisoners. Outside of the typical prison environment, such as in the prison's hospital, the prisoners could use a more relaxed *half-freedom* bajera and and could address suckers with the more neutral term of "non-grypsmen." In such a place, a sucker's relationship with grypsmen could also be friendlier.

The most significant and most mythologized offense against the grypsmen rules concerned prisoners' penises: a prisoner was never to touch another man's penis, nor was he allowed to be touched by another prisoner's penis. A grypsman doing so intentionally, or even accidentally—typically, in a bathhouse—was immediately demoted to the fag caste. Downgrading could also occur by agreeing to satisfy another prisoner sexually or by committing some other serious *bending* (misconduct). An estimated 1–2 percent of inmates belonged to this lowest category.

Becoming a fag was a grypsman's greatest fear. A fag was often treated as a male prostitute and exploited to satisfy the sexual needs of the grypsmen as well as forced to endure various minor and major humiliations. He was often given a woman's name and told to dress in female clothes. He was not allowed to leave the vicinity of the toilet bowl—aptly called a *jaruzel*, after the name of the first secretary of the Central Committee, General Wojciech Jaruzelski.[3] In the evenings, the fags had to entertain the grypsmen with singing and dancing (see fig. 3.3).

A *rookie*—a new *first-time-caught* prisoner—who wanted to become a grypsman usually had to go through several complicated tests, which could include *fagotization* and *baptism*. Both tests, as well as less formal *little games*, put the unsuspecting rookie in situations where he had to make a decision that was supposed to reveal his *character* and *smartness*. A smart and tough rookie would pass those tests while a dumb and soft one would fail (see Kaminski 2003, 2004a for detailed analysis). Those who failed the tests, depending on the magnitude of the failure, became either suckers or fags.

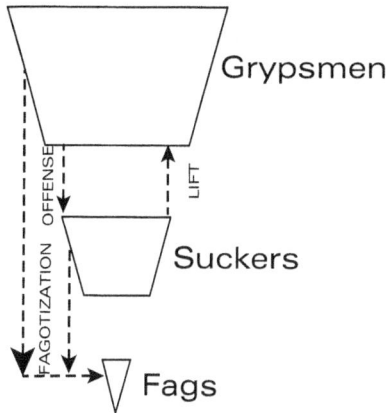

3.3. Relations among prison castes in Rakowiecka Jail. The areas of the rectangles are proportional to the estimated sizes of the castes in the Rakowiecka Jail in 1985. The arrows show the possible directions of inter-cast mobility. *Source*: Kaminski (2004a).

The last stage was to study and pass a final exam on the principles, behaviors, and bajera of the grypsmen. As mentioned, a grypsman who significantly broke important grypsmen norms could be demoted to one of the lower groups. On the other hand, a sucker who performed exceptionally noble acts, such as severe self-injury in defense of his honor or a serious sacrifice in the interests of his cell, could sometimes be *raised* to the position of grypsman. Sadly, a fag had no chance to change his miserable fate.

Bajera was probably the most extraordinary feature of grypsman subculture. Standard bajera had many forbidden words, which were not allowed to be spoken against other grypsmen under the threat of violence by the offended inmate. For instance, disallowed *cursing* could occur by comparing a grypsman to a woman, a communist, a fag, and so on. The rules banned even slight allusions in this direction. Therefore, one grypsman could not say to another that he was a "pretty boy," as only a woman or a fag could be called pretty. Furthermore, the word "boy" without any qualifying adjective could also refer to a fag. One had to talk about a "handsome boy," or even better, a "handsome man" or "handsome lad" instead. In another example of bajera restrictions, one could not say to a grypsman with a flushed face that he was "red," you could only use the word "red" to describe communists. One needed to *finalize*—that is, complete the phrase, such as with "You are red in the face," or use one of many more or less witty substitutes, such as *brick-colored*.

The rules forbade the use of several dozen words because they were associated with the penis. To say about someone that he "sucked juice from a bottle" or that he "played a trumpet" (or flute, pipe, trombone, etc.) meant either that the speaker had committed a serious, thoughtless offense or was mounting a deliberate verbal attack. In fact, it was prudent to avoid talking about objects with phallic shapes altogether. Overall, the list of banned terms was very long, and grypsman candidates were motivated to study hard by teachers who eagerly mounted plates for the slightest mistake.

In some prisons, or even particular cells, the adherence to argot standards was more restrictive than elsewhere. In turn, the prison hospital allowed for less restrictive, *loose bajera* or *loose code*. In these places, a grypsman could eat with suckers at the same table, and minor offenses were often forgiven. The elders in ordinary cells could also temporarily introduce loose bajera on special occasions, such as on Christmas Eve.

Interestingly, almost all criminal prisoners were "viciously anticommunist."[4] Even the formal rules of eligibility for grypsmen explicitly excluded communists and other regime functionaries from membership. Admittedly, the pejorative adjective "communist" referred more to the cruel and crude reality of the penitentiary than the political system of the Soviet Bloc. A "communist organization," then, meant simply an "evil organization" or even a "poorly managed organization."

Anticommunism was also present in artifacts of grypsman culture that prisoners created to occupy their time. While at Rakowiecka Jail, the Student's cellmates would proudly show him their poems, carefully written into precious, fat notebooks full of prison art of such a quality that it would redefine the concept of graphomania (Kaminski 1985a, April 4). The Student's buddy, a prisoner called "Kazik," in his poem describes his anticommunist heroism (the translation has attempted to preserve the flavor of the original spelling):

It is noting, it is hardt–
the blow falls after the blow–
I am from those who cold bravery
throw lighting in the communist fortress

Among the most remarkable features of Polish prisons in 1985 was an incredibly complex and ingenious system for exchanging information and trading small goods. *Grypses* (secret messages) circulated steadily in Polish prisons. It is no wonder, then, that the name of the highest caste was derived from this word. Sending, distribution and receipt of the secret messages were at the very center of inmate activity. Each gryps was written concisely, rolled into a small tube, and sometimes sealed with a drop of hot plastic. It was passed on, usually with the help of *corridormen* (inmates who worked mainly in the corridor dispensing meals, newspapers, books, and other items), but also through barbers or even guards. Secret messages conveyed arrangements between accomplices, details of commercial transactions, and love letters, as well as occasional birthday wishes and ordinary greetings. Gryps—like the one sent by Korycki to the Student, described later—could also announce the passage of the most precious object for a smoker, a cigarette lighter; this preliminary information sent via a gryps that spoke about an upcoming shipment provided an extra security layer against theft.

Local, in-house grypses constituted the bulk of information turnover, but some grypses also traveled to other prisons or even out into the world. Transmission of such long-distance secret messages was more complicated and required the collaboration of family members, lawyers, medical service personnel, prison colleagues about to be released, or even guards. Typically, long-distance grypses verified the identity of new inmates or were used to send important notes to partners in crime.

The most extraordinary channel for transmitting not only secret messages, but also money and goods, such as cigarettes and tea, was a system of *get-throughs* (holes in the walls, floors, and ceilings used for sending grypses). All of the cells at the Rakowiecka and Białołęka Jails where the Student stayed were connected with neighboring cells, and often with the cells both above and below, by small tunnels that had been hollowed out laboriously by patient prisoners. The staff tolerated get-throughs as long as their diameters remained small. If the prisoners increased the diameter past a certain point, all the inmates would be moved to a new cell and inmate masons would be ordered to seal the get-through. In *barns*—large cells holding forty or fifty prisoners—a designated rookie or sucker, called a *get-throughman,* would service the get-throughs and spend his whole busy day moving from one hole to another, receiving secret messages and parcels, shouting the names of final recipients, and forwarding on secret messages.

Figure 3.4 shows the most important communication methods used at Rakowiecka.

In some prisons, there were also other castes, such as those termed *ladybugs* or *fests*, who fought for power with the grypsmen and employed modified norms and bajera, or the *Swiss*, who—naturally—claimed neutrality during inter-caste conflicts.[5] However, the standards set by the grypsmen governed the behavior of prisoners in Rakowiecka

3.4. Major methods of communication at Rakowiecka in 1985. Clockwise from the top: telephone (used only by political prisoners); pipe ringing (sender and receiver); get-through; gryps via corridormen; window-shouting; hand alphabet; horse. Drawing by Mirek Andrzejewski. *Source*: Kaminski (2004a).

Jail. Korycki's unique situation led to some modifications, including a more flexible treatment of important grypsman rules and taboos.

## DOWN BUT NOT OUT

During the final manhunt described in the last chapter, Korycki survived the fatal shot. Later, he told the Student that in the heat of the moment, he had made a mistake. He had placed the revolver too close to his temple, and because of that, the bullet did not explode properly and thus did not kill him.

The militia brought the unconscious man to the hospital in Międzyrzec Podlaski. From daybreak on, the tension in this city was palpable. The militia forces who had gathered there set up their base at the facilities of the Państwowe Gospodarstwo Rolne (State Agricultural Farm, PGR) on Lubelska Street. There were many militia cars, even armored vehicles, and numerous officers around the PGR. The army was also there. The local health service remained on alert.

By the afternoon, the news of Korycki's capture had electrified the town. A crowd of curious onlookers filled the square in front of the hospital. Everyone wanted to see the famous Janosik of Podlasie. The head of the MO Commissariat in Międzyrzec, Captain Łys, recalled, "My civilian phones [lines] were getting red-hot. They were constantly ringing, with people asking if it was true about Korycki, had he been caught?" (Borkowski 1982, 10).

At the hospital, Korycki eventually regained consciousness. He was able to speak logically and clearly. During a conversation with the doctor, he smoked quite a few cigarettes. When it turned out that he would have surgery, probably expecting that he might not survive, he shouted, "Long live Poland!" He wanted these to be his final words. He did not answer the doctor who, wanting to please the militiamen who were present, asked Korycki, "Which Poland? That of bandits?" (Borkowski 1982, 10). Korycki did not succumb to the doctor's provocation even though he certainly considered the "People's" Poland of the communists to be "that of bandits."

In the Surgical Ward, Korycki underwent two operations conducted by the head of the surgical team, Doctor Stanisław Gaszewski. The surgeon removed the bullets from the patient's right hand and left groin. However, he did not remove the bullet from his head, instead only cleaning the wound. He found that this bullet had damaged the right hemisphere of Korycki's brain, resulting in paralysis on the left side of his body (Borkowski 1982, 10). Neither the head surgeon nor any other surgeon at Międzyrzec was able to remove the bullet from the patient's head safely, and nobody wanted to take the risk that Korycki would die on the operating table.

Four days later, the prosecutor read Korycki the verdict on his "temporary arrest." The following day, an ambulance took him to the Rakowiecka Jail. Prison doctors assigned Korycki to the Surgical Ward of the hospital in Rakowiecka in *Trójka*, Cell No. 3, which was set aside for the most severe cases. In addition to his partial paralysis, Korycki had a broken right arm and a deep wound in his left leg near the groin. The humerus in his arm had been fractured as a result of a gunshot traveling through the bone. Still, even with a bullet lodged between the two hemispheres of his brain, he miraculously survived. He was bedridden, however, and could not even prop himself up enough to sit. He could only lie in bed (Kaminski 1985b).

Although Korycki survived the shooting, he still had a dramatic fight for survival on his hands. The prosecutor conducting the investigation, anticipating procedural complications, decided to make things easier for himself. He ordered the prison health service to put a mentally handicapped non-grypsman inmate in the hospital cell with Korycki. As Korycki later described him, he was "a *freak* [mentally ill person] who strangled his whole family" (Kaminski 1985b).[6] The prosecutor promised this man freedom in exchange for strangling the paralyzed Korycki, who was "as helpless as a baby" at the time. Korycki later told the Student that he saw the prosecutor point him out to the freak and make a hand gesture around his neck, meaning, "strangle him too." The young man later confessed the truth to Korycki (Kaminski 1985b; Kaminski 2004a, 176).

Why would the prosecutor want to murder an inmate? Contrary to popular belief, even in the PRL's imperfect judicial system, a death sentence for Korycki would have been unlikely. In 1980s Poland, primarily serial killers or perpetrators of extremely cruel crimes received such sentences (see Infor.pl 2020b). The most serious of Korycki's charges, the accidental killing of Wojciech Dąbrowski at the Łuków train station, was based on circumstantial evidence. Colonel Płócienniczak, who predicted *kaes* (the death penalty) in the trial, perhaps expected that the political pressure would lead to this sentence. The PRL often broke its own laws—one of numerous cases was the unlawful detention

of the Student. However, with each passing decade, the loose communist attitude toward the law faced ever-increasing resistance from non-
governmental organizations. In 1971, the prominent opposition leader
Jacek Kuroń appealed for "a new program whose goal would be to create a united front for those who oppose the current system. ... Let us
enter socio-cultural associations and transform them ... into a league
of human rights defenses and  ...  political prisoners' rights" (Friszke
2011, 38). These words were soon translated by Kuroń into the concise
"Do not burn committees, set up your own," in reference to the Gdańsk
workers' strike of 1970, when the local communist party committee
building was burned.

In the 1980s, activists took up and operationalized Kuroń's ideas into
a variety of legal and underground "committees." The Polish division
of Amnesty International supported the PRL's political prisoners with
great commitment. (Using parcels received from AI in prison, the Student was able to donate some of the vitamin supplements he obtained
to Korycki.) The Primate's Committee organized charitable help for political prisoners both during and after their imprisonment.[7] In 1982, the
Helsinki Committee, associated with the opposition, was founded. The
Helsinki Committee oversaw Poland's compliance with the 1975 Helsinki Accords, which committed the socialist states to respect human
rights and fundamental freedoms. Soon opposition organizations blos-
somed, claiming legality by referring to the Helsinki Accords.

All such changes imposed certain constraints on communist prosecutors in the 1980s. The grypsman community quickly learned—probably from the corridormen who were servicing the cells—about the
prosecutor's plan to have Korycki assassinated. Korycki's arrival at Rakowiecka Jail was enormously important for the local grypsmen: "No
grypsman could doubt that Janosik was a fine robber, fierce anticommunist, loyal to the death, tougher than rock, that he was the incar-
nation of all grypsman values. His record was transparent, confirmed
by TV broadcasts and newspaper stories. He clearly deserved help"
(Kaminski 2004a, 177). Out of all the mythologized grypsman values,
perhaps the most impressive for the grypsmen was that they perceived
Korycki to be a tough and decisive fighter who would not hesitate to
use deadly force if needed. While this perception was imprecise—in
the opinion of his fellow inmate, the Student—it helped to mobilize
the Rakowiecka grypsmen. They reacted firmly and immediately announced that Korycki's death would result in the automatic execution of
the killer.

Consequently, the potential assassin quickly abandoned his assassination plans. Even further, he immediately began to help and look after Korycki. Korycki later reported to the Student that "he was a good boy. ... He even helped to put my dick in the bedpan and washed it." (Kaminski 1985b). Paralyzed and bedridden, Korycki was still able to convert a serial murderer into a dedicated Good Samaritan.

To understand the uniqueness of Korycki's would-be killer's behavior and Korycki's accomplishment in taming this dangerous man, it is important to recall the strongest taboo of the grypsman subculture: at all costs, one had to avoid touching the penis of another inmate or being touched by another's penis. One had to be careful, for example, in the bathhouse, where the prisoners went once a week, or while undressing before sleep. The rules even prohibited a handshake with another grypsman immediately after nighttime, as grypsmen had to first wash their hands in the event that they had masturbated the night before. Even referring to another grypsman in a manner alluding to the penis or, even worse, suggesting an activity reserved for a fag, for example, "pull this cable," was extremely dangerous. If any such fateful transgression occurred, the offended grypsman was compelled to fight to fiercely defend his tarnished honor. Otherwise, he might be immediately demoted. Clearly, then, helping another prisoner with putting his "dick in the bedpan" was an extremely heavy offense in the rulebook of grypsman transgressions.

However, the non-grypsman cellmate who helped Korycki humanely meet his physiological needs apparently did not suffer any consequences. It is possible nobody learned the extent to which the man helped Korycki, or perhaps his fellow inmates mercifully overlooked the information. Most likely, Korycki told only the Student about the man's assistance. In any case, no other inmate with whom the Student talked about Korycki repeated this part of Korycki's prison story.

After Korycki had recovered somewhat, doctors transferred him to a regular multi-person hospital cell, mostly staffed by grypsmen (Kaminski 1985b). Later, in a similar cell, Korycki met the Student. Paradoxically, his situation worsened, as there was no longer a friendly assistant to help him discreetly with his needs. Even if the helpful inmate were in the same cell with Korycki, he would have been too scared of punishment by the grypsmen to continue helping him in the same way as when they were in just a two-inmate cell.

The prison staff made Korycki's life difficult in every possible way. The nurses employed by the prison punished him in accordance with the expectations of the jail's administration, to the point where they ignored his requests for a bedpan.[8] The nurses' direct superiors did not react either. Therefore, Korycki, due to his incapacitated arms and partial paralysis, defecated and urinated in bed. Both the prison medical staff and the administration remained indifferent. Their interventions were limited to daily changes of linen and bedding (Kaminski 2004a, 176).

Korycki's treatment, albeit particularly malicious, was not an exception in penal history. The inhumane treatment of patient-inmates has gone on for centuries, including during the cruelest periods of penitentiary history, when torturing inmates' bodies regularly accompanied imprisonment (Foucault 2012). Yet the prison medical service at Rakowiecka was not so much deliberately cruel as apathetic and lazy. The staff's "treatment" was often limited to dispensing a huge number of pills, up to forty per day, partly dissolved in water so that prisoners would not accumulate psychotropic drugs. The administration feared that such drugs could be traded and used for self-injuries and simulating sickness.

In the Student's cell, "a lad came one day after surgery. He had swallowed some iron crosses and held them inside for over a year; finally, they pierced his intestines. ... They took him for a second surgery for peritonitis. ... He asked the nurse for a bedpan. She refused. A fellow prisoner wanted to give him one, but he refused: [he said,] 'No, the nurse.' She did not come, so he shat under himself. She returned the joke and didn't clean it up. He lay there and rang her all night" (Kaminski 1985a, May 23).

Another inmate reported, "Marek, a lad from my cell, has a ... cast on his upper torso and an arm. His hand is immobilized in a splint. This splint is no longer needed, but Marek wears it because 'there is no key' to unscrew it. Perhaps the key was lost forever?" The Student witnessed many other situations of the medical staff's indifference and apathy, for example, when the "buddies of another guy removed his stitches after the surgery and not one of the doctors noticed." He further described the situation in which Korycki found himself several times: "An older man after a heart attack, with a weak heart, asked 'Berta' [the nurse's nickname] for some nitroglycerin. Her answer: 'Count sheep up to a thousand, lie on your right side, it will pass'" (Kaminski 1985a, May 19 and May 23).

There were times when this type of negligence had more severe consequences. In one such case, the Student recorded the following story:

A few weeks ago, a guy was under my cell who had his x-rays mixed up before the surgery. Instead of hemorrhoids, they operated on his *samara* (stomach). They cut him open, checked that everything was OK, and stitched him up. He wakes up, and his stomach is upset. He tears the bandages off: there is a cut. He reaches down to the obvious place—everything healthy, except the hole, as it had been tight, so it remains. ... He accepted the prosecutor's offer to release him from arrest. (Kaminski 1985a, May 23)

In such cases, waiving the inmate's temporary arrest and releasing him was a bribe by the prosecutor to stop the inmate from making potentially embarrassing accusations regarding the prison personnel's extreme negligence. It was common knowledge that a defendant's trial prospects were better when he was not arrested.

Korycki suffered in prison. Subculture rules forbid the grypsmen from aiding him in relieving his physiological needs. He knew the rules. Despite suffering, he never uttered a word of complaint. In the Student's words, "He was one of the toughest people I met in my life. He gave the impression of being so tough that nothing can break him. He was a man of iron character and immense self-discipline. Without this, leading a life like he lived would not have been possible" (Kaminski 2018, email 2).

Korycki's dramatic fate posed a serious dilemma for the grypsmen elders at Rakowiecka. A tough gangster and a staunch anticommunist fighter—the communists' "Public Enemy No. 1"—Korycki was the double epitome of all mythologized grypsmen values (Kaminski 2004a, 277). Prisoners told and retold legends, often exaggerating Korycki's fantastical raids and adventures. Within the prison, he had an impeccable reputation and enjoyed the respect of his fellow prisoners, almost as if he were a mythical figure, and not a man of flesh and blood. Both "rookies" and experienced prisoners, and even the elders, secretly wrote to him for his opinion on matters. He issued balanced and measured judgments, based on convincing reasoning. In various prison dilemmas, the grypsmen considered his verdict to be conclusive. Even incapacitated, he was an asset to prison life (Kaminski 1985a, May 23).

"Książę" (Prince), a non-grypsman with whom Kaminski spent time in a hospital cell at Rakowiecka Jail, stated that when he was in prison in Chełm, in the years 1980–81, he already knew of "Korycki's legend," which, he said, was still fresh and going strong. The Chełm prisoners admired Korycki for his uncompromising treatment of the militia and because in every confrontation—like a true gangster—he just fired on them ("Książę" 2018).

Yet the legendary robber and anticommunist fighter was helpless and at the mercy of others while in prison. In the opinion of the grypsmen leaders, Korycki, systematically humiliated through the mistreatment of the medical staff, undoubtedly deserved their help. However, helping him with his physiological needs would mean breaking the fundamental norm of the grypsman subculture "do not touch the penis of another man." The grypsmen were concerned that the suspension of such a fundamental norm was very risky, and could bring the wholesale degradation of all the grypsmen within the cell, or even within the whole cellblock.

Finally, the grypsmen openly conversed about helping Korycki. For several days, the "issue of Korycki's penis" was the only topic discussed via the grypses sent secretly through corridormen. In the end, the elders of Rakowiecka decided that the humiliation of the "prince of robbers" was more insulting for the grypsmen than breaking the principle of not touching the intimate body parts of another prisoner. Thus, they decided to establish precise instructions for prisoners who were to take on the role of temporary nurses. If the cell happened to house a prisoner degraded to the lowest status—a fag—then the prisoners should compel him to serve the paralyzed Korycki. Otherwise, a designated prisoner had to firmly inform the hospital staff about Korycki's need, and only in the absence of a response from the staff could he begin assisting Korycki. If the prisoners in the cell were physically in good condition, they could move Korycki to the *corner* (toilet behind a metal screen) so that he could relieve himself. If they could not lift Korycki, one of them brought him a bedpan, and they were allowed to touch the penis of the paralyzed man through toilet tissue. For months, until Korycki's right arm bone healed, the grypsmen in his cell alternated and performed these nursing duties (Kaminski 2004a, 177).

## FOUR YEARS WITHOUT A SENTENCE

After his initial dramatic fight for life, Korycki's situation in prison stabilized. His days slowly filled up with the tiny routines that are essential for prison survival. He broke the cast on his right arm himself and tried to regain use of it through exercise. During these attempts, he broke his left, limp arm. Medical personnel also failed to react to this situation, so his left arm healed very slowly (Kaminski 2004a, 176). The Student noted the progress in the rehabilitation of Korycki's right arm and hand in his secret records: "He clenched his teeth and practiced. After three months of pain, he regained use [of his right arm]. Now he can reach for a cigarette and a match. If he has to, he will even light it himself" (Kaminski 1985b).

Among the hospital staff, some doctors did remain faithful to the Hippocratic Oath. As the Student recollected, "The head of the surgical department at Rakowiecka, Dr. Jerzy Possart, always chatted with Józek in a friendly manner during rounds."[9] The initial negative attitude of the medical staff toward Korycki was likely due to their exposure to communist propaganda, which only presented Korycki in the worst possible light. Later, however, perhaps influenced by Dr. Possart's friendly manner, Korycki's treatment became less biased.

In the Student's experience, medical staff both in and outside of prison were usually friendly toward political prisoners, and even sometimes made subtle fun of communist-regime functionaries. A hilarious situation occurred when three SB officers escorted the Student to the Marie Skłodowska-Curie Institute of Oncology outside the prison to get an X-ray. The radiologist warned the commanding officer to leave the X-ray room but the esbek did not obey. After the X-ray, she grumpily informed the increasingly more frightened esbek "You swallowed a lot of radiation," and asked him, "How far do you live from Rakowiecka? Ten kilometers? Good. You need to walk to work for a month to ventilate your body from radiation. And do not even think about approaching your wife earlier!" As the Student learned later, the radiologist was grumpy because she had wanted to secretly give him a bar of chocolate to cheer him up and was unhappy that the esbek made it impossible. Korycki and other cellmates laughed heartily when they heard the story.

The grypsmen's dilemmas with Korycki and their way of solving them set precedents in grypsman subculture norms and had some impact on the norms' subsequent evolution. This subculture, despite its conservative and hermetic structure, was always slowly evolving, along with some periods of speedy change that usually coincided with political thunderstorms. The first such moment was in 1956 during the post-Stalinist thaw. Control in the penitentiary was relaxed, and the inmates obtained greater freedom and more rights. There was also rapid expansion and democratization of the subculture, which allowed almost anyone to become a grypsman, not just thieves—the former criminal elite. Several decades later, the years 1980–81 and the Carnival of Solidarity brought the easing of rigors and the abolishment of the most brutal punishment of *hard bed* or *belts*.[10] The fall of communism in 1989 brought further relaxation of both administrative constraints and subculture punishments.

It is not clear whether Korycki received formal grypsman training, but during his last stay at Rakowiecka Jail, he had a good knowledge of the basics. As discussed earlier, all new grypsmen apprentices had to undergo such training, while veteran prisoners additionally tested young prisoners without experience in a juvenile reformatory or via their reputations as career criminals for bravery and intelligence. Testing Korycki would have been pointless. During the twenty-four days the Student spent with Korycki in the cell, the question of whether Korycki was a grypsman was never raised in conversations due to the extraordinary esteem that he enjoyed. As a seriously ailing super-robber, Korycki had a separate, high status, usually reserved only for the elders at the top of the prison hierarchy. The elders thus released Korycki from the most orthodox rules of the grypsmen. Obviously, he could not comply with certain hygiene requirements. Moreover, the prohibition against frequently signing up for meetings with a rehabilitation officer—which, in fact, could have been meetings with a prosecutor or penitentiary personnel to spy on someone—was considered irrelevant for him. He could not walk, and no guard would normally move his bed or carry him outside his cell. Thus, he only had to follow the most basic principles, such as "do not inform" and "do not offend other inmates." When asked by prison staff, he did not have to declare that he was a grypsman; this was important because revealing one's grypsman membership was required as it was part of the *behaviors*. In any event, no one would have asked him such a question anyway.

The language requirements were probably the only norms that were technically relevant for Korycki. Due to the unusual nature of his history and situation, the bajera's standard rules of "political correctness" were reduced for him. He could use phrases that, for another prisoner, would have caused immediate protest and would have resulted in a mounted plate. Basically, he could use "freedom language," including forbidden words, when describing his adventures outside of prison. For instance, he once spoke about his partner, Mirosław Kaliński, whom he took in; instead of using words like "lad" or "man," he called him a "boy," which, as discussed earlier, has specific connotations in prison, but his fellow prisoners disregarded this and let the story continue. Of course, Korycki's linguistic freedom did not include intentional insults toward grypsmen, but he obviously did not intend to test the boundaries or break every basic rule. In the cell with the Student and Korycki were two expert grypsmen who had an extraordinary grasp of bajera and other criminal slang; both inmates were supportive and supplemented Korycki's knowledge of bajera rules so that he did not make a big mistake.

Eventually, Korycki started functioning relatively independently and comfortably. In time, the authorities placed him in larger cells, with a few *walking* inmates (physically fit prisoners who were able to walk normally). When he needed help, his cellmates carried him to the corner, and then he was then able to use his hand and relieve himself. When the Student carried him a few times, he needed only one additional helper to move Korycki quickly and safely. The Student noted in his secret notes: "Guys carry him onto the toilet. They take him under the armpits and carry him out. He's very light. His right leg was 'curved in a claw,' and his left leg was 'thin as a stick.' And this left leg, after one of his visits in the corner, once slipped off the bed and broke." The Student explained, "They had laid him unevenly. He saw as [the leg] was sliding down the sheets, but he couldn't do anything" (Kaminski 1985b). His reliance on the help of the other prisoners distressed Korycki. He did not want to be a burden on his fellow inmates. As he explained to his sister-in-law, he purposefully ate little in order to minimize the frequency of his bathroom visits (Korycka 2020).

During this time, overall Korycki's spirit was good, but his body was deteriorating. In the prison hospital, he lost a lot of weight—down to 106 pounds from the 192 he weighed before the arrest. In his words, he had "shrunk." He was also balding, with only sparse tufts of hair on the sides of his head.

While the Student had also "shrunk," from about 176 pounds to about 123 pounds, losing weight at first often reversed in time into gaining more weight among long-term prisoners. Convicted inmates who came to terms with the prospect of long sentences survived the early prison period of overwhelming stress that caused weight loss. Later, while the prison menu was poor, three regular meals a day helped prisoners gain weight. Food parcels provided vital supplements to the prison menu for inmates who were lucky enough to have family members mail such parcels. For parcels, which had a weight limit of three kilograms (6.6 pounds), the inmates needed discretionary vouchers (see fig. 3.5).

Despite the bullet in his head, Korycki retained his mental powers. He spoke slowly but clearly, with no slurring of his speech; every word

3.5. A standard voucher for a food parcel. *Source*: Archive of Marek Kaminski.

was measured. He remained a rational, mentally strong, and principled man. He wanted to keep fighting the hated system. As the Student recalled, "I remembered his total obsession with Poland and its liberation from communism. It certainly brought us closer, because I was probably making a similar impression [on him]. … Communism was his obsession on a scale that impressed even me. He was interested in every detail of the functioning of the anticommunist underground. He also asked me several times to greet the student community from him" (Kaminski 2018, email 6). The greetings were the result of conversations in which the Student described to Korycki—without disclosing sensitive details—the strong anticommunist feelings dominating most universities and the organization of the underground publishing movement, which was largely based on students' volunteer labor.

Even with his poor health, Korycki himself was able to send and receive secret messages to and from various sources, which he did from time to time to attend to various types of small business. Typically, he dictated his messages to some volunteer helper. Writing even a short text with his own hand was very tiring and required some help from another inmate. Figure 3.6 shows a copy of a personally handwritten gryps, with words of sympathy and encouragement sent by Korycki to the Student, who at that time was in the adjacent cell in the Surgery Ward.

3.6. A gryps from Korycki to the Student in June or July 1985 (Korycki 1985): "Hi Mareczek [affectionate form of Marek]—As you depart, you will leave the best memories of yourself, and a realistic assessment of reality fills me with belief that you will wisely and usefully guide your life.—I wish you the best with it and, above all, a lot of health. The university ethos has its rights and no statute will pervert it, yet a wise one can support, expand, and consolidate it. As for the lighter, Andrzej will pass it on at the first opportunity. That you will be released won't be any favor. Thank you for the vitamins, regards and most cordial goodbye once again.–J. When you are released, please give my greetings to the college youth." *Source*: Archive of Marek Kaminski.

This memorable note, written with beautiful handwriting, still inspires emotions after all these decades. It condenses a few traits of Korycki's personality well. He addresses his friend warmly ("Mareczek") and speaks with a high level of reflection. He formulates a considered prediction and avoids discussing trivia; the wording and effort invested in the message suggest that he assumed this to be his farewell letter. An everyday business issue ("the lighter") is interspersed among noble verses. This was often done in order to trick the guards, who could intercept a gryps and then take a casual look at the first few sentences to check to see if they contained any reference to forbidden barter. If a guard learned about the lighter—an object prohibited under the cell— he could have ordered a *kipisz* (a comprehensive search of an inmate and/or his cell), which would have inconvenienced the entire cell and could have resulted in the loss of the precious item, as well as other punitive measures. The letter ends with regards to the university students and signals Korycki's high esteem for them.

The gryps was probably sent to comfort and support the Student at the end of his disciplinary transfer to *Trójka* (i.e., Cell No. 3, an ICU cell meant for seriously sick inmates) where he was transferred as a disciplinary measure for shouting at night "Good Night Solidarity!" Inmates in a prison hospital could not be punished with solitary confinement. The few available disciplinary actions for such patient-inmates included a transfer to an inferior cell or the withdrawal of food vouchers. While not a place of formal punishment, Trójka, where Korycki spent his initial time at Rakowiecka, was the worst cell in the Surgery Ward due to its poor conditions and the repellent smell from the seriously sick inmates housed there. When there was no walking inmate in Trójka, nurses tried to take rookies for a ride:

> They would say: take your blanket, bedsheet, and pillow and come with us. They would move him to Trójka. [ … Inside Trójka is] a guy with a festering wound in his lung (injection of feces). There's stink, cruel stench; nobody walks, everyone pukes, shits, and pisses under himself, and you need an inmate inside to pass them a bedpan. So he would be running in that stench all night [unable to sleep], and the sister would have a peace of mind. And in the morning (or even in the evening) would come the prize—[a shot of] one hundred grams of salicyl alcohol. I saw how a nurse tried to take "Rysio" for a ride, but he just laughed: it is his fifth month in the hospital. (Kaminski 1985a, May 23)

Receiving a handwritten gryps signaling close friendship with the prince of the prison aristocracy was a sensation and helped raise the position of the Student in the new cell where he had been transferred. It was a source of prestige and aroused respect. Later, the Student publicly read the gryps to the curious audience. It also sparked requests to retell Korycki's adventures, which the Student agreed to, editing out some of the more private parts of the narrative. After providing great escapist entertainment—so highly valued in prison—that filled out the entire evening, the Student cemented his position in the new cell.

Reading newspapers and listening to radio news demarcated Józef's days in prison. In prison, inmates were offered a free copy of *Trybuna Ludu* (*People's Tribune*), a Polish version of the Soviet Union's *Pravda*. *Trybuna* was the major vehicle of communist media propaganda, not deviating an inch from the orthodox party line, and providing manipulated general information mixed with irrelevant communist factoids and ideological opinion pieces. Since nothing else was available, readers tried to read between the lines. Whenever corridormen brought the daily copy (one copy for several prison cells), Korycki always received it first. He read it cover to cover. He tried to extract the smallest details heralding the twilight of the hated system, and intelligently commented on what he found there. The Student remembered how much Korycki was interested in the article about the American program called "Star Wars," which was President Ronald Reagan's famous initiative for a global system of strategic defense against Soviet intercontinental ballistic missiles. "Now President Reagan will fuck the communists up," Korycki said delightedly (Kaminski 1985b). He also listened attentively to political news from the *driller* (prison radio station broadcasting in the cells). The Student recalled, "When driller announces the daily news, conversations quiet down under the cell—Józek listens!" This was the entirety of Korycki's life routine at that time: the newspaper, the radio news, a cigarette, and conversations over *czajura* (strong infusion of tea). The joke that made Korycki laugh to tears was the one that goes, "A woman comes to the doctor with a bullet in her head. And he goes: what popped into your head?"

Family visits provided rare breaks from the everyday monotony of prison life. Korycki did not have many of them. During his four-year stay at Rakowiecka, his life partner—the person closest to him—only once obtained permission to visit, even though she traveled to the Warsaw prosecutor's office five times in attempts to get such permission. Since Korycki formally had the status of "temporarily arrested," the prosecutor had arbitrary power to issue or deny permissions. Oksiejuk (2018a) remembered her prison visit, which was in the company of watchful prison guards, well:

> When he was in prison in Warsaw, I went to see him. I went to the prosecutor and got the permission to visit. Only once. Józek's brother, Jan, also went with me, but they did not let him in, he did not get permission. They led me there through all these pavilions, how many were there, and in one of them, in the corridor, when I was already there, they put up a bed with Józek. And this is how I saw him; he couldn't even move. There were guards beside, and militia all around, so that it was impossible to talk freely, to say what I wanted. I smuggled only two packets of cigarettes for him, tucked them under the blanket, although everything was searched before. And that was it.

Despite apparent suffering, Korycki did not complain. He said to her, "It will get better," and that "we would meet soon, that he would come back to us … but that's not what happened, he returned forever, only dead" (Oksiejuk 1986). She never saw her "dearest friend and husband" alive again.

Korycki's mother, his brother Władysław, and sister-in-law Barbara were luckier. The courts permitted them to have a few family meetings. They first had to go to the Regional Court on Świętokrzyska Street in Warsaw and ask for a visitation permit. Once at the prison, they had to wait as he was prepared for the visit. As Barbara Korycka (2020) recalls,

> When Józek was in a better shape, they were bringing him in a sort of wheelchair. He was partially seating. He was behind the glass, he had a phone receiver, and we all had our receivers on the other side. And I did not know what to say. The stress was such that I wanted it to end it as soon as possible. When he was in worse shape [in his last year], those meetings were at [the Surgery Ward … ]. You walked down a corridor, and then there was a booth where a militiaman was sitting. They were moving him with the bed and giving us a chair. When we visited him in [the] prison hospital, he enjoyed it very much. He asked about his brothers, the children, how everything was at home.

Many inmates ask family not to visit them, since the visits are often followed by a period of depression. And everybody wants the hostile time to pass quickly. As the Student wrote, "in prison, where the basic unit of time is a week, Józek's time flows even slower. It is measured by months and years" (Kaminski 1985b).

Korycki spent most of his four years at Rakowiecka in the Surgery Ward, with about a six-week break when doctors placed him in the Internal Medicine Ward. As Barbara Korycka discusses it, "it was a whole trip, they moved him to another pavilion a hundred meters away," and "for a while, he was also with the crazies, one floor above." For a year and a half, the courts refused visitation from his family members. He did not receive parcels since he did not want to be a burden to anyone. He only asked for a thousand zlotys every month for *wypiska* (bimonthly shopping in the prison's store)—to buy cigarettes and matches. The money was indeed useful. Those who were "temporarily arrested" could use money deposited in their prison accounts to order products like "Sport" cigarettes, matches, notebooks, envelopes, stamps, and pens, as well as salt, sugar, canned pâté, and chicken in broth. In 1985, the average monthly salary in Poland was about 20,005 zlotys (Infor.pl 2020a).

## NO TRIAL FOR JÓZEF K.

The major, anxiously awaited event for a "temporarily arrested" inmate is the trial. All other activities and events are time-fillers. In his prison records, the Student noted the devastating lethargy in Korycki's life:

> It has been like this for years; it will be for years. Józiek is waiting for what comes first: the trial or death. He knows that "they" are waiting until he dies. He would be out of their hair. They are in no hurry. One year, five years, ten years. Józiek will be lying there for days, years. Sometimes, he repeats his court speech. Not a word can be changed. Each has its own place and meaning. It has been polished over the years like stones on the beach. Józiek will have it out with them. He fought the communists for his rights. He did not kill anyone. He does not feel guilty. He will be the accuser. (Kaminski 1985b)

In the end, Korycki never faced a trial, although the authorities had started formal proceedings. The evidence we have for the initiation of the proceedings is a pencil annotation on an Easter card that Korycki received from Krystyna Oksiejuk and her daughter, Agnieszka, which he later gave to Kaminski as a souvenir. Next to the "Censored" stamp, there is a handwritten note with two signatures: the first one for the prison files, starting with SW ... [the rest illegible]; the second one for the court—"I VK 186/83." The second note means that the court initiated proceedings in 1983 in the Fourth Criminal Department.[11] The signatures were probably added since a copy or a transcript of the postcard had to be included in Korycki's file (see fig. 3.7).

The postcard contained Krystyna Oksiejuk's name and address, and Korycki gave it to the Student so he could contact Oksiejuk in person and prove to her that he was friends with Korycki. Korycki added that Oksiejuk could tell the Student more but he neither revealed her role in his life nor the fact that she hid him for a long time. The postcard was a secure carrier of that sensitive information. While the prison

3.7. Easter postcard that Korycki gave to the Student in early May 1985, which included the name and address of Krystyna Oksiejuk. *Source*: Archive of Marek Kaminski.

administration or inmates could confiscate or destroy notes with an address, no one would be motivated to confiscate (due to the "Censored" stamp) or to steal (no market value) a used postcard.

Until his death, Korycki remained in prison with the legal status of "temporarily arrested." Prison surgeons repeatedly recommended the removal of the bullet from the prisoner's head; however, since it was a life-threatening operation, his consent was necessary. He always refused. Consequently, every three months, the prosecutor extended his "temporary arrest"—probably about seventeen or eighteen times in total (see fig. 3.8).

Korycki's decision to refuse the surgery to remove the bullet from his head may seem irrational, but he had, in fact, thoughtfully and strategically analyzed the situation. When one fully understands the context of his decision, it seems to be the only sensible one. Before discussing his specific rationale, it is worth devoting some space to the general problem of inmates' strategic utilization of health problems (for a comprehensive analysis, see Kaminski 2004a, 145–68). Korycki's refusal to undergo surgery did not appear in a vacuum but was a logical action taken within the broader context of the grypsman subculture.

3.8. A standard prosecutor's note that extended a "temporary arrest" by three months. The generic "justification" provided for the extension was an "obvious anticipation of lying." *Source*: Archive of Marek Kaminski.

Prisoners quickly learn that their health problems are valuable assets that they can use in prison games. General institutional prison norms, as well as informal norms, determine the value of health problems. These norms direct prison personnel to treat a patient-prisoner better than a healthy inmate, to follow humanitarian procedures imposed by supervisory and monitoring organizations, and to address the health issue as quickly as possible because of the high cost of treatment in a prison hospital. The imperative of keeping the prison free from epidemics and riots is also important, as is a warden's desire to keep negative indicators of the quality of his or her work, like mortality rates, as low as possible.

The specific purposes for a strategic illness include putting pressure on the prosecutor, court, or prison staff; drawing public attention to one's situation; the symbolic cleansing of a curse cast by another grypsman; or because one needs to escape from a hostile cell. Simpler rewards received in a prison hospital, such as greater comfort, a daily glass of milk, slightly better food, an extra half hour of walking time, or gentler treatment by the guards, can also motivate inmates. Those who are most efficient in running this game can obtain an early release, a break in punishment, the suspension of their sentence, or a change in their indictment.

The most common type of strategic illness is *self-injury*. For example, a relatively simple self-injury, *pochlastanie,* involves the cutting of one's skin on the forearm and the inside of the wrist—which is most common—or on the abdomen, chest, thighs, back, cheeks, or neck, sometimes including veins, to cause heavy bleeding. In another popular type of self-injury, the spectacular *połyk* (swallow), inmates swallow various metal and other objects, such as cutlery, bedsprings, nails, wires, needles, ballpoint pen springs, safety pins, thermometers, razor blades, or metal bucket hoops. The catalog of the most popular self-injuries is, in fact, quite long (Kaminski 2004a, 150–52; see fig. 3.9).

The second type of strategic illness is *simulation*. The most unusual example of simulation is probably *seesawing*, meaning to simulate suicide by hanging. A prearranged partner who carefully watches his fellow inmate's hanging body quickly cuts off the seesawer from the rope at the proper moment. Unconscious, but still alive, the seesawer is transported to the hospital. Simulation can also be part of an elaborate game conducted with the help of bribed physicians or specialists from freedom clinics who conduct complex tests on the prisoner-patient to help him leave prison "due to health reasons."

Korycki's case is an example of a simple strategic illness of a third type: the *refusal* to take action or to deny consent to actions that the prison administration or health services consider beneficial or even necessary for an inmate's health or life. A simple example is a prisoner refusing consent for surgery to remove a tumor. Another common form is a *hunger strike*—refusing to eat—that may also be combined with simulation (e.g., stealthy eating of small meals) and self-injury (e.g., tearing out an IV drip).

Every refusal comes from a prisoner's calculation of expected costs

3.9. Most popular techniques for self-injury around 1985. Clockwise from top left: *seesawing, cutting, swallowing, scalding, torching, injections,* and *nailing.* Drawing by Mirek Andrzejewski. *Source:* Kaminski (2004a).

and benefits. Likewise, Korycki's refusal to allow doctors to remove the bullet from his head resulted from his personal calculation. He assumed that if he were to have the surgery, only one of two scenarios was likely to materialize. First, he could die during the operation, which, of course, would be a situation worse than remaining alive in partial paralysis. Second, the surgery could be successful and he would recover the use of his body, at least in part. He believed that in this scenario, the authorities would quickly put him on trial, sentence him to death, and execute him. By refusing his consent to the operation, he hoped to survive until the fall of communism and see a rapid amnesty or the dismissal of the charges against him. Korycki revealed his strategy to the Student at the end of April or beginning of May in 1985.

While Korycki's case and his situation in prison were uncommon in comparison to those of other inmates, his strategic utilization of the state of his health was typical. According to the Student's assessment, almost all prisoners contemplate self-injuries, and many decide to go ahead and enact them. The consequence of Korycki's refusal was that the prison physicians, when asked about his condition by the court, invariably stated, "The accused is not able to attend the trial." As a result, the medical examiner blocked the trial (Kaminski 2018, emails 2 and 6).

Regardless of Korycki's lack of consent, the prison physicians were also reluctant to undertake such a risky surgery. At some point, the authorities summoned Korycki's mother and sister-and-law to Warsaw to discuss the possible removal of the bullet. A medical council took place, and a physician informed Janina Korycka that they would not go ahead since, unfortunately, the location of the bullet was in such a place that its removal would kill the patient. They called them to Warsaw because they wanted to inform Korycki's mother personally (Korycka 2020).

The complexity of Korycki's situation was apparent to both the militiamen who arrested him and the prosecutors. Like others, Colonel Płócienniczak thought that Korycki would probably "have received at that time the death penalty and probably would have been executed." He agreed that Korycki "escaped with his life by not agreeing to the operation, for which his consent was needed" (Bodasiński and Osipowski 2015, Płócienniczak, 22'41"). Thus, ironically, the authorities agreed with Korycki's assessment that his refusal to consent to the brain surgery prevented his trial and death sentence. The trial—and even more so, his death sentence—would have been a communist propaganda triumph. The events would also have resonated throughout the underground opposition press.

In many cases, journalists have confused the issues of Korycki's trial and sentence. For example, a police officer and journalist, Przemysław Kacak, improperly cited Kaminski's book when he wrote the following: "In turn, according to Professor Kaminski, Korycki was tried and sentenced to death, only the sentencing was delayed due to his health condition" (Kacak 2011, 42). Apart from the false information that the trial took place, Kacak's statement confused the legal definitions of a person's sentencing and the execution of their sentence. If the authorities had tried Korycki and sentenced him to death, this would mean that the court had imposed a sentence, and only the execution could have been delayed. On this same issue, another author, Pytlakowski, without providing any sources, stated that Korycki "was sentenced to death, but the execution was delayed because the convict's health did not allow for it" (Pytlakowski 2006).

However, in Kaminski's writing, he stated unequivocally that Korycki avoided trial by refusing surgery. Certainly, Korycki's trial did not take place before the Student left prison—that is, before August 9,

1985—and neither Korycki's family nor his partner, Krystyna Oksiejuk, heard about any such trial afterward. Korycki died on August 21, 1986. Therefore, there is a probability bordering on certainty that a trial never took place (Kaminski 2018, emails 2–4).

## THE DEMISE OF JANOSIK

The communist courts convicted Józef Korycki six times for criminal offenses. He received relatively short individual sentences, usually two or three years each. In total, although his various sentences added up to thirteen and a half years, he spent almost twenty years in penitentiary units. This figure covers the periods of his "temporary arrests," including the more than four years from the start of his last detention to his death. His longest period in jail was his last. While he was never tried for the offenses that landed him in jail for the final time and no death penalty was ever imposed, the poor conditions of his imprisonment amounted to a prolonged execution.

In mid-1984, Korycki had his first heart attack. In critical condition, prison doctors transferred him to a freedom hospital in Warsaw. Then, since the doctors there confirmed that he was dying, the authorities transported him to his family home in Radzyń Podlaski a week later. The medical council at the Rakowiecka Jail hospital formally requested his release from detention despite the prosecutor's strong opposition. Kacak reported, "According to militia accounts, he left it [prison] only once, already as an aging man, for a temporary release. Apparently his (fully innocent, this time) appearance in his hometown resulted in a storm of phone calls to the 'organs' in Warsaw" (Kacak 2011, 42). It remains unclear what the official basis was for his release, but quite possibly, the warden, fearing that Korycki would die in his care, may have acted on impulse and accepted the medical council's advice.

The transfer came as a surprise to everyone. Barbara Korycka was alone when a delivery van stopped in front of her home, with Korycki tossed like a sack of potatoes in the back (Korycka 2020). The driver had initially transported Korycki to his mother's place, but since nobody was at home, he then went to the alternative address he had been given, the home of Barbara Korycka. The neighbors helped Barbara move Józef to her apartment and lay him on the sofa. He was thin, dirty, paralyzed, and had a broken leg. She was shocked: "My God, what did they do to a human being?" (Korycka 2020). Still, despite his physical condition, he was in good mental shape and was clearly very happy to be back with his loved ones. The driver left Barbara with a hospital referral for Korycki's broken leg and departed. After two nights, his relatives moved Józef to a local hospital, where he spent another two days.

Korycki, however, did not die. After several days at his mother's home, he was transported back to Rakowiecka. His sister-in-law remembers the events clearly:

> When his mother went shopping, they suddenly took him. She left the door unlocked since she was going to come back quickly from the store. As she returned, her son was not there; there was no note as to what happened, where he was, who took him. Just as they brought him suddenly, so they suddenly took him away. It was Saturday. Two days later, on Monday, there was TV reportage from Radzyń, on prime time, that the prison released a dangerous criminal, Józef Korycki. But because he walked in the town with weapons and frightened people, the residents called for the authorities to take him back. That's all. (Korycka 2020)

Thus, the family learned from the TV that the authorities had imprisoned Korycki again. The prosecution provided an absurd motivation for their decision to take him back to jail—the neighbors' fear of a dangerous criminal wandering about. In reality, bedridden and with a broken leg, Korycki spent all this time either under his mother's care or in the local hospital.

Why did the prison release Korycki in the first place? A seemingly minor, but, in fact, crucial detail was that Korycki was "in critical condition" when the van transported him to freedom. It was very common for prison authorities to get rid of seriously ill prisoners just before they died, as this reduced their official prison mortality rates. Prisoners understood this phenomenon well. They sometimes attempted to simulate a severe illness or serious depression, or they even tried to contract a highly infectious disease like Hepatitis A, to create the impression that they were dying, that they were likely to commit suicide because of their depression, or that their sickness was a real threat to the safety of the prison. The propaganda value of Korycki's case was probably so high that the permanent lifting of pre-trial detention by the prosecutor or the court due to his critical state was blocked at a higher decision-making level.

Back in prison, Korycki was seriously ill but still alive. In either March or April 1985, he suffered a second heart attack, just weeks before he met the Student. The exact day of the cardiac arrest is impossible to determine since doctors discovered it a few weeks later, only after they carried out further medical exams. After this heart attack, they placed him in the Internal Medicine Ward of the prison hospital, where, for twenty-four days, his time in the cell overlapped with that of the Student's incarceration there. The medical council again asked for the release of the patient to his home. This time the authorities denied the application. This may be the only case in the history of the PRL's prison system when a prosecutor's office repeatedly refused to release a prisoner who was so gravely ill (Kaminski 1985b).

The Student, immediately after his own release, tried to get the public's attention focused on Korycki's serious situation. He passed information about Korycki's fate to two institutions involved in helping political prisoners: the Primate's Committee and, in a special letter, *Tygodnik Mazowsze*.[12] Despite expectations, no intervention occurred, or at least, nothing happened that had any official effects.

Korycki did not live to see what he dreamt about for so long: the first partially free elections in postwar Poland and the downfall of communism. At the age of fifty-two, tormented by imprisonment and sickness, Korycki died on August 21, 1986, behind bars in Rakowiecka Jail, still a "temporarily arrested" inmate and still without a sentence. The Polish communist system entered a phase of rapid liberalization only three weeks later, when General Kiszczak announced a broad amnesty for political prisoners on September 11, 1986. Within three years, the entire system fell apart.

Korycki's family received the telegram with the news stating that he had died of a heart attack. It is unclear if he died suddenly or whether his condition gradually worsened after what would have been a third heart attack. The exact circumstances and details of his death remain unknown. Barbara Korycka and her husband, Władysław, who was weak after a heart attack of his own, had to travel to Warsaw to collect the body and the proper documentation for the funeral. The authorities treated them poorly, directing them to go from the prison to the militia, from the militia to the prosecutor, and then back again. The militia informally interrogated them and questioned them about the family. Their trip turned out to be unsuccessful, and they returned to Radzyń empty-handed. They bought a coffin and waited. Finally, they received a call that they could return to Warsaw to retrieve the body and the documents they needed.

The body was at the Institute of Court Medicine on Oczki Street, where an autopsy had been performed. During the autopsy, the bullet was removed from Józef's head, but the physician denied the family's request to tell them whether the bullet was from a revolver—supporting Korycki's claim that he shot himself—or from a machine gun—as the militia claimed. So this part of Korycki's mystery remains unanswered, although, in light of the coroner's refusal to discuss it, Korycki's version seems to gain some corroborative weight. We may hypothesize that if the militia's version of the events were true, the authorities would have revealed the type of bullet found. Barbara Korycka and two of Józef's brothers brought him back home:

> It turned out that the casket was too short since Józef was a tall man. Despite removing the padding from both sides, the body fit inside only when we bent the knees, and the lid was leaning on those knees. This is how we rode home, again on a "Żuk" delivery van. I was next to the driver's seat; Józek's brothers were in the back, holding the unclosed lid. In Radzyń, we had to buy another coffin, to which all the family had to contribute since this was a substantial expense for us. We had an appointment with a priest, who treated Józef as every other man, did not judge him. We moved the body to the new coffin and lay it in the chapel near the belfry of the Holy Trinity Church. I changed Józek's head dressing since it was bandaged after his skull had been opened. Everything was covered in blood. In the morning at 8:00, there was a mass and we buried Józek. (Korycka 2020)

Thanks to the efforts of his family and of Krystyna Oksiejuk, Józef Korycki was buried in his hometown of Radzyń Podlaski. His body was laid in a grave where, later, his two brothers, Władysław and Stanisław, would also be put to rest. Władysław died at age forty-eight and Stanisław at sixty-two (see fig. 3.10). Józef's third brother, Henryk, died the youngest of all of them, at forty-six.

Oksiejuk helped to carry out all the necessary formalities. She also contributed to the costs of transporting Józef's body and the burial, which amounted to 52,000 zlotys (Oksiejuk 1986). Janina, Józef's mother, spent her whole life savings on the transport of his body, casket, and funeral.

Krystyna Oksiejuk mourned Korycki deeply and still felt strongly connected emotionally with her life partner. In a touching letter to the Student, she wrote:

> Believe me, how hard it is for me, how I have suffered this terrible news, how terrible it was for me because nothing was ever said about death, he always comforted me, always said that we would meet soon, that he would come back to us, only that he always worried that he would be a burden to us, that is not what happened, he returned forever, only dead. … My dear God, what a difficult parting, no one could understand. (Oksiejuk 1986)

3.10. The grave of Józef, Stanisław, and Władysław Korycki in Radzyń Podlaski. Photo by Ernest Szum.

3.11. Józef Korycki's son, Sławomir, around 1968. *Source*: Archive of Barbara Korycka. Photo of the original by Ernest Szum.

3.12. Józef Korycki (wearing a beret) with son Sławomir and brother Henryk, around 1966. *Source*: Archive of Barbara Korycka. Photo of the original by Ernest Szum.

Apparently, Korycki's arrest and condition deeply affected his quiet son, Sławomir Korycki, as well (see figs. 3.11 and 3.12). As one person said of him, he "worked in a hospital. ... He was a spotless boy, well-mannered and nice, always very polite." (Korycka 2020) However, Płócienniczak publicized a story that "in the mid-eighties," the son of Korycki "using a knife, tried to hijack a ferry from Świnoujście to the [Danish] island of Bornholm" (Bodasiński and Osipowski 2015, Płócienniczak, 23'39"). In turn, Kacak stated that "a few months after Korycki was busted and canned, his son tried to terrorize the crew of a ferry [sailing] to Bornholm with a knife" (Kacak 2011, 42).

Thanks to the declassified archives of the KWMO Szczecin, we can verify both statements. Once we disregard sloppy reporting related to the timing and other mixed-up details, we find that it is true that on July 30, 1983, Sławomir Korycki, en route from Świnoujście to Szczecin, attempted to hijack a seaplane, the *Daria*, and head to Sweden with passengers on board. He was arrested, but it is unclear how his criminal case ended. Successful hijackers—even in absentia—were punished severely by communist courts, sometimes even with the death penalty (Bortlik-Dźwierzyńska and Niedurny 2009). This level of sentencing was in violation of Article 13 of the Universal Declaration of Human Rights (1948), which states, "Everyone has the right to leave any country, including their own."

Sławomir's aunt recalled, "[When hijacking the plane] He probably went nuts over alcohol. ... There was no political context to that [as opposed to his father's activity]. Later he drank a lot, too much. But he worked for Franciszek Stadnicki's business, on Międzyrzecka St., who knew Józek and employed him because of his father. ... Even when he overdrank, when he had weeklong binges, Mr. Stadnicki never fired him. His son escorted Sławomir to a rehab" (Korycka 2020). The family's curse of the early deaths of Józef and his three brothers continued with Sławomir; he died in 2011 at the age of forty-nine.

# Conclusion

## Bandit or Partisan?

A social psychologist, Philip Zimbardo (2007), argues that situations and group pressures are responsible for the "evils" of human behavior. He states that good people may commit wrongdoing when certain important situations, perhaps randomly created, push them in the wrong direction. While Zimbardo's best-known research in his Stanford Prison Experiment was recently subjected to substantial criticism, his argument still helps us to understand Korycki's case. A significant event in Korycki's life was the university's refusal to admit him. However, the incident in the mine may have been even more significant and was the event that was most responsible for redirecting his life onto the criminal path. A young, intelligent, and sensitive person, moved by strong emotions stemming from the harm inflicted on his close friend, reacted impulsively. Beating his tyrannical superior resulted in his desertion from the army, and it also caused Korycki's first contact with prison. This episode started a sequence of events that eventually catapulted Józef from a normal existence to a life at society's margins. As Oksiejuk summarized Korycki's situation after his first prison sentence, "At the time, he already had problems because he had been in prison for escaping from the army. He could not live a normal life anymore" (Oksiejuk 2018a). Korycki, wanting to remain true to his ideals, had limited choices, and his moral imperative forced him to follow a path opposing the political and legal order. Even Płócienniczak said, "Korycki was created to some extent by the situation" (Bodasiński and Osipowski 2015, Płócienniczak, 1'20"). This is how the "bandit" was born.

We can understand Korycki's biography only within the political context. His anticommunist attitude aligned him with nonviolent activists seeking change by encouraging the regime's authorities to democratize the system. However, the Polish opposition occupied an entire spectrum of approaches toward the fight with communism, from nonviolence to the acceptance of restricted violence. Kaminski's underground publishing house STOP, similarly to almost all other underground publishers, worked mostly in the "entryway" (to the communist system) by using workers in the so-called shadow economy. It obtained paper and ink for printing mostly by stealing them from state enterprises. It even printed some of its books in such incredible places as the print shops of the Rakowiecka Jail or the Central Committee of the PZPR's headquarters.

Several of the opposition leaders in the 1980s found the more reserved methods of the nonviolent part of their movement ineffective and were thus attracted to more violent and, in their view, effective measures. Leszek Moczulski's group, Confederation of Independent Poland, and Kornel Morawiecki's organization, Fighting Solidarity, repeatedly participated in street fights with ZOMO and went beyond nonviolence in their actions (Dudek and Marszałkowski 1999). Mateusz Morawiecki, the son of Kornel and the present prime minister of Poland, openly described violent struggles with the communists in the 1980s: "Many times, I tossed Molotov cocktails … at militia vans and water cannons, which pacified strikes" (Redakcja 2020; see the interview in Tompson and Ney 2020). Other oppositionists sometimes spontaneously used even more radical and violent methods in the fight against the communists. For example, in September 1982, after the massacre of demonstrators in Lubin in the so-called Polish Copper Belt, miners formed an informal group to avenge those who had been murdered. They gathered explosives and planned to place them under the headquarters of PZPR committees and in the flats of particularly hated communist party activists. Before they were arrested, they were able to carry out several attacks, including planting a bomb under the building of the PZPR in Legnica, which did not explode (Kamiński 2001). Against this backdrop, Korycki fits in the catalog of Polish anticommunist opposition. One historian opined that Korycki was a "bandit-recidivist who became a symbol of resistance to the communist authorities" (Pietrzak 2013).

## ON REBELS AND BANDITS

The Enlightenment social philosopher Thomas Hobbes was likely the first to consider the trade-off between societal safety and freedom.[1] States, or in Hobbes's parlance, "Leviathans," emerged from an unstructured state of nature—"the war of all against all"—and offered assurances of personal safety against threats from others. The price for the safety that the state provided was restriction on personal liberty.

Therefore, various forms of states evolved that were based on a self-centered calculation that responded to people's longing for security (Hobbes 2018).

In modern societies, whether centralized or decentralized, contemporary Leviathans exert social pressures via the institutions of the state, but also pressures come from business corporations and religious organizations. "Good" and "successful" citizens are socialized to consume goods and take part in pleasurable activities, provide for their families, and sometimes be killed in incomprehensible wars. Individuals are provided with handy patterns of behavior to give their lives meaning (Fromm 1997). Paradoxically, the propaganda of submission and humble consumption most aggressively confronted citizens in societies that were far from consumerist—communist societies, with economies of permanent scarcity.

There is hardly one universally accepted level of trade-off between freedom and safety. While for Hobbes, the submission to Leviathan was total, the scope of the state's power is debatable. Legitimate "law and order" for one person may be an oppressive regime for another. Among the important traditions of modern Europe is the struggle to shed what some perceive as the social, political, economic, and mental shackles imposed on them by existing regimes. Such struggles include communist and other radical parties' attempts to install another centralized "brave new world," but also the counter-efforts to restore an *ancien régime* destroyed by a revolution. Entire nations, social groups, and individuals have long fought against what they have perceived as oppression. The oppressors may be foreign invaders or internal enemies. And sometimes, rebels believe that they fight in the name of all of humanity (Fromm 1994).

Every person living in an organized state inevitably faces some form of "rebel's dilemma," which may involve an often-dramatic choice between safety—which implies some amount of submission and subordination—and greater freedom—associated with more uncertainty and a greater threat to the quality of life. This "rebel's dilemma" is equally valid now, within any social system, as it was as in the time of the writing of Hobbes's *Leviathan*. Rebels reject the comfort of personal safety in a quest for more freedom. Theories of "civil disobedience" or "the laws of history" may be born to justify opposing existing regimes in the name of higher values (Thoreau 2009; Marx and Engels 1848; Kaczmarczyk 2010). Insurgents, dissidents, or revolutionaries take on the challenge.

## Ideological Banditry: Beyond Anarchism

Among rebels, "social bandits" justify their activities with reference to social justice (Hobsbawm 1969). Korycki, who robbed the communist state and distributed the property to poor peasants, undoubtedly fits into the social bandit model. Like Hobsbawm's ideal types of social bandits, Korycki's criminal career begins with injustice; while on the run, locals protect him, and he becomes ever more strongly attached emotionally to his home region; and his capture follows a betrayal—the carelessness of an associate—with his captors then trying to desecrate his limp body. In addition, today there are still some locals who have immortalized the rebel, refusing to believe in his death.

Korycki can claim association with all three Hobsbawmian subcategories of "social bandits." He was clearly a "redistributive" noble robber. However, just as Robin Hood and Janosik did, Korycki stood against the power of a usurper who lacked legitimacy; he remained loyal to what he believed was the legitimate sovereign, in his case, the Polish nation. This would make him closer to Hobsbawm's second type, that of a "primitive resistance" fighter. Yet Korycki also had some features of the third category, the "avenger," dispensing vigilante justice to village mayors and communist officials.

The similarities to Hobsbawm's three categories of social bandits also help us to better understand the differences. Korycki's rebellion was persistent, comprehensive, and based on a strong moral foundation. It involved constrained robbery, but also the printing and distributing of manifestos and the writing of letters to officials. His enemy was not a local satrap but a large and complex state apparatus. He was also task-motivated. The firm foundation of his activity was the enormous gap between the "official" communist ideology and "unofficial" legal and moral norms—the latter shared by the vast majority of the society. Korycki's mature individualism, extreme attachment to personal freedom, and contestation of state rules at the fundamental level put him closer to anarchism. This makes his case worthy of analyzing in the context of his ideological cousins, practitioners of anarchic *illégalisme* or "illegalists."

Among many types of "rebels," those that fall under the rubric of *illégalisme* assume a prominent place due to their extreme position on individual freedom and a disdain for any state or normative societal constraints. Derived from French libertarian thought, the concept of *illégalisme* translates into English as "illegalism" or, with some poetic license, as "ideological banditry" (Laskowski 2006, 359). Dating back to the turn of the twentieth century, the phenomenon of illegalism was born in Western Europe, but appeared also in the territory of the Russian Empire. It was a radical form of individualist anarchism. It embraced criminal behavior as justified by society's misdeeds. It fit into the broader perspective of the *propaganda of the deed*, where insurgent fighting was replaced by individual violent action.

Unlike the classic propaganda of the deed, ideological banditry is characterized by a combination of altruistic and personal—even selfish—motives of the activists. The actions are regular and professional, and they are pragmatically calculated, planned, and systematically implemented (Grinberg 1994, 302). In practice, individuals or small collectives, which the authorities usually called "bands," typically carried out well-planned acts of violence. In all of the historical situations described in this book, the squads of the January Uprising, the partisan units during the Nazi occupation, and the independent underground after the end of World War II were called "bands" by Russian Tsarist authorities, German Nazi occupiers, and the PRL's communist rulers, respectively. Similarly, while his activity was obviously criminal under the PRL's law, the militia officers chose to call Korycki a "bandit." The disparaging terminology of "bandit" and "bands" represents an attempt of the "legals" to discredit "illegals" whom they saw as undermining the main feature of modern states: a sanctioned monopoly to use violence against citizens.

From the very beginning, ideological banditry aroused controversy and sparked theoretical discussion, even within anarchist circles. It was criticized by libertarian leaders, such as Pyotr Kropotkin and Errico Malatesta, who believed that ideological bandits were pushing the libertarian movement into the gutter (Grinberg 1994). According to another early twentieth-century libertarian philosopher, Jean Grave, ideological banditry was a denial of the anarchist ethos—a retreat from its values and moral norms. In his opinion, ideologically motivated bandits did not differ in their practices from bourgeois thieves; they were not rebels, but merely another kind of product of society (Laskowski 2006, 362). Nevertheless, the majority of the leaders of the anarchist movement supported, or at least tolerated, ideological banditry and morally endorsed groups who used this tactic.

Critics of ideological banditry primarily accused illegalists of disrespect for human beings, violations of fundamental ethical principles, and nihilism. Despite this criticism, the idea of ideological banditry quickly became the driving force and the moral alibi for many individuals and small anarchist groups.

## Who Were the Illegalists?

Ideological banditry may be traced back to popular benefactors of the poor, such as the American gunslingers Jesse James and his brother, Frank; the hero of medieval English legends Robin Hood; or, closer to Slavic culture, the Slovak Janosik. In each of these narratives, the redistribution among the poor of loot stolen from the rich was a common feature (Hobsbawm 1969; Racięski and Kabiesz 1996; Sroka 2004; Knight 1994).

However, the universe of illegals is much vaster than a few robbers from folklore. With the advent of ideological banditry, a new era of terrorism began. The explosion—both literally and metaphorically—occurred on French soil a hundred years after the Parisians' capture of the Bastille. It was then that an anarchist, François Koënigstein, known as Ravachol, began his activity. The man quickly found a large group of followers. The years of *la belle époque* turned into the golden age of dynamite, revolvers, and daggers. In the years around 1900, many died, and this violence claimed the lives of not only men of authority, entrepreneurs, and members of the bourgeoisie but also casual bystanders (Tuchman 1996).

Not only anarchists but also subversives of other orientations, including socialists, committed ideologically motivated violence. In Poland, many "expropriations," a term that denotes robberies claiming moral and legal justification, and violent attacks were carried out by members of the Organizacja Bojowa Polskiej Partii Socjalistycznej (Combat Organization of the Polish Socialist Party, OB PPS). The most famous act of "expropriation" in Poland was the assault on the Russian postal train near Bezdany in 1908, executed under the command of Józef Piłsudski, considered the father of the Second Polish Republic.

In general, during wars, occupations, uprisings, and partitions, the agents of armed organizations of resistance movements in occupied lands do not shun ideologically motivated violence. In World War II Poland, these agents included members of both the Home Army (AK) and the communist People's Army (AL). Several decades later, in spring 1969 in Poland, members of the underground anticommunist movement Ruch attempted a rather grotesque expropriation by attacking a saleswoman on Źródłowa Street in Łódź who was carrying cash, in order to acquire money for their organization. The woman loudly screamed for help, so the attackers fled (Byszewski 2008).

Of course, there have been numerous insurgent paramilitary separatist organizations throughout the years, such as the Irish Republican Army (IRA) or the Euskadi Ta Askatasuna (Basque Homeland and Liberty, ETA), groups which terrorized Great Britain and Spain, respectively. Presently, many militant and terrorist groups around the world act as non-anarchist ideological bandits, including Hamas, which operates on a national level, and Al-Qaida, which operates internationally.

For his part, Korycki's activity is much more closely linked to the more individualistic actions of anarchists than to mass paramilitary or terrorist organizations. Although Korycki never described himself as an anarchist, his activity certainly shared some features with anarchism, as it was aimed at bringing about the fall of the communist Polish state. An anarchist theorist, Rafał Górski (2009), expressed his appreciation for Korycki and considered him a seasoned conspirator. Korycki was even explicitly called an "anarchist" in 1954, when he served in a mine as part of his disciplinary punishment during his military service. His commander, who was a Soviet officer, yelled at him at the time, "You anarchist!" (Kaminski 1985b). Of course, the name-calling of an outraged communist does not mean that Korycki was a true anarchist. For centuries, officials of every sociopolitical system have tossed various epithets at troublemaking rebels. Anarchist ideological bandits and Korycki differed in claimed legitimacy, declared goals, and the means they used; these differences are sufficiently prominent to warrant some discussion.

## Claims of Legitimacy

Probably the most important characteristic distinguishing ideological banditry from ordinary banditry is the justification of the robber's activities. Common bandits do not justify their actions with any consistent ideology. They may produce ad hoc justifications (Kaminski 2004a), but the ideological aspect of their crimes is weak. Their justifications simply rationalize private appropriations. Conversely, the criminal actions of an ideological bandit are ideologically motivated and are aimed at capturing the wealth of individuals and privileged groups, regardless of the existing legal order. Anarchists who perform ideologically motivated robberies repeatedly protest against calling their activities ordinary plunder, claiming the moral legitimacy of their actions that provide for the restitution or redistribution of property (Laskowski 2006, 359–60).

Some justifications here refer to simple claims that "everybody is stealing," or that "we steal what was stolen earlier." Paul Reclus (1964), for example, justified the right to steal by the fact that the loot had been stolen earlier through the acts of selling and buying, while Lenin called openly for "robbing what had been robbed," as he was convinced that the existing property rights had no legitimacy, and therefore could be dispensed with (Michalkiewicz 2017). As one ideological bandit wrote, "We, anarchists, do not have to follow any rules. It's enough that the ideas that guide us are right" (Grinberg 1994).

Illegalism has occurred in all social strata, with variable justifications. For peasants, illegalism has often been an accepted lifestyle, with the poverty of the lower classes providing sufficient legitimacy. That is why the seizure of property—necessarily from the members of wealthy classes—has often been met with spontaneous appreciation from the poor. For those in the lowest social strata, it is a natural manifestation of class struggle, regardless of the prevailing form of government (Foucault 2012; Hobsbawm 1969). A 1913 article in a sociopolitical journal states that "banditry arises from the living conditions of the broad masses of the proletariat in the same way as the enormous dishonesty, roguery and speculation, and the whole banditry of profiteers arises from the living conditions and the atmosphere in which the kinglets of capital live" (Złotowski 1913, 3).

In the twentieth century, the redistributive illegalism of the poor competed with the refined illegalism of the privileged. The more complex justifications of the latter have varied from personal enrichment to political change. The intense activities of the illegalists in the early twentieth century in both Western Europe and the Russian Empire often treated a temporary destabilization of the state and society as an end in and of itself, and not a prologue to revolutionary social change. The activity of the 1890s anarchist bombers, who were led by the infamous Ravachol, provided some inspiration for the twentieth-century illegalists. Their focus on practical actions explains the scarcity of source texts presenting their ideology during the heyday of ideological banditry.

Korycki, in opposition to the anarchist ideological bandits, did not reject the legitimacy of all states while he used redistribution as justification; his actions were directed against the *sui generis* communist state. He fought against a specific state that he considered illegal and that had no popular legitimacy, not for the abolition of government in general.[2] He shared the prevailing sentiment that the communist state had been imposed on the Poles with the help of the Red Army and that it stayed alive only due to the threat of Soviet intervention and through the collaboration of a relatively small group of local opportunists. In fact, the PRL's legitimacy was founded on the naked power of its enforcement apparatus and the menace of Soviet intervention. As Stalin once soberly observed, "Communism fits Poles like a saddle fits a cow."

Although the Polish communist state was widely recognized internationally, it had no internal democratic legitimacy. While a substantial part of the population gradually and reluctantly accepted the status quo as a "lesser evil" than bloody Soviet tyranny, undoubtedly no communist party would have stood a chance at winning in free elections. The results of the elections in 1947, as well as the preceding 1946 "referendum" on the shape of the political system, were dramatically falsified (Paczkowski 2010). Indeed, when Mikhail Gorbachev abolished the Brezhnev doctrine of intervention in July 1989, communist regimes in Poland and other Eastern Bloc countries soon collapsed (Kaminski 1999). In short order, the communist party entirely disappeared and its former functionaries jumped ship, becoming social—and sometimes even Christian—democrats.

The lack of internal legitimacy of communism in Poland was supported by the continuity of prewar political institutions that functioned mostly in France, the United Kingdom, and the United States. Poland's "government in exile" was established in London in 1939, and functioned to delegitimize the communist usurpers in Warsaw. This exiled Polish government body was only dissolved when President Kaczorowski handed the insignia of power to President Wałęsa after the first free presidential elections in 1990.

## Ends and Means

Korycki's use of violence and terror against the institutional violence of the state is consistent with the practices and assumptions of anarchist ideological banditry. The catalog of criminal activities of ideological bandits includes burglary, assault, blackmail, intimidation, kidnapping, and sometimes even murder (Grinberg 1994). Korycki was indeed said to have committed all of these acts, with homicide being an unclear case, since the accidental manslaughter was attributed to an unidentified member of his group and the question of who was responsible remained unanswered.

Extreme ideological banditry builds on the freedom of the individual and liberation from social, and, especially, legal norms. However, in addition to earlier anarchist justifications of violence in the name of freedom and social change, ideological banditry allows for personal motivation and interest. For some illegalists, their activity was almost exclusively a means for enrichment and for obtaining a livelihood. For others, they were forced into ideological banditry by their living situations; these people, harassed by the police and portrayed as dangerous bandits, could not find employment to earn a living legally (Grinberg 1994). Their solitary actions targeted the institutions and officers of the existing social system as an effective alternative to the permanent impotence of ordinary politics. The violent destruction of the state's repressive apparatus was considered the most effective—and only realistic—way to revolutionary social change (Grinberg 1994).

Korycki shared the anarchists' adoration of freedom. Both his sympathizers and his opponents repeatedly talked about his independence and his refusal to submit his freedom to societal limitations (Bodasiński and Osipowski 2015, Dudziak, 7'14"). However, he acted within clear normative constraints. For example, he rejected personal enrichment as a goal of his activity. He did not gather any personal wealth, and all his loot was either redistributed among the poor or used to arm and feed the paramilitary groups that he created. He explicitly rejected stealing any private property—not only money and goods belonging to the "people" but also that belonging to state officials. "I take only Bolshevik" became a widely repeated slogan. His loot was exclusively "communist" property, including household goods, tax money, and even groceries from the state grocery chain.

Other crucial differences concern the scale of the violence and its targets. When organizing attacks, Korycki always tried to avoid unnecessary violence as his intended victim was only supposed to be the communist Leviathan. Here, it is likely that the popular nonviolent ideology of the trade union Solidarity and the teaching of Pope John Paul II, who came from Poland, affected his limited use of violence. He rejected terror as a means for reaching his goals. The closest he came to mass terror was when martial law was introduced in Poland on December 13, 1981. Depressed, he considered blowing up the Soviet Moscow–Berlin Mitropa express train but finally decided against it. The prospective victims were Soviet military personnel and their families, but Korycki decided that the indiscriminate killing of the occupiers' families was unacceptable. When compared to the violent and often chaotic actions of anarchist ideological bandits, Korycki's actions are restrained and focused on the functionaries of the regime, which was widely considered illegitimate.

## JACEK KUROŃ'S OPINION

Interestingly, possibly the most important opposition politician of the immediate pre-Solidarity era, Jacek Kuroń, expressed a different opinion about Korycki. He knew Korycki personally from the prison for recidivists in Wronki, where Kuroń and Korycki were together in the years 1970–71. As a co-organizer of the 1968 March protests, and earlier, a co-author with Karol Modzelewski of the famous "Open Letter to the Party," Kuroń was initially housed in a single cell due to the authorities' fear of his potential "negative political influence on other prisoners." However, on weekdays, he worked in the laundry, and thus he had contact with the other prisoners there. Kuroń and Korycki likely met in the laundry room, and as Korycki recalled later, while in prison, Kuroń gave him his Żoliborz address so that after they got out, they could meet up (Kaminski 1985b). In 1970, Kuroń and Korycki jointly refused parole so as not to give the communists the satisfaction that they were receiving some special favor. However, through the efforts of his parents, Kuroń did eventually get out on parole, leaving prison on September 17, 1971, even though his sentence was supposed to conclude on July 25, 1972 (Friszke 2011, 32).

Kuroń, however, stated later that "Korycki is an ordinary bandit." Kuroń branded him as a bandit when, after leaving prison, the Student tried to interest the underground press in Korycki's story (even though Korycki himself did not ask for this). The Student sent a report about Korycki's fate to the most influential underground newspaper, *Tygodnik Mazowsze*. At that time, Kuroń, whose voice was decisive in that newspaper's editorial office, opposed the publication of the Student's article about Korycki. He did so, even though he was sensitive to the fate of all prisoners, including criminal ones, whom he called "crime professionals," to differentiate them from political prisoners (Friszke 2011, 24; Kaminski 2018, emails 2, 6, 8).

In striking contrast with his opinion about Korycki, Kuroń, in his programmatic declarations, recognized as political opposition "all those who consciously and actively oppose totalitarianism, fighting for the sovereignty of the Nation and Polish State" (Kuroń 1977). We hypothesize that Kuroń's opinion about Korycki could have been motivated by personal negative experience with prison subculture as well as his former political afilliations.

First, despite his unquestionable achievement in building the anticommunist opposition in Poland, especially in the 1970s, when Kuroń was arguably the most important opposition leader, it is important to remember that Kuroń was hardly an impartial observer. In the 1950s, he had been an enthusiastic and quite important builder of the communist "bright future," and at the time, he considered those people who fought against communism as "bandits." Some of the older opposition activists with whom Marek Kaminski had worked in the underground remembered young Kuroń's early fanaticism and the damage that he did to the Polish boy-scout movement; they could not forgive him. It was only later, in the 1960s, that Kuroń became disillusioned with communism. After its fall, Kuroń wrote a critical account of his youth infatuation under the title "Faith and Guilt: Toward and Away from Communism" (Kuroń 1995). Nonetheless, it is possible that Kuroń held on to some of his old sentiments about armed anticommunist resistance being "banditry."

Second, Kuroń and Korycki had different positions within the prison subculture, and quite different experiences of it (Kaminski 2018, email 2). Kuroń was an outsider while Korycki was one of its revered leaders. Kuroń felt strongly about the significance of prison subculture. So, when he was the editor in charge of *Tygodnik Mazowsze*, against the fierce opposition from the rest of the editorial board (as reported to the author, the discussion was very heated), he forced them to publish another text by Kaminski (Mikołaj 1985). That article describes harsh aspects of prison life, including the test of "fagotization," which lures an uninformed inmate into consenting to his own rape. The article was later elected by the readers of *Tygodnik Mazowsze* as the most controversial text ever published by this weekly, since it won the most votes for both the "best" and "worst" categories.


## WAS KORYCKI A SECURITY SERVICE INFORMER?

Korycki spent almost twenty years behind bars. Before his final fight in 1979, he received relatively short sentences and was always released on parole due to "good behavior." The briefness of his incarcerations raised suspicions of collaboration with the communist SB. But there may have been two less mysterious reasons for his "luck." The first one was amnesties. He got his first sentence near the end of the Stalinist period, when the courts were much more lenient than just a year or two prior. He was released on an amnesty, and the sentence was likely annulled, or at least not considered a significant black mark on his record. His half-year sentence for a long escape seems not so unbelievable when compared to another deserter from a penal mine at the same time: in 1955, Zdzisław Celebrak received a three-month sentence at about that same time for escape, and four additional months for stealing civilian clothing (Stwora 1993, 27–28). Korycki was again lucky in 1969, when he was released due to another amnesty.

The second reason for the shortness of Korycki's prison stays was his good behavior there, which seemed to be a deliberate strategy on his part. After 1956, the courts became less punitive and more open to releasing inmates due to their exemplary behavior. Prison wardens even promised the most active inmates, "if you work well, … you will get a chance for parole" (Stwora 1993, 26). Once, for example, as a reward, Korycki was appointed to be leader of a group of prisoners going outside for supplies. Wardens always asked for Korycki's conditional early release as soon as he became eligible. Captain Romuald Dudziak, the head of the Criminal Department of the MO Provincial Headquarters in Siedlce, offered the following explanation, using language that suggested respect, as he called Korycki an "ideal man" (Bodasiński and Osipowski 2015, Dudziak, 4'10"):

> [Korycki] was released early due to—I said once that he had two faces. In prison, he was the ideal man. In prison, he was able to organize the inmates so that they listened to him like their mother. There were no brawls, rows, strikes, and hunger strikes in prison. … [Korycki] had a wonderful reputation among the guards, and when the legal date came, when he was eligible to apply for early release, he wrote the application, and practically [always] prison wardens accepted and supported his applications for early release from prison.

Most likely, Korycki intelligently manipulated prison staff by assuming a strategy of being the "perfect inmate." It worked. Korycki's sister-in-law, who visited him in prison many times, stated, "Those earlier imprisonments were not as painful for him [as the last one], since he was very respected there" (Korycka 2020). Similarly, Korycki showed an amazing ability to influence people. For instance, as described in Chapter 3, during his last stay in prison a prosecutor told a mentally disturbed murderer, who had earlier strangled his whole family, to strangle Korycki. The paralyzed Korycki befriended this prisoner, who then started kindly helping Korycki with his physiological needs and, later, confessed to him that he had been asked to kill him.

Still, all the early releases raise a valid doubt: Was Korycki an informer of the Security Service—at least at some moment—who thus received more lenient treatment from the courts, prosecutors, and prison officials? On the one hand, it is hard to imagine that an "informer" would inevitably and immediately return to crime after being released, and then quickly return to prison. Nonetheless, the communist Security Service repeatedly accused Korycki of collaboration. The most elaborate was the attempt to discredit him against public opinion by accusing him of cooperating with the UB, and then with the SB.

Colonel Jan Płócienniczak, the chief propagandist of the communist media, publicized the hypothesis that the SB in Lublin had recruited Korycki in the 1950s. He provided no evidence, but his words were repeated many times later in statements by MO officers and by militia journalists or other publicists (Bodasiński and Osipowski 2015, Płócienniczak, 1'43"; Bodasiński and Osipowski 2015, passim; Kacak 2011; Wasiluk 2014). Płócienniczak described Korycki's assignment as an alleged secret collaborator when he was part of an organization of illegal youth groups, "often even armed" (Bodasiński and Osipowski 2015, Płócienniczak, 1'40"). According to the militia propagandist, after organizing a given group, Korycki would denounce its members to the militia, who would then arrest them (Bodasiński and Osipowski 2015, Płócienniczak, 1'43"). This statement paints Korycki as a traitor to the young people who trusted him, and for whom he was not only a leader and an organizer but also a figure of authority and a protector. There were other militia sources, as well, who stated that the SB used Korycki's groups to infiltrate local criminal gangs (Zajączkowska 2012; Wasiluk 2014, 8). According to these accounts, Korycki had acted as agent provocateur.

In Korycki's own words, he defined his small groups—the largest had thirteen members—as "armed units," whose ultimate objective was "the people's administration of justice" (Kacak 2011, 41). To the people in those units, Korycki justified opposing the communist state by using classic subversive reasoning: he saw his conflict with the law and social order as justified by the view that only a fool adheres to the rules established by the torturer to keep his victim in check (Gray 2004). All those people joined Korycki's units solely because of his personal organizational efforts; without him, they would have remained inactive. The goal of an agent provaceteur is usually to pacify dangerous or potentially dangerous people. It is unclear what value the SB would derive from converting more or less dormant and harmless individuals into dangerous bandits.

Yet the authorities frequently ascribed collaboration to Korycki. For instance, former militia officer Jan Skrzypiec reported that, at the behest of the provincial headquarters of the MO in Siedlce, he was in contact with Korycki, who was supposedly cooperating with the militia. The main goal of the communist authorities was to "disarm the area," which was allegedly made possible by their informal contact with Korycki.

We find these allegations unconvincing. The Polish communist Security Service has a record of fiercely defending its own collaborators and falsely exposing its enemies. Communist SB luminaries, including Minister of the Interior Czesław Kiszczak, the last communist in Poland to hold this post, repeated the maxim of "not exposing their own" many times. The justification for this rule was simple: exposing their own people, even those who went rogue, would be likely to expose the Security Service's recruitment methods and the supervision procedures of their agents. It would also undermine the confidence of the SB's agents in their own organization.

Most importantly, a secret informer would have to be registered with the SB. Informers were registered liberally, since every new one was considered a success story for the SB officer who signed up that person. In extreme cases, even a casual conversation with the SB could sometimes result in registering a person as an "informer" without his or her knowledge. After the fall of communism, removing such documents from the SB archives turned out to be extremely difficult, even for high-profile politicians. For someone like Korycki, who died before the fall of communism and who had no political connections, such removal would essentially have been impossible.

The archival resources of the Institute of National Remembrance (IPN) contain SB files documenting two persons with the names "Józef Korycki" (see Lista IPN n.d.; IPN n.d.).[3] The reference numbers are IPNBU 002082/484 and IPNBU 002086/1371; the two zeros at the beginning of the code indicate the level of information classification was marked as top secret in the SB's files. However, neither of these men was our Józef Korycki, that is, the son of Zygmunt, born in Radzyń Podlaski. One of the people named Józef Korycki in the files was registered in the Wojewódzki Urząd Spraw Wewnętrznych (Provincial Office of the Interior, WUSW) in Gdańsk as Józef Korycki, son of Jan, born on June 18, 1935, with the reference number of the personal file on him as IPN Gd 464/13664. The other person in the files was registered in the WUSW in Zielona Góra as Józef Korycki, son of Józef, born on October 11, 1953, with the file reference number IPN Po 668/618. Thus, the accusation made by Jan Płócienniczak, that Korycki was a secret collaborator, finds no support in the IPN files and is only based on his unverifiable statements and those of other militiamen.

Further, analysis of Korycki's overall activity, personality type, value system, and political sympathies also supports the conclusion that MO officers likely promoted his alleged cooperation with the militia in order to discredit him. Remembering Korycki, the Student stated, "He made an impression of a completely honest, reliable, and just man" (Kaminski 2018, email 1). The Student, who knew and quickly came to trust Korycki's personality, character, anticommunist attitude, and background, and who conducted many biographical conversations with him in prison, felt that Korycki's cooperating with the SB would have been entirely inconsistent with his personal profile. Moreover, Korycki ended up in prison as a man who was extremely fragile, partially paralyzed, and with a bullet in his head. Despite those vulnerabilities, he was incredibly disciplined, composed, and even cheerful. Under the worst possible circumstances, he never showed a single sign of weakness or regretted his life choices. It seems highly unlikely that he would have broken under much lighter duress (Kaminski 2018, email 2).

Płócienniczak's other thesis, according to which Korycki "decided to become a militiaman," also seems unreliable. Korycki's niece confirmed that she heard rumors, for example, such as that he was riding with the militia to Lublin. However, Korycki's sister-in-law, who knew Korycki much better, emphatically denied the possibility of anything like that (Boreczek 2020; Korycka 2020). Moreover, his brother, Władysław, who worked with Korycki in the forestry service, and even lived with him for a while in a company flat, said it was much more likely that Korycki had some routine official relationship with the militia, as he was a forestry officer (Korycka 2020). Such contacts were common and normal for forestry workers and rangers.

The documentary film *Janosik z Podlasia* about Korycki implies that "because he could not fulfill his dream of becoming a militiaman, he decided to join the other side" (Bodasiński and Osipowski 2015, 2'35"). In this argument, the motivation for Korycki's fierce anticommunism and his illegal activity was his inability to become a regime soldier. Not only is this utterly unbelievable but also the documentary offers no support of any kind for this allegation. First, becoming a militia officer would have been entirely incongruous with Korycki's background and early anticommunist activity. Although there are cases of former members of the communist militia, SB, or Communist Army who switched sides—for instance, Józef ("Lalek") Franczak, described earlier, who deserted the Communist Army and joined the underground—this happened in the formative years of the PRL, and the deserters were either compulsorily recruited or were trying to infiltrate the communist structures. Second, after Korycki had received his first sentence for desertion, joining the militia was not possible for legal reasons due to his criminal record, as well as because his father's Home Army past caused the communist authorities to label him as an adversary. His brother Władysław was later denied the opportunity to become a professional soldier because he was related to Korycki. In fact, such restrictions had an effect on Korycki's life from a very early age, when the stamp of "inappropriate background" prevented him from being admitted to college, a career path with fewer restrictions than admission to the militia.

The allegations that at some point in his criminal career Korycki accepted an offer made by the SB for some sort of mutually beneficial transaction may be more plausible. There is a story that, while in prison in the early 1970s, the militia offered Korycki an early release in exchange for information on where a criminal group he knew was hiding weapons. In his statement, Skrzypiec said that he was to hand over illegal weapons obtained by Korycki to the provincial headquarters (Bodasiński and Osipowski 2015, Skrzypiec, 2'22"). Allegedly, Korycki pinpointed the location of the arsenal, but was not released from prison in accordance with the deal (Czajka 2018; Bodasiński and Osipowski 2015, Skrzypiec, 2'22"). However, even if such an event actually occurred, Korycki could have accepted such a deal without becoming a secret collaborator of the SB or a full-time militia officer.

The accusations that Korycki betrayed his young partners also seem unfounded and contrary to evidence. The citizens of the villages where he lived remember his attitude toward his young subordinates well. He always tried to protect them and often took the blame for their actions (Kaliński 2018). Once, when twelve of his accomplices and helpers were supposed to go to trial, Korycki called the court and mailed threatening letters to stop the trial from moving forward, ultimately causing the relocation of the trial to Warsaw (Borkowski 1982). It is unbelievable that Korycki would first betray his accomplices and then take a great personal risk to defend them from the court. Similarly, when he and his partner, Mirosław Kaliński, were apprehended in the final manhunt on May 14, 1982, despite the fact that Mirosław's imprudence caused his arrest, he took all the blame for their joint robberies, as well as their acts of hiding and acquiring illegal weapons, and testified that Kaliński was under pressure from him to follow his orders. Because of this testimony, Korycki's young accomplice received a relatively lenient sentence (Kaliński 2018).

One of Korycki's fellow inmates offered an interesting argument against his collaboration. Most militia informers very quickly acquired bad reputations in prison, and their true identities were quickly revealed. Prisoners were incredibly ingenious at uncovering a person's collaboration efforts, since "rats" were the greatest threat for their prison well-being. Due to the active inmate inter-prison communication system, if an informer was transferred to a new prison, such information about him would be obtained within few weeks from his previous place of incarceration. It was practically impossible for a communist collaborator to reemerge in a new prison with an unblemished name (Kaminski 2004a). While in prison, no one ever accused Korycki of collaboration.[4]

Finally, former communist functionaries had a powerful motive to present their adversaries as nothing more than ordinary criminals. After the fall of communism, former militia and Security Service officers—implicitly or explicitly—assumed the line of defense that "they were only involved in fighting crime." For instance, the former militiaman Wojciech Raczuk, whom Korycki injured, used such a defense. Raczuk fought in court for the restoration of his pension, which was lowered by the 2016 parliamentary bill (Wiktorowska 2019). The image of Korycki as a communist informer and ordinary bandit comfortably bolstered his case for a higher pension. The militiamen could even say a few nice words about Korycki, calling him the local Janosik. However, naming Korycki an anticommunist fighter would destroy the rationalizations that they were "only fighting ordinary bandits," rather than propping up the communist system.

Ultimately, in light of the facts that we collected and analyzed, we believe that Korycki's alleged collaboration with the UB, SB, or militia was a deliberate smear campaign prepared by communist propagandists.

## SO WHO WAS THE REAL BANDIT?

On January 12, 2012, the Warsaw Regional Court ruled on behalf of the Republic of Poland that Wojciech Jaruzelski, Czesław Kiszczak, Florian Siwicki, and Tadeusz Tuczapski had formed an armed criminal association, which prepared for and illegally imposed martial law in Poland. In the opinion of the court, "the actual motive of the members of the criminal association to unlawfully impose martial law was to preserve the existing political system and [their] personal position in the hierarchy of the party and state apparatus" (Kazimierczak 2018). In addition, the court stated that when Kiszczak was appointed to the position of minister of the interior, "the hierarchy of the association members in the structures of the state apparatus and party corresponded to their hierarchy in the criminal association" (Kazimierczak 2018). Thus, in the opinion of the court, the leaders of the Polish communist state— General Jaruzelski, minister of national defense, and General Kiszczak, minister of the interior—who had viciously pursued the "ideological bandit" Korycki, were nothing less than "ideological bandits" themselves; however, they were the ones who had more powerful state instruments of violence at their disposal.

Lenin famously predicted that capitalists would sell communists a rope to hang themselves. Ironically, the PRL and other "socialist democracies"—communist exemplifications of states—collapsed when they started experimenting with classic instruments of democracy, parliamentary elections. Paradoxically, Jaruzelski, Kiszczak, and their associates initiated this process and turned out to be the PRL's undertakers (Kaminski 1999).

The anticommunist Korycki, strenuously fighting for the fall of Poland's communist regime, did not live long enough to see it come about. However, the memory of him and his uncompromising fight remains alive in the collective memory of those who knew him. It is our hope that this book, rather than communist propaganda, can serve as part of his memorial.

# EPILOGUE

Rysio picked me up from the Warsaw Hilton. He gave me a bottle of water and introduced me to his little dog resting in the back of his dark green Mercedes. My high-school best friend, presently a director and owner of a prosperous studio that makes TV commercials, wanted to make a film about Janosik. It would be another one in his portfolio of documentaries on prison subculture and juvenile delinquents. A few years ago, we had a brief recording session at the nearby Rakowiecka Jail, which had just been converted into a Museum of Political Prisoners. Now, the Polish edition of my book with Ernest Szum was out. We were going to Radzyń Podlaski, Józek's hometown, for a meet-the-author event in the Potocki Palace. On our way, we planned a stop at the house where Józef Korycki was hiding from late 1979 to his arrest on May 14, 1982. Ernest had arranged a recording session with Krystyna Oksiejuk, Janosik's life partner, and promised to meet us at Misie.

Years ago, Rysio started and soon paused shooting a documentary about my 1985 imprisonment. There were no sponsors. Too many high-profile political prisoners had diluted the dramatic potential in prison stories. Now, although the expressways to Siedlce and Radzyń were not built yet—eastern Poland was a little bit behind the rest of the country—the road was still pretty good, and Rysio was speeding. Two rows of colorful green, blue, and brown houses surrounded by freshly painted fences were moving past us in an orderly way on both sides of the road. Changing the A/C and tuning the radio with one hand, Rysio was complaining about stingy film sponsors and the rising cost of running a business. The current Polish government had antagonized transition winners like Rysio. Massive redistribution programs inflated his employee salaries and deflated his profit margin. The back seat of his car was covered with the usual messy goulash of papers and clothing; his little dog was barking loudly; small plastic handcuffs were hanging from the back mirror. Nothing could distract Rysio.

We grabbed a forgettable bite at McDonalds. Rysio took his dog for a pee. At a nearby flower shop, I bought a bouquet of red roses for Ms. Oksiejuk, paying 100 zlotys, which was quite steep. The owner must have noticed a Mercedes and Warsaw plates. Or perhaps the prices had gone up. A policeman entered the store, and I shuddered, an uncontrollable leftover reflex from communism. He smiled at me.

Abandoned by our helpless GPS, we drove through Misie's newly asphalted main street a couple of times before we found Korycki's hideout, five minutes late. No wonder that the communist secret police couldn't find him! Ernest was waiting by the short wooden fence. He was a slim fortyish guy of medium height, already a grandfather. A historian with several publications, he was presently working as a high-school teacher. It would be the first time I would meet him in person. We had planned and completed our book via email without ever seeing or speaking to each other.

The smell of *babka drożdżowa* greeted us at the door. Our eighty-four-year-old host waited for us inside her one-bedroom wooden hut. Jovial, she showed us in, wiping her big hands on her apron. I gave her the roses and the promised copy of the book, and Ernest and I signed it. Inside her big room, with the obligatory worn-out *wersalka*, a memento of the PRL, a massive wooden table was competing for space with a high bed. The interior probably hadn't changed a lot from Józek's times. We squeezed inside with Rysio's equipment.

Krystyna performed well in front of camera, better than I did. She retold the story of how she met Józek and answered our questions. The barn where she found him was gone. The hole dug in the sand under the floor of the smaller room where he hid when she had an unexpected client was also gone. Sometimes he had to spend an hour or two there. Motionless. His papers, his memoir, all was lost. My letter to Krystyna from 1986 was lost. Ernest gave her a scan of her reply to me that broke the news of Józek's death. She was scared to keep any papers at home after they arrested him.

Rysio was recording. "Please, take a seat, a chair is better than the *wersalka*." Ernest and I sat with our glasses of tea on the *wersalka*. Light, angles, window, all routine. "Please look into the camera." The confident professional. In the mid-1980s, I showed him my attempts at photography taken at an anticommunist demonstration in Warsaw. He took a careful look at the photos, and quipped, "Marek, you are such a lucky man! You can still learn so much."

Krystyna spoke about Józiek with love. Józef-Józek-Józiek, in the Polish language, those names denote increasing familiarity and intimacy. It was clear that she wasn't acting. Her words described her life, her deepest emotions. Before speaking to us, she hadn't told her story to anybody. She talked about Józiek's obsession with communism, about his disregard for gathering "things," about his Spartan life. She repeated a few times that he gave away everything that he stole, that he didn't bring anything to her except for some occasional food, that she had to feed him. Fortunately, she had a good job—she was a hair stylist. There was always a line of clients.

What was Korycki's deepest motivation in his lone war with communism? Was he a clever but common criminal who used anticommunism as an alibi? This is what some of communist propagandists maintained. But many of his fiercest enemies still called him Janosik and seemed to buy into his legend. We, the authors, were not dispassionate researchers looking for answers. I joined this project motivated by a sense of duty to a departed friend. Ernest built his sentiments through his own research and conversations with the locals who knew Józek. I agreed to write a book with an unknown co-author after he asked me in one of his first emails "Was Korycki a good man?" I believed that he was, and that the question was spot on. But I also believed that all questions about motivation were fundamentally undecidable. When I left prison, and my involvement in underground publishing became public knowledge at the Institute of Sociology, I wrote a term paper that analyzed the motivations of underground Solidarity activists. It generated some interest, but I wasn't happy with it and never tried to publish it. I felt that I was unable to provide a satisfactory answer.

Have we found definite evidence that Józek's motivations were exclusively political? Certainly not. But this was impossible from the very beginning. However, we gathered substantial evidence that corroborated our working "good man" hypothesis. He had a long and consistent record of anticommunist activity. We haven't found a single report documenting a common theft of private property. According to the testimonies, Józek distributed the stolen goods almost in their entirety, sometimes using the paltry remainder to satisfy only his basic life necessities. Did he enjoy robbing village mayors and taking over the village for a few hours? Did he feel powerful? Most certainly. When I was a student, along with thousands of my compatriots, I enjoyed tossing stones at the militia's Nyska vans. Should fighting for a cause be sterile of ordinary feelings? Should we suppress our minor human emotions when facing bigger ethical dilemmas? As we become socialized to life in the anticommunist underground, communist guerilla cadre, or gang of robbers, our more noble motivations may be fused and unseparable from a proclivity toward the illegal.

Guided by Ernest, Rysio drove into the giant courtyard of the pastel Potocki Palace in Radzyń Podlaski. The Potocki family initially built the beautiful rococo palace in 1566–67 as a castle, and later remodeled it with a moat as a *palazzo in fortezza*. Rundown in the PRL as many similar buildings of the Polish-Lithuanian Commonwealth became, it was slowly coming back to life in post-communist Poland.

Our host, a friendly local historian and university professor, Dariusz Magier, advertised the meet-the-author event widely, and invited the local press as well as a photographer. I hoped to meet some militiamen who had hunted Korycki. They didn't come. Later, under the online account of the meet-the-author event in a local newspaper, I found comments that possibly came from a militiaman. "Those two authors of this book should pay dearly for what they wrote." Sorry, different times. Among the fifty participants, there were some from Józek's remote family, an inmate who overlapped with him in various prisons, local and Polish Academy of Sciences historians, a forest ranger who was forced to help in a manhunt for Korycki, and many others who either knew Korycki personally or from frightening communist newspaper passages.

The Palace's aseptic interior was not as impressive as the façade. Large halls and chambers were devastated in a big fire in July 1944 when the Red Army was chasing the Wehrmacht, and finally destroyed by forty-five years of the PRL. Nothing valuable survived and a true renovation was still in the future. The meeting took over three hours and we signed almost as many books as there were participants. We alternated with our narrations. This was the only meet-the-author event that I planned, so we hadn't gotten bored with repeating the same stories and anecdotes.

When we finished our presentations, the more interesting part began with the questions and contributions from the audience. We got our first—except for the one on the arrest warrant—photo of Józek. Later, thanks to the publication of the book, Józek's sister-in-law, Barbara Korycka, offered access to the family archive. Józek's fellow-inmate—never was with him in the same cell but overlapped for long time in a few prisons—assured me that Korycki couldn't be an informer, that the grypsmen would have decoded him. Right, inmates are incredibly good in *rozkminianie*—identifying moles and rats. A historian told us that he had identified the place where Korycki was caught. A local woman described to us how scared of Korycki she was as a child when the local communist press and media demonized him. We realized that there was more to the story than we had related in the Polish version of our book.

Have we proved that Józek was not a communist informer who survived thanks to his double identity? We haven't. Again, it is impossible to contradict this kind of hearsay. But the reasons to believe Józek rather than his opponents are compelling. The accusations are what is called in game theory, my field, "cheap talk," a type of cost-free slander routinely fabricated by communist secret police. Anybody can be accused that way. Most importantly, and decisively for me, there was no record of Józek's collaboration in the IPN archives. Such records survived the fall of the system that generated them and were practically impossible to remove. A few years ago, I found in the IPN archives the painfully preserved records of the secret police involvement of two members of my extended family.

There is a downside to all inconclusive statements. Making them lumps a vast array of characters, attitudes, and lives into the same "what-is-truth" bin. Adopting a truly *Rashomon* perspective absolves us from the risk of making a moral judgement. Certainly, there exists the unremovable limitation of uncertainty that we must have about the motivations of all humans, including our own motivations. Certainly, our moral virtues and character may fluctuate in time, may even dramatically change over our lifetimes. With these human constraints in mind, I still believed Józek.

There was a specific moment in prison when I stopped thinking about Józef Korycki as a bandit, undoubtedly anticommunist, but a bandit. Initially, this is how I perceived him. Like many young oppositionists, I thought about communist functionaries with the utmost contempt. Korycki didn't. He tried to understand militiamen and *esbeks*, and didn't deny their human qualities. During one of our conversations, he said, "Marek, they are victims too." I was speechless when I heard those words from *him*. This was not an ambiguous and potentially reversible bon mot. Korycki believed what he said.

Devoid of hatred, Korycki's slow, measured, magnanimous words forgiving the communist apparatchiks and militiamen, spoken by a paralyzed man in a prison bunk, stunned me and long resonated with me. Bedridden, Korycki maintained his dignity and radiated a charisma that elicited the respect of ordinary thugs and thieves. In prison,

Korycki resembled Conrad's Lord Jim—a damaged hero stubbornly fighting his lone battle for honor—rather than an immobilized bandit. And that is how I remember him: an honorable, honest man whose life was turned by communism into a tragedy.

—Marek Kaminski

# ACKNOWLEDGMENTS

Special thanks are due to Krystyna Oksiejuk, who helped us reconstruct the last dramatic years of Józef Korycki's life. From 1979 until Korycki's death in 1986, Ms. Oksiejuk remained his closest confidante and life partner. He hid in her home most of the time between 1979 and 1982. We are also indebted to Barbara Korycka, Józef's sister-in-law, for her detailed account of his family history and reactions to Józef's activities.

Mirosław Andrzejewski shared two secret prison messages, as well as various documents and contacts from his own political internment and then imprisonment. Antoni Kamiński, who reviewed the Polish edition of the book, and three anonymous reviewers of the English edition, suggested many valuable changes. Hanna Bajkowska helped with the reproduction of archival texts about Korycki that were published in the local press in 1982. Russ Dalton read the Polish version with the help of Google Translate and convinced Marek Kaminski to properly translate it and publish in English. We also thank Dorota Boreczek, Waldemar Czajka, Leszek Grochowski, Jerzy Jezierski, Waldemar Kaliński, Barbara Kamińska, Mikołaj Kamiński, Grzegorz Karpiński, Jerzy Kędzior, Andrzej "Książę," Mariusz Mazurek, Wiesława Mleczek, Andrzej Sadowski, Marianna Sójka, and Franciszek Trochimiak for help in establishing facts and gathering useful information.

We'd sincerely like to thank Basia Kaminski, who translated the Polish version of the book and all quoted passages. The publication of the Polish edition resulted in many additional stories and contacts that greatly enriched the factual basis of the narrative. The final English edition, prepared by Marek Kaminski on the basis of the translation, is substantially more accurate and detailed because of those people who got in touch with us. We are grateful to Donald Woodward for initial language editing. Kathleen Cioffi of PIASA Books was a very patient editor and provided final language editing.

Finally, we are grateful to all the people and institutions that helped the paralyzed Józef Korycki to live in some comfort and dignity. Dr. Jerzy Possart, the head of the Surgical Ward at the Rakowiecka Jail, always treated him with friendliness and care. Amnesty International sent generous parcels to Marek Kaminski while he was in prison via the Primate's Charity and Social Committee. The content of these parcels also aided Korycki.

# GLOSSARY

AK (Armia Krajowa, Home Army): the biggest underground resistance structure in Poland during World War II.

Esbek: member of secret security service SB.

IPN: The Instytut Pamięci Narodowej (Institute of National Remembrance). The Polish government institution that investigates and prosecutes Nazi and communist crimes.

MO: Milicjia Obywatelska, also called the milicja or militia in this volume. The Communist-era name for the police.

MSW: Ministerstwo Spraw Wewnętrznych (Ministry of the Interior).

NKVD: Наро́дный комиссариа́т вну́тренних дел (People's Commissariat for Internal Affairs), Soviet secret political police that consolidated the entire apparatus of the USSR's police repression.

PPR: Polska Partia Robotnicza (Polish Workers' Party). The communist party that took over power in Poland after World War II. It absorbed the PPS in 1948, forming the PZPR.

PPS: Polska Partia Socjalistyczna (Polish Socialist Party) that was absorbed by PPR in 1948.

PPSh: (Pepesha). Popular Soviet submachine gun used by Korycki.

PRL: Polska Rzeczpospolita Ludowa (Polish People's Republic). The name of the Polish communist state that existed from 1947 to 1989.

PZPR: Polska Zjednoczona Partia Robotnicza (Polish United Worker's Party). The official name of the communist party in Poland, which formally ruled the country from 1948 to 1989.

SB: Służba Bezpieczeństwa (Security Service, *esbecja*). The secret Polish political service established in 1956 and dissolved on July 31, 1990.

UB: Urząd Bezpieczeństwa Publicznego (Urząd Bezpieczeństwa, *ubecja*, Office of Public Safety, the Security Office). The secret Polish political service that existed 1945–54.

Ubek: member of secret security service UB.

WMB: Walka Młodych Bojowników (Struggle of Young Warriors), a short-lived anticommunist organization founded by Korycki in 1952.

*Word of Podlasie (Słowo Podlasia)*: local official newspaper of the PZPR that reported extensively on Korycki's activities in 1982.

WRON: Wojskowa Rada Ocalenia Narodowego (Military Council of National Salvation). Non-constitutional military communist group that introduced the martial law in Poland on December 13, 1981.

ZOMO: Zmotoryzowane Odwody Milicji Obywatelskiej (Motorized Reserves of the Citizens' Militia). Branches of the militia established in 1956 to "eliminate collective violations of public order." In fact, they pacified opposition members and supporters.

# NOTES

## INTRODUCTION

1. In this book, the words "communism," "communist," and "anticommunist" are used in their colloquial meaning, and commonly applied in relation to the period of the Polska Rzeczpospolita Ludowa (Polish People's Republic, PRL). Paczkowski (2002, 7) has provided many synonyms of "communism": real socialism, state socialism, post-totalitarian authoritarianism, and post-communist authoritarianism. Poles didn't use terms such as these in the strictly ideological sense, but rather as handy shortcuts describing the social reality of the PRL.
2. See Kenney (2017) for a comparative analysis of different cases of political prisoners.
3. See, e.g., Włodarek and Ziółkowski (1990).
4. For a rare systematic analysis of communist-era crime in political contexts see Heinzen (2016).
5. The Instytut Pamięci Narodowej (Institute of National Remembrance, IPN) is the Polish government institution that investigates and prosecutes Nazi and communist crimes. It houses extensive archives. In addition, its work also encompasses education and the lustration of communist collaborators.
6. The Milicja Obywatelska (Citizens Militia), frequently shortened to just the *milicja* (militia), was the equivalent of the police force in the Polish People's Republic. On April 6, 1990, the government changed the name "militia" back to *policja* (police).
7. The Zmotoryzowane Odwody Milicji Obywatelskiej (Motorized Reserves of the Citizens' Militia, ZOMO) were branches of the militia established in 1956 after the events of the "Poznań June" to "eliminate collective violations of public order." In fact, they terrorized Polish society and pacified opposition members and supporters. Due to its continual use of brutal violence by its young commando officers, Poles ironically called it the "beating heart of

the party" (see Dudek 2001, 28–30; Dudek and Marszałkowski 1999; Górski 2009).

8. In Kaminski's (2004a) book, the cell that Kaminski shared with Korycki was mistakenly identified as a cell in the Surgical Ward, and the dates mistakenly identified as June 3–17, 1985.

9. The account "The Story of Józef Korycki's Life," the interviews with Korycki's partner, Krystyna Oksiejuk, and the interview with Korycki's sister-in-law are published with comments in Kaminski and Szum (2020).

10. More detailed information on the methodology of Kaminski's prison research can be found in the introduction of his 2004 book (see Kaminski 2004a, 1–15).

11. For the distinction between a participating observer and an observing participant, see Kaminski 2004a, 1–15.

12. *Esbeks* are members of the Esbecja, or the Służba Bezpieczeństwa (Security Service, SB). The SB was the secret political service established in the PRL in 1956 that followed the reorganization of the units of the Komitet do Spraw Bezpieczeństwa Publicznego (Committee for Public Security) on November 28, 1956. The SB was dissolved on July 31, 1990.

13. As a side note, it is worth noting the inadequacy of the journal's name. About 90 percent of those in the militia were members of the communist party and constituted the apparatus of repression: the political Security Service (the SB) and the Motorized Reserves of the Citizens' Militia (the ZOMO). These formations were the communist regime's main enforcers of repression.

14. An extreme case is a 2017 piece by Małgorzata Lipczyńska, with the misleading title "The True Story of Janosik from Podlasie."

15. The Polska Zjednoczona Partia Robotnicza (Polish United Worker's Party, PZPR) was the official name of the communist party in Poland, which formally ruled the country from 1948 to 1989.

## CHAPTER 1

1. In 1982, Korycki would contemplate a similar action to derail the Moscow–Berlin express train.

2. The Polska Partia Robotnicza (Polish Workers' Party, PPR) was the communist party that took over power in Poland after World War II. It absorbed the Polska Partia Socjalistyczna (Polish Socialist Party) in 1948, forming the PZPR.

3. The Russian Наро́дный комиссариа́т вну́тренних дел (People's Commissariat for Internal Affairs, NKVD) consolidated the entire apparatus of the USSR's police repression, from criminal militia, intelligence and

counterintelligence, border protection troops, and administrative ad hoc courts to its system of concentration camps Gulag (see Kołakowski 2002).

4. The Urząd Bezpieczeństwa Publicznego, or more simply, the Urząd Bezpieczeństwa (Office of Public Safety, commonly, the Security Office, UB), was formally established in order to protect national security. In reality, it was tasked with the liquidation of resistance during the consolidation of the communist regime in Poland. The UB was made up hierarchically of field units at the Voivodeship (WUBP), county (PUBP), and city (MUBP) levels. At the central level, the UB functioned as the (Ministry of Public Security, MBP), from December 31, 1944 to December 7, 1954, and then as the Komitet do spraw Bezpieczeństwa Publicznego (Committee for Public Security, KdsBP), from December 14, 1954 to November 28, 1956. After the liquidation of the KdSBP, during the so-called thaw of 1956, the UB was reorganized and incorporated into the structure of the Ministerstwa Spraw Wewnętrznych (Ministry of the Interior, MSW) as part of the SB, which operated from November 28, 1956 to July 31, 1990 (Dominiczak 1997).

5. See "Józef Korycki" [1981?]; Oksiejuk 2018a; Kaminski and Szum 2020; Kaliński 2018; Kaminski 1985b, 2004a, 2004b, 2006; Kopka 1982.

6. In the words of Korejwo (2014, 273), the communists intended eventually to take over all aspects of social, political, and economic life and "it did not matter whether it was a scout organization, blueberry plantation, or political opposition."

7. These figures come from Nation Master (n.d.); Ivanstat (n.d.); and World Bank Public Data (n.d.).

8. See Kaminski (1985a). After leaving prison, the impression of a fairy-tale free world was common among inmates who had been subjected to sensory deprivation in grey prison facilities. According to the Student: "[After the consultation in a freedom clinic,] I was unable to pull myself together. People walk in all directions instead of just in a circle. … Girls—all incredibly beautiful; older gentlemen—distinguished. Even an intensively red tram that stopped by SGPiS [an economics college] seemed to be the eighth wonder of the world."

9. Hanna Guz, personal communication, Radzyń Podlaski, September 30, 2019.

10. As per a phone conversation between Krystyna Oksiejuk and Ernest Szum, November 29, 2019, based on a letter that she had received from a history teacher, Janina Jarczyńska. We were unable to locate Ms. Jarczyńska.

11. Among others, this group included Jerzy Jezierski, who overlapped in prison with Korycki; Mariusz Mazurek, whose grandmother reconstructed Korycki's place of capture (Mazurek 2018); Wiesława Mleczek, who offered us Korycki's photo; Grzegorz Karpiński; and three unidentified members of Korycki's extended family.

CHAPTER 2

1. We could not independently verify this claim. However, the participants of the meet-the-author event in Radzyń Podlaski on September 30, 2019, confirmed that such situations took place.
2. GS stores were a popular co-op chain of village stores controlled by the communists.
3. In his article, Paluch described a series of burglaries and robberies committed by Korycki, Kaliński, and others. Since the names of the perpetrators at that time were apparently unknown, or at least uncertain, Paluch used the fictional names of "Klemens J." and "Kalina," and also embellished his story with products of his own fantasy.
4. See Raczuk (Bodasiński and Osipowski 2015, 16'20") and Brzuszkiewicz (2018). After the action, Raczuk stayed in the hospital for two months, where he underwent complex surgery. As he said later, "I had to give up a full-time job in the criminal department and I was transferred to the deputy head of the militia police station for political and educational affairs." In fact, his transfer was a promotion, awarding him the rank of officer, which allowed for higher disability benefits. Raczuk was placed on sick leave for a long time, and then granted a disability pension. He never returned to work in the militia, which he had joined in 1972 "to solve criminal riddles, hunt down criminals, work out gangs. Just like in the movies" (as quoted in Brzuszkiewicz 2018).
5. In a comment on the interview, an Internet user with nickname "Glina," which translates as "Cop," expressed the sentiment of many Poles: "Who ever served Moscow—zero scruples—all their property should be confiscated, their houses put on auction and the money given to the victims. They knew what system it was and they had the choice to be in the Militia, UB, etc. or work elsewhere."
6. Jacek Kuroń (1991, 119) described the mechanism of short-term, forty-eight-hour arrests of dissidents. The MO repeatedly and cyclically detained Kuroń in this way. After each forty-eight-hour detention period, he was released from the militia detention center and then quickly detained again in front of the station for another forty-eight hours "for explanations." The procedure was repeated again and again, sometimes four times in a row. In Warsaw, dissidents were most often held in the Mostowski Palace, in front of which was a fountain. When released, arresting officers were waiting for the hapless detainees at the fountain. In the opposition lingo, "I got four fountains" meant that a person was detained for the "normal" forty-eight hours and then four additional times.
7. Some members of WRON, such as Mirosław Hermaszewski (the only astronaut in the PRL), later reported that they found out about their presence in this group from, of all places, television. In this way, Hermaszewski later

tried to downplay his participation in this body, which was widely hated by the Poles. He also claimed "the council did not make any decision" (api 2018). Sławomir Cenckiewicz, the head of the Wojskowe Biuro Historyczne (Military Historical Bureau) believes that the documents that have been preserved demonstrate that Hermaszewski was deeply involved in "building communism" in many roles (Cenckiewicz 2018, 62–65). Therefore, dividing WRON into the "bad" part, with Jaruzelski at the head, and the "passive" part, with Hermaszewski and possibly others, is unjustified (see also Ligarski and Majchrzak 2018).

8. The code name for the Jodła campaign was changed in autumn 1981, since it had been "burned" by Ryszard Kukliński—the deputy head of the operational board of the general staff of the Polish Army who escaped from the PRL, and who was also a Central Intelligence Agency spy under the pseudonym "Jack Strong" (Majchrzak 2016b, 121; Cenckiewicz 2014; Weiser 2004). In 2016, President Andrzej Duda posthumously promoted Kukliński, who was often called "the first Polish officer in NATO," to the rank of brigadier general.

9. Górski (2009, 104) wrote about Korycki during the time of martial law as a conspiracy veteran of the 1950s. Pietrzak (2013, 53) wrote that Korycki "increasingly was considered a partisan rather than an ordinary bandit."

10. The German-Austro-Hungarian company Mitropa, founded in 1916, serviced restaurant and sleeping compartment cars. The name is an acronym of the German name Mitteleuropäische Schlaf- und Speisewagen Aktiengesellschaft (Central European Sleeping and Restaurant Car Corporation). After World War II, Mitropa AG, based in East Berlin and working for the East German State Railroad, became Mitropa's heir in the Soviet occupation zone. Korycki probably meant a nonstop special military train that traveled the Berlin–Moscow route until 1994; it had sleeping cars managed by Mitropa AG.

11. Korycki highly valued and trusted former Home Army soldiers. For him, they were a model of patriotism and steadfastness in the fight against communism, as well as moral support in difficult times. He always carried a white and red armband characteristic of the AK, which served him as a kind of talisman (Kaliński 2018).

12. Two brothers of Mirosław Kaliński, Zdzisław and Waldemar, were interned on February 11, 1982. They were arrested preventively so they would not attempt to help Mirosław or Korycki. In the decision on the imprisonment of Waldemar Kaliński, the provincial commandant of the MO in Biała Podlaska stated, "allowing this citizen to stay free would threaten the security of the State and public order by the fact that he could participate in the organization of an armed criminal group of a criminal nature [sic] and hide the wanted J. Korycki" (Komendant Wojewódzki 1982). Mirosław Andrzejewski, who was in a cell in Kwidzyń Prison with the Kaliński brothers, recalled

years later that he had "never talked to them about Janosik, but we all knew in prison why they were there" (Andrzejewski 2018). The Kaliński brothers were released from prison on May 24, 1982, soon after Korycki's arrest (Kaliński 2018).

13. See Kaminski (2004a, 176). The list of items in the militia and army arsenal even included tanks; however, no tanks were actually used in manhunts. Most likely, when Korycki was speaking about "tanks," he had in mind the armed personnel carriers called BTR-60s.

14. Kaliński was later tried and sentenced to five-and-a-half years in prison. The sentence covered only the burglaries and thefts because Korycki took all the blame for the "banditry." Korycki made a statement that he was the one who illegally acquired the weapon and equipped Kaliński with it, and that Kaliński, under his influence, only carried out instructions. Kaliński served just two years and two months since, as a first-time offender, he was covered by the amnesty of July 21, 1984. After his release, he got married and had two children. He took a job on the railroad. However, the period of hiding and prison had damaged his psyche. "He locked himself in, pondered his past, abused alcohol. And that lost him"; he died in 1995 at the age of thirty-seven (Kaliński 2018).

15. The name *Rashomon*, the title that Akira Kurosawa gave to one of his films—one of most influential movies in the history of cinema—comes from the historical city gate where the film was shot. Four people—two crime victims, the perpetrator, and a witness—reported four fundamentally different and contradictory accounts of the event.

16. A note on Korycki's weapons: According to the militia report, at the time of his capture, Korycki had a PPSz submachine gun with twenty pieces of ammunition and a Nagant revolver with fifteen pieces of ammunition as well as a compass, flashlight, and Dana transistor radio (ch 1982; Bodasiński and Osipowski 2015, Skrzypiec 22'10"; Kacak 2011, 42). Kaminski (2004a, 176), describing the submachine gun, stated in his book that it was a "Kalashnikov," the colloquial name for the AK-47 submachine gun, also known as a "kałach" (Kochański 1991, 26). In prison argot, the words "kałach" or "Kalashnikov" simply meant a submachine gun, without distinguishing the type. The Student found in his prison notes of conversations with Korycki a record containing the crossed-out word "pepesha," as he noted originally, and then changed, probably because he used the term "Kalashnikov" in other places. The terms "kałach" and "Kalashnikov" were also used by Oksiejuk, reporting the visit of the militia to her home, as well as when describing Korycki's weapons, which meant that they were commonly used (Oksiejuk 2018a). Additionally, in their texts, Kaminski and Kacak used the colloquial name of Korycki's revolver, "nagan," derived from the Russian name Наган. The correct dictionary Polish name "Nagant" comes from the name of the Belgian designer Emil Nagant (Ciepliński and Woźniak 1994, 159).

CHAPTER 3

1. The description of grypsman subculture is almost entirely based on the accounts of Marek M. Kaminski, who was given the nickname "the Student" in prison; more information on grypsman subculture can be found in Kaminski's publications (2003, 2004a, 2004b, 2006).

2. Bajera words and phrases—secret prison argot—as well as more general prison slang, are italicized and explained when they appear for the first time. The popular prison phrase "freedom x," where x may be world, woman, hospital, etc., in this text emphasizes that "x is coming from the other world, called freedom."

3. In the time of the PRL, the toilet bowl in prison was given the abbreviated name of the first secretary of the Central Committee of the communist party PZPR. In the Gierek era, it was called "gier," and when General Jaruzelski came to power, Polish prisoners called the toilet bowl the "jaruzel," and talked about "feeding the jaruzel" or "watering the jaruzel" depending on what toileting need was being performed. In addition, the portable vessel used as a toilet in some cells was named after General Jaruzelski's first name, "Wojtek" (Kaminski 2004a). After the fall of communism, the clumsy name "jaruzel" finally lost out to the revived "gier," which returned to circulation at the turn of the millennium. However, the origin of the name "gier" has already been forgotten (Miszewski 2007, 2015). The minister of the interior, General Czesław Kiszczak, was also popular among the grypsmen. In a word game, his surname Kiszczak, or the diminutive of his first name, Czesio, denoted especially smelly gases produced by the human body (Kaminski 2004a).

4. Quote from Kaminski's prison notes (Kaminski, 1985a, April 4). The strong anticommunist sentiment of criminal prisoners sometimes resulted in a tolerant treatment of non-grypsman political prisoners. Even if they were non-grypsmen, people who had been part of Solidarity were often allowed to sit at the table with the grypsmen (Kozera 2014, Frasyniuk, 6'54). The leader of the prisoners' rebellion in Nowogard, Poland, a man named Zbigniew Orzechowski, stated, "We at this time ... were attracted to the movement of 'Solidarity'" (Kozera 2014, Orzechowski, 13'20"). In Kaminski's opinion, being a political prisoner, called a "for Solidarity" prisoner, was usually an asset in prison.

5. See Moczydłowski (1992). The non-grypsman political prisoner Stefan Niesiołowski expressed a typical opinion on prison caste division from the view of a rookie intellectual prisoner. In his memoirs, Niesiołowski wrote, "Gradually, I learned about the existence of divisions and groups fighting with each other. At first, I couldn't believe it, but later I got to know it too well" (Niesiołowski 1989, 139–40) He summed up the issue bitterly: "eaters, fags, fests, all the damned underclass, with which I unfortunately have to live

together for so long. In fact, all these punks can only bully the vulnerable" (Niesiołowski 1989, 101–2).

6. In bajera, the situational context of using a word often determined its meaning. A "freak" primarily denoted a mentally ill prisoner; however, it could also mean an inmate simulating a mentally ill person or a habitual joker.

7. The Prymasowski Komitet Pomocy Osobom Pozbawionym Wolności i ich Rodzinom (Primate's Committee for Assistance to Persons Deprived of Freedom and their Families) was a church charity institution established by the primate, Cardinal Józef Glemp, on December 17, 1981, at the Warsaw Church of St. Martin in response to the internment of anticommunist opposition members during martial law. Between 1981 and 1983, the Committee served the interned prisoners and their families with material, legal, and medical assistance. In September 1983, it was renamed the Prymasowski Komitet Charytatywno-Społeczny (Primate's Charity and Social Committee), and eventually ended its activities when General Kiszczak announced a wide amnesty and liberalization in September 1986 (Micewski 1987). Thanks to the Committee, the Student received valuable vitamin supplements and other critical goods that he shared with Korycki and other prisoners.

8. Niesiołowski (1989, 24, 32, 96–97) also remembered with disgust the "mean prison nurses" ("because doctors are a separate story"), who "looked at him and other prisoners with such eyes, as if we were dead and unbridled rats, which for some reason disturb their work" and spoke the inmates' names "as if they were some absolutely unimportant, long dead animals."

9. From Kaminski (2018, email 5). Dr. Possart was in contact with Kaminski's father, who was also a surgeon, and kept him apprised of his son's situation. Possart proposed a complex scheme using fake documentation, which required the cooperation of several doctors from the non-prison Oncology Center, located at 15 Wawelska Street. The plan worked, and Kaminski was released early "due to health reasons."

10. In the PRL in the 1970s, torture was used as a common punishment. The worst was the "hard bed," also called "belts." The prisoner would be forced to lie down on a wooden board, and when he exhaled, the guards would secure his chest and legs to the board with a pair of strong leather belts. They would then leave the prisoner on the hard bed, often for a few hours, but sometimes up to a full twenty-four hours. The hard bed was abolished with the advent of Solidarity (Leski 2007).

11. We were not able to determine in which court.

12. As found in Kaminski's notes (1985a, May 6). The Student sent a secret message with contact information to Ms. Oksiejuk, asking friends for help for Korycki. There was also one secret message describing Korycki's situation, which was lost without reaching the addressee, namely, Barbara Kamińska, the Student's sister (Kamińska 2018). During a prison visit in May 1985, the Student gave Korycki's data to his parents, who later talked to two female

employees of the Primate's Committee. They decided that Korycki was a criminal rather than a political prisoner and refused help. There was no other real effect, and nobody contacted Ms. Oksiejuk (Oksiejuk 2018a). *Tygodnik Mazowsze* published a note about the arrest of the Student, and the editors also contacted Nobel-winning poet and writer Czesław Miłosz, who wrote to the Student—his underground publisher—with a letter of support that was delivered to Kaminski in prison and which stunned the guards.

## CONCLUSION

1. This chapter is based on work by Szum (2019).
2. Arguments about the illegality of the communist system of the PRL were raised many times by scientists and opposition activists (for a review, see Kaminski and Nalepa 2006).
3. The source listing basic information about secret collaborators of the SB (and other categories) is the so-called Wildstein's List that is available from various servers; for instance, (Lista IPN n.d.). It lists the name of a person, Józef Korycki, and the associated signature. The Archival Resources of the IPN lists all records that include the name "Józef" and the surname "Korycki" (IPN n.d.). Those records include additional information about the name of father, place and date of birth, etc.
4. Jerzy Jezierski, personal communication, September 30, 2019, Radzyń Podlaski. Jezierski was a frequent prisoner in the 1960s and 1970s, and his time overlapped with that of Korycki's in some prisons. Marek Kaminski's 1985 experience also supports Jezierski's reasoning.

# BIBLIOGRAPHY

Ambroziewicz, Piotr. 2016. "Nieuchwytny z pepeszą." *NewsBook* (blog). October 9, 2016. https://newsbook.pl/2016/10/09/nieuchwytny-z -pepesza-2/.

Andrzejewski, Mirosław. 2018. Email to Marek M. Kaminski: "Janosik," May 31, 2018.

Baczyński, Jerzy. 1984. "Ile za dolara." *Polityka* 34 (1425).

Baczyński, Mateusz, and Janusz Schwertner. 2018. "O 'ustawie dezubekizacyjnej' w Brukseli." *Onet Wiadomości*, February 28. Accessed: February 15, 2020. https://wiadomosci.onet.pl/tylko-w-onecie/o-ustawie -dezubekizacyjnej-w-brukseli-byly-szef-msw-represjonowany-w -prl-staje-w/x054qlr.

Biłgorajski, Franciszek. 1956. *Pamiętniki o sprawie chłopskiej w 1863 roku*. Wrocław: Zakład im. Ossolińskich.

Bodasiński, Maciej, and Damian Osipowski (dirs.). 2005. *Janosik z Podlasia*. Documentary film. Warsaw: TVP.

Boreczek, Dorota. 2019. Email to Marek Kaminski: "Józef Korycki," December 26.

———. 2020. "Józek podbił moje serce—wspomnienie o Józefie Koryckim." Interview conducted by Ernest Szum in Radzyń Podlaski on January 3.

Borkowski, Andrzej. 1982. "Śladem Koryckiego." *Słowo Podlasia*, June 3.

Bortlik-Dźwierzyńska, Monika, and Marcin Niedurny. 2009. *Uciekinierzy z PRL*. Katowice: Instytut Pamięci Narodowej. Komisja Ścigania Zbrodni przeciwko Narodowi Polskiemu.

Brzuszkiewicz, Jacek. 2017. "Podczas próby zatrzymania zabójcy dostał sześć kul." gazeta.pl. September 9. Accessed January 27, 2020. http:// wiadomosci.gazeta.pl/wiadomosci/7,114883,22345849,podczas -proby-zatrzymania-zabojcy-dostal-szesc-kul-dla-pis.html.

Byszewski, Piotr, ed. 2008. *Działania służby bezpieczeństwa wobec organizacji "Ruch."* Warsaw: Instytut Pamięci Narodowej-Komisja Ścigania Zbrodni przeciwko Narodowi Polskiemu.

Cenckiewicz, Sławomir. 2014. *Atomowy szpieg: Ryszard Kukliński i wojna wywiadów*. Poznań: Zysk i S-ka.

———. 2018. "Towarzysz Kosmonauta. Mirosław Hermaszewski—nieprzypadkowy członek WRON." *Do Rzeczy* 15: 62–65.

(ch). 1982. "Groźny przestępca ujęty." *Słowo Podlasia*, May 20.

Charczuk, Wiesław. 2006. "Działalność radzieckiego aparatu bezpieczeństwa i kontrwywiadu (NKWD i Smiersz) przeciwko podziemiu niepodległościowemu na Podlasiu i Wschodnim Mazowszu, lipiec 1944–grudzień 1945." *Wschodni Rocznik Humanistyczny* 3: 313–33.

Chociej, Czesław. 2012. "Armia Krajowa okręg Białystok." Accessed January 27, 2020. http://www.armiakrajowa.org.pl/pdf/okreg bialystok.pdf.

Ciepliński, Andrzej, and Ryszard Woźniak. 1994. *Encyklopedia współczesnej broni palnej: od połowy XIX wieku*. Warsaw: WIS.

Conrad, Joseph. 1977 (orig. 1900). *Lord Jim*, with introduction by Nicholas Monsarrat. Norwalk, CT: Easton Press.

Czajka, Waldemar. 2018. Interview conducted by Ernest Szum in Brzozowica Duża on August 5.

Dąbrowski, Marcin. 2008. "Śladami komunistycznych zbrodni na Lubelszczyźnie." *Radzyński Rocznik Humanistyczny* 6:312–34.

Deskur, Bronisław. 1966. "Dla moich wnuków." In *Powstanie styczniowe na Lubelszczyźnie. Pamiętniki*, edited by Tadeusz Mencel, 71–120. Lublin: Wydawnictwo Lubelskie.

Dobroński, Adam. 2010. "Powstanie styczniowe 1863–1864 i jego konsekwencje." In *Historia Województwa Podlaskiego*, edited by Adam Dobroński, 142–146. Białystok: Instytut Wydawniczy "Kreator."

dodek777. 2012. "Janosik z Podlasia." Blog. January 21. https://dodek777.flog .pl/wpis/4161002/wykleci-.

Dominiczak, Henryk. 1997. *Organy bezpieczeństwa PRL, 1944–1990: rozwój i działalność w świetle dokumentów MSW*. Warsaw: Dom Wydawniczy Bellona.

Dudek, Antoni. 2001. "Bijące serce partii." *Wprost* 30:28–30.

———. 2002. "Obóz władzy w okresie Stanu Wojennego." *Pamięć i Sprawiedliwość* 1 (2): 233–43.

Dudek, Antoni, and Tomasz Marszałkowski. 1999. *Walki uliczne w PRL 1956–1989*. Kraków: Wydawnictwo Geo.

Dudek, Antoni, and Zdzisław Zblewski. 2008. *Utopia nad Wisłą: historia Peerelu*. Warsaw-Bielsko-Biała: Wydawnictwo Szkolne PWN.

Dziennik Ustaw. 1981. *Uchwała Rady Państwa z dnia 12 grudnia 1981 r. w sprawie wprowadzenia Stanu Wojennego ze względu na bezpieczeństwo państwa*. Dz. U. 1981, nr 29, poz. 155.

Eisler, Jerzy. 1992. *Zarys dziejów politycznych Polski: 1944–1989*. Warsaw: Polska Oficyna Wydawnicza "BGW."

Engels, Friedrich. 1962, first ed. 1878. *Werke: Anti-Dühring*. Institut für Marxismus-Leninismus bein ZK der SED. 20. Berlin: Dietz Verlag.

Forsyth, Frederick. 1971. *The Day of the Jackal*. London: Hutchinson.

Foucault, Michel. 2012 (orig. 1975). *Discipline and Punish: The Birth of the Prison*. New York: Knopf Doubleday Publishing Group.

Friszke, Andrzej. 2003. *Polska: losy państwa i narodu 1939–1989*. Warsaw: ISKRY.

———. 2011. *Czas KOR-u: Jacek Kuroń a geneza Solidarności*. Kraków: Wydawnictwo Znak Instytut Studiow Politycznych Polskiej Akademii Nauk.

Fromm, Erich. 1994 (orig. 1941). *Escape from Freedom*. New York: Macmillan.

———. 1997 (orig. 1973). *The Anatomy of Human Destructiveness*. London: Pimlico.

Gesket, S., A. K Puzyrewski, Włodzimierz Sawicz Semeka, and Katarzyna Stołoska-Fuz. 2013. *Działania wojenne w guberni płockiej w 1863 roku*. Muzeum Mazowieckie w Płocku.

Głos. 1982. "Kalendarium polskie." *Niezależny Miesięcznik Społeczno-Polityczny Głos* 2/3: 10–12.

Głowacki, Witold. 2014. "Stan wojenny. Plutony specjalne ZOMO, SS Batalion Hempel, 'Czarne diabły'. Bezwzględni pałkarze Jaruzelskiego." *Polska Times*. December 13. https://polskatimes.pl/stan-wojenny-plutony-specjalne-zomo-ss-batalion-hempel-czarne-diably-bezwgledni-palkarze-jaruzelskiego/ar/3682924.

Gomułka, Władysław. 1945. "Speech for the Members of the PSL." June 18.

Góra, Stanisław. 1965. "Działalność powstańcza Romana Rogińskiego na Podlasiu." *Rocznik Białostocki* 6:361–404.

Górski, Rafał. 2009. "Opór społeczny w Polsce w latach 1944–1989." *Przegląd Anarchistyczny* 6:100–119.

Gray, Marcus. 2004. 2nd ed. *The Clash: Return of the Last Gang in Town*. Milwaukee: Hal Leonard Corporation.

Grinberg, Daniel. 1994. *Ruch anarchistyczny w Europe zachodniej: 1870–1914*. Warsaw: Wydawnictwo Naukowe PWN.

Halicz, Emanuel. 1955. *Kwestia chłopska w Królestwie Polskim w dobie powstania styczniowego*. Warsaw: Książka i Wiedza.

Heinzen, James W. 2016. *The Art of the Bribe: Corruption under Stalin, 1943–1953*. New Haven, CT: Yale University Press.

Hobbes, Thomas. 1982 (orig. 1651, revised 1668). *Leviathan*. London: Penguin Classics.

Hobsbawm, Eric John Ernest. 1969. *Bandits*. London: Weidenfeld & Nicolson.

Holland, Agnieszka, and Kasia Adamik (dirs.). 2009. *Janosik. Prawdziwa Historia*. Documentary film. Syrena Films.

IMF (International Monetary Fund). 2018. Accessed January 27, 2020. https://www.imf.org/external/index.htm.

Infor.pl. 2020a. "Miesięczne zarobki w Polsce." January 10. https://www.infor
.pl/prawo/zarobki/zarobki-w-polsce/686166,Przecietne-miesieczne
wynagrodzenie-w-latach-19502008.html.

Infor.pl. 2020b. "Kara śmierci w PRL." Accessed January 27, 2020. https://
www.infor.pl/prawo/prawo-karne/ciekawostki/87633,Kara-smierci
-w-PRL.html.

IPN. n.d. "Inwentarz archiwalny IPN." Accessed January 27, 2020. https://
inwentarz.ipn.gov.pl/#.

Ivanstat. n.d. Accessed February 16, 2020. http://ivanstat.com/en/.

Janowski, Józef Kajetan. 1923. *Pamiętniki o powstaniu styczniowem. T. 1.*
Lwów: s.n.

Jasiak, Henryk. 1989a. "Superglina z ulicy Małej (1)." *Jan Włodarek i przyjaciele.* Accessed January 27, 2020. http://www.jwip.pl/readarticle
.php?article_id=437.

———. 1989b. "Superglina z ulicy Małej (2)." *Jan Włodarek i przyjaciele.* Accessed January 27, 2020. http://www.jwip.pl/readarticle.php
?article_id=442.

Jasienica, Paweł. 1960. *Dwie drogi.* Warsaw: PIW.

(jch). 1982. "Groźny przestępca na Podlasiu." *Słowo Podlasia*, April 8.

"Józef Korycki." [1981?]. Biographical note in the arrest warrant of Józef Korycki, published by MO in late 1980, 1981 or early 1982.

Kacak, Przemysław. 2011. "Podlaski Janosik." *Policja 997* 4:40–42.

Kaczmarczyk, Michał Roch. 2010. *Nieposłuszeństwo obywatelskie a pojęcie
prawa.* Warsaw: Oficyna Naukowa.

Kaliński, Waldemar. 2018. Interview conducted by Ernest Szum in Brzozowica
Duża on August 4.

Kamińska, Barbara. 2018. Personal communication to Marek M. Kaminski on
May 9.

Kamiński, Łukasz. 2001. "Jak partia szła na wojnę." *Tygodnik Powszechny* 50:3.

Kaminski, Marek Mikołaj. 1985a. "Dziennik Studenta." A manuscript containing the author's daily notes from prison.

———. 1985b. "Historia życia Józefa Koryckiego." A manuscript containing a
record of conversations with Józef Korycki in the cell at Rakowiecka.

———. 1999. "How Communism Could Have Been Saved: Formal Analysis of
Electoral Bargaining in Poland in 1989." *Public Choice* 98 (1–2): 83–109.

———. 2003. "Games Prisoners Play: Allocation of Social Roles in a Total
Institution." *Rationality and Society* 15 (2): 188–217.

———. 2004a. *Games Prisoners Play: The Tragicomic Worlds of Polish Prison.*
Princeton, NJ: Princeton University Press.

———. 2004b. "Gry więźniów. podział ról społecznych w instytucji totalnej."
*Studia Socjologiczne*, no. 3: 92–120.

———. 2006. *Gry więzienne.* Warsaw: Oficyna Naukowa.

———. 2018. Emails to Ernest Szum. "Józef Korycki (a series of emails: 1–11)," April.

Kaminski, Marek Mikołaj, and Don C. Gibbons. 1994. "Prison Subculture in Poland." *Crime & Delinquency* 40 (1): 105–19.

Kaminski, Marek Mikołaj, and Monika Nalepa. 2006. "Judging Transitional Justice: A New Criterion for Evaluating Truth Revelation Procedures." *Journal of Conflict Resolution* 50 (3): 383–408.

Kaminski, Marek Mikołaj, and Ernest Szum. 2019. *Janosik Podlaski. Józefa Koryckiego prywatna wojna z komunizmem.* Warsaw: Oficyna Naukowa.

———. 2020. "Prometeizm Janosika Podlaskiego w relacjach przyjaciół. Źródła do biografii Józefa Koryckiego." *Radzyński Rocznik Humanistyczny* 18:1–23. https://doi.org/10.36121/RRH.KAMINSKI_SZUM.18.2020.

Kamiński, Mikołaj. 1985. "Z tej strony bramy, czyli 150 dni z życia rodziny Kamińskich." Typescript. Tomaszów Mazowiecki.

Kazimierczak, Włodzimierz. 2012. "Sąd: stan wojenny—Kiszczak winny, Kania niewinny." January 12, 2012. Accessed February 16, 2020. https://www.prawo.pl/prawnicy-sady/sad-stan-wojenny-kiszczak-winny-kania-niewinny,43096.html.

Kenney, Padraic. 2017. *Dance in Chains: Political Imprisonment in the Modern World.* Oxford: Oxford University Press.

Kieniewicz, Stefan. 1953. *Sprawa włościańska w powstaniu styczniowym.* Wrocław: Zakład imienia Ossolińskich.

———, ed. 1983. *Roman Rogiński powstaniec 1963 r. Zeznania i wspomnienia.* Warsaw: PWN.

———. 1989. "Roman Rogiński." In *Polski słownik biograficzny. T. 31 z. 3 [og. zb.],* edited by Emanuel Rostworowski, 429–30. Kraków and Wrocław: Polska Akademia Umiejętności and Zakład Narodowy im. Ossolińskich.

———. 2009. *Powstanie styczniowe.* Warsaw: Wydawnictwo Naukowe PWN.

Knight, Stephen. 1994. *Robin Hood: A Complete Study of the English Outlaw.* Oxford: Blackwell.

Kochański, Stanisław. 1991. *Automatyczna broń strzelecka.* Warsaw: Sigma NOT.

Kołakowski, Piotr. 2002. *NKWD i GRU na ziemiach polskich, 1939–1945.* Warsaw: Dom Wydawniczy Bellona.

Komendant Wojewódzki MO w Białej Podlaskiej. 1982. *Decyzja Nr 3/82 o Internowaniu.* Biała Podlaska.

Kopiński, Jarosław. 1998. *Konspiracja akowska i poakowska na terenie Inspektoratu Rejonowego "Radzyń Podlaski" w latach 1944–1956.* Biała Podlaska: s.n.

Kopka, Sławoj. 1982. "Szakal." *W Służbie Narodu* 25:26–28.

Korejwo, Mariusz Tomasz. 2014. "Oddziaływanie PZPR na aparat administracji państwowej." In *Partia komunistyczna w Polsce. Struktury, ludzie, dokumentacja,* edited by Dariusz Magier, 273–304. Lublin: Archiwum Państwowe–Radzyńskie Stowarzyszenie Inicjatyw Lokalnych.

Korycka, Barbara. 2020. "To był bardzo mądry człowiek—Józef Korycki w mojej pamięci." Interview conducted by Ernest Szum in Radzyń Podlaski on January 3, 2020.

Korycki, Józef. 1985. "Sala 7 Student, gryps do studenta" (Secret letter to Marek Kaminski). June or July.

Kosztyła, Zygmunt, ed. 1985. *Obok Orła znak Pogoni: powstańcy styczniowi na Białostocczyźnie*. Ośrodek Badań Historii Wojskowej. Białystok: Krajowa Agencja Wydawnicza.

Kozera, Małgorzata (dir.). 2014. *Był bunt*. Documentary film. Warsaw: TVP.

Kozłowski, Patryk. 2013. *Zygmunt Szendzielarz "Łupaszko": 1910–1951*. Warsaw: Rytm.

Krawczak, Tadeusz. 1995. *Ksiądz generał Stanisław Brzóska: kapelan i dowódca*. Pruszków: Oficyna Wydawnicza "Ajaks."

Książę (alias). 2018. Email to Marek M. Kaminski. 2018. "Janosik," May 28.

Kunicki, Kazimierz, and Tomasz Ławecki. 2017. *Zagadki kryminalne PRL*. Warsaw: Bellona.

Kuroń, Jacek. 1977. "Myśli o programie działania." *Aneks* 13/14:4–32.

———. 1982. "Tezy o wyjściu z sytuacji bez wyjścia." *Tygodnik Mazowsze* 8:3. March 31.

———. 1991. *Gwiezdny czas: "Wiary i winy" dalszy ciąg*. Londyn: Aneks.

———. 1995. *Wiara i wina: do i od komunizmu*. Wrocław: Wydawnictwo Dolnośląskie.

Kurosawa, Akira (dir.). 1950. *Rashomon*. Film. Daiei Motion Picture Company.

Laskowski, Piotr. 2006. *Szkice z dziejow anarchizmu*. Warsaw: Muza.

Leski, Krzysztof. 2007. "Solidarność, Zeki i twarde łoże." salon24.pl. October 24. Accessed January 27, 2020. http://krzysztofleski.salon24 .pl/1588,solidarnosc-zeki-i-twarde-loze.

Lewandowska, Stanisława. 1982. *Ruch oporu na Podlasiu, 1939–1944*. 2nd ed., corrected and supplemented. Warsaw: Wydawnictwo Ministerstwa Obrony Narodowej.

Ligarski, Sebastian, and Grzegorz Majchrzak. 2018. "WRON od kulis." *Do Rzeczy* 15:66–69.

Lipczyńska, Małgorzata. 2017. "Prawdziwa Historia Janosika z Podlasia." *Detektyw Extra* 4:4–10.

"Lista IPN." n.d. Accessed January 27, 2020. http://www.listaipn.pl/kor.php.

luq. 2018. "Postrzelony podczas służby milicjant żyje za 30 zł." *Polsat News*. February 14, 2018. Accessed January 27, 2020. https://www.polsatnews. pl/wiadomosc/2018-02-14/postrzelony-podczas-sluzby-milicjant-zyje -za-30-zl-objela-go-dezubekizacja/.

Łaniec, Stanisław. 1978. *Konspiracja i czyn zbrojny kolejarzy w powstaniu styczniowym*. Olsztyn: Wyższa Szkoła Pedagogiczna.

Magier, Dariusz. 2018. "Jak Bialskopodlaska partia komunistyczna się w Stanie Wojennym reformowała." *Podlaski Kwartalnik Kulturalny*, no. 1: 51–60.

Majchrzak, Grzegorz. 2016a. *Solidarnosc na celowniku*. Poznań: Zysk i S-ka.

———. 2016b. *Tajemnice stanu wojennego*. Warsaw: Zona Zero.

———. 2011. "Obóz władzy w stanie wojennym." *forumemjot* (blog). December 12, 2011. Accessed January 27, 2020. http://emjot.blogx.pl/2011/12/12 /oboz-wladzy-w-stanie-wojennym-grzegorz-majchrzak/.

Makus, Grzegorz. 2008. *"Jastrząb" i "Żelazny". Ostatni partyzanci Polesia Lubelskiego 1945–1951.* Włodawa: IPN.

Malinowski, Jerzy Cezary. 1998. "Działalność Zrzeszenia 'Wolność i Niezawisłość' w Obwodzie Siedlce." *Szkice Podlaskie*, no. 6: 74–82.

Maroszek, Józef. 1992. "Konfiskaty mienia mieszkańców białostocczyzny po wojnie z Rosją 1812 r." *Rubieże*, no. 1: 101–7.

Marx, Karl, and Friedrich Engels. 1848. *The Communist Manifesto.* Translated by Samuel Moore. London: Penguin.

Mazurek, Mariusz. 2018. Emails to Ernest Szum. "Józef Korycki." July 5 and July 9.

Mencel, Tadeusz. 1963. "Walenty Lewandowski i początki Powstania Styczniowego na Podlasiu." *Rocznik Lubelski*, no. 6: 71–120.

Micewski, Andrzej. 1987. *Kościół wobec "Solidarności" i stanu wojennego.* Paris: Éditions du Dialogue.

Michalkiewicz, Stanisław. 2017. "Czarny sztandar anarchii czerwieni się ze wstydu." *Bibuła Pismo Niezależne.* April 12. http://www.bibula .com/?p=95078.

Mikołaj (Marek Mikołaj Kaminski). 1985. "Sokrates pierze skarpetki." *Tygodnik Mazowsze* 149: 4. December 5.

Miszewski, Kamil. 2007. "Uniwersytet więzienny." *Studia Socjologiczne* 184 (1): 163–71.

———. 2015. *Zabójcy w więzieniu.* Warsaw: Oficyna Naukowa.

Moczydłowski, Paweł. 1992. *The Hidden Life of Polish Prisons.* Bloomington: Indiana University Press.

Morozowa, Olga. 1982. *Bronisław Szwarce.* Wrocław: Zakład Narodowy im. Ossolinskich.

"Nation Master: Global Industry Market Sizing." n.d. NationMaster. Accessed January 27, 2020. https://www.nationmaster.com/.

Niebelski, Eugeniusz. 1993. *Zmierzch Powstania Styczniowego w Lubelskiem w Podlasiu (1864–1872).* Lublin: Lubelskie Towarzystwo Naukowe.

Niesiołowski, Stefan. 1989. *Wysoki brzeg.* Poznań: W drodze.

Oksiejuk, Krystyna. 1986. "Szanowny Panie Marku." Letter to Marek M. Kaminski. October 14.

———. 2018a. "Był dobrym człowiekiem. Moje wspomnienia o Józefie Koryckim." Interview conducted by Ernest Szum in Misie on April 21.

———. 2018b. Personal communications to Ernest Szum on April 21 and May 9.

Oksiejuk, Krystyna, and Agnieszka Oksiejuk. 1985. "'Wesołych Świąt.' A Postcard to Józef Korycki (given to Marek M. Kaminski)." March 31.

Paczkowski, Andrzej. 2002. *Droga do "mniejszego zła". Strategia i taktyka obozu władzy, lipiec 1980–styczeń 1982.* Kraków: Wydawnictwo Literackie.

————. 2003. *Strajki, bunty, manifestacje jako "polska droga" przez socjalizm.* Poznań: Poznańskie Towarzystwo Przyjaciół Nauk.

————. 2006. *Wojna polsko-jaruzelska.* Warsaw: Prószyński.

————. 2010. *Spring Will Be Ours: Poland and the Poles from Occupation to Freedom.* University Park: Penn State University Press.

Paluch, Porucznik. 1981. "Napady z Bronią." *Słowo Podlasia.* May 7.

Pietrzak, Leszek. 2013. "Podlaski 'Szakal.'" *Uważam Rze Historia* 7:53–55.

Piotrowski, Mirosław. 2004. "Władze bezpieczeństwa wobec niepodległo-ściowych dążeń społeczeństwa powiatu Radzyń Podlaski po II Wojnie Światowej." *Wschodni Rocznik Humanistyczny,* no. 1: 215–28.

Piskunowicz, Henryk. 1990. "Działalność zbrojna ZWZ-AK na Podlasiu." In *Z nieznanej przeszłości Białej i Podlasia,* edited by Tadeusz Wasilewski and Tadeusz Krawczak. Biała Podlaska: PTS-K.

Pytlakowski, Piotr. 2006. "Pitawal PRL." *Polityka* 51/52:46–49.

Racięski, Jarosław, and Edward Kabiesz. 1996. *Encyklopedia Dzikiego Zachodu.* Katowice: Videograf II.

Ramotowska, Franciszka. 1971. *Rząd carski wobec manifestacji patriotycznych w Królestwie Polskim w latach 1860–1862.* Wrocław: Zakład Narodowy im. Ossolińskich.

Reclus, Paul. 1964. *Les frères Élie et Élisée Reclus où du Protestantisme à l'anarchisme.* Paris: Les Amis d'Élisée Reclus.

red. 2014. "Janosik z pepeszą." Międzyrzec.Info. August 7. Accessed January 27, 2020. https://miedzyrzec.info/artykuly/janosik-z-pepesza/.

Redakcja. 2020. "Zderzyły się dwie pamięci Stanu Wojennego." Accessed February 15, 2020. https://niezalezna.pl/311142-zderzyly-sie-dwie -pamieci-stanu-wojennego-glos-solidarnosci-walczacej-po-slowach -premiera.

Rogaska, Karolina. 2018. "W PRL polował na groźnego przestępcę, został postrzelony." WP Wiadomości. April 13. Accessed January 27, 2020. https:// wiadomosci.wp.pl/w-prl-polowal-na-groznego-przestepce-zostal -postrzelony-przez-ustawe-blaszczaka-obniza-mu-rente-6141606008 322177a.

Rogiński, Roman. 1898. *Z pamiętnika Romana: 1859–1863.* Edited by Aleksander Kraushar. Kraków: W. L. Anczyc i Spółka.

————. 1966. "Kartki z pamiętnika (1861–1863)." In *Powstanie styczniowe na Lubelszczyźnie. Pamiętniki,* edited by Tadeusz Mencel, 9–70. Lublin: Wydawnictwo Lubelskie.

Rostworowski, Emanuel, and Marian Tyrowicz, eds. 1972. "Walenty Teofil Lewandowski." In *Polski słownik biograficzny.* Vol. 17. Wrocław: Zakład Narodowy im. Ossolińskich; Wydawnictwo Polskiej Akademii Nauk.

Ryżewski, Grzegorz. 2013. "Zarys dziejów powstania styczniowego na terenie dzisiejszego województwa podlaskiego." In *1983. Katalog miejsc pamięci powstania styczniowego w województwie podlaskim,* edited by Iwona Górska, 8–16. Białystok: Towarzystwo Opieki nad Zabytkami.

Schwertner, Janusz, and Mateusz Baczyński. 2019. *Antyterroryści. Polskie elitarne Siły Specjalne w akcji*. Kraków: Społeczny Instytut Wydawniczy Znak.

Sikora, Dariusz. 2005. *Ruch oporu w powiecie bialskim 1939–1944: szkice z dziejów ZWZ-AK, BCh, GL-AL*. Biała Podlaska: Starostwo Powiatowe.

Skowronek, Jerzy. 1990. "Ziemia bialska w polskim ruchu narodowym do 1864 r." In *Z nieznanej przeszłości Białej i Podlasia*, edited by Tadeusz Wasilewski and Tadeusz Krawczak, 281–308. Biała Podlaska: Podlaskie Towarzystwo Społeczno-Kulturalne.

Smolarek, Dariusz. 2005. *Władze komunistyczne wobec opozycji na południowym Podlasiu w latach 1944–1947*. Siedlce: Instytut Historii Akademii Podlaskiej.

Sroka, Stanisław Andrzej. 2004. *Janosik: prawdziwa historia karpackiego zbójnika*. Kraków: Homini.

Stwora, Jacek. 1993. *Co jest za tym murem?* Warsaw: Seta Enterprises Ltd.

Szum, Ernest. 2012a. "Anarchiści na Białostocczyźnie w okresie Rewolucji 1905–1907. Przyczynek do dziejów ideologii anarchizmu i działalności organizacji anarchistycznych na Podlasiu."

———. 2012b. "Pułkownik Władysław Cichorski 'Zameczek'. Studium przywództwa." *Studia z Dziejów Wojskowości* 1:213–56.

———. 2013. "Wróg publiczny—wrogiem społeczeństwa czy państwa? Józefa Koryckiego wojna z PRL-Em." *Radzyński Rocznik Humanistyczny* 11:127–141.

———. 2014. *Bitwa siemiatycka w powstaniu styczniowym (6–7 II 1863). Studium historyczno-socjologiczne*. Biała Podlaska: Biblioteczka Regionalna.

———. 2018. "Bez wyroku. Postscriptum do losów Józefa Koryckiego." *Radzyński Rocznik Humanistyczny* 16 (2): 573–84.

———. 2019. "Crimen Józefa Koryckiego w świetle koncepcji bandytyzmu ideowego." *Radzyński Rocznik Humanistyczny* 17:293–304.

Śladkowski, Wiesław. 1973. "Z powstania styczniowego na Lubelszczyźnie." In *Kalendarz lubelski 1973*, 130–43. Lublin: Wydawnictwo Lubelskie.

Thoreau, Henry David. 2009 (orig. 1849). *Civil Disobedience: Resistance to Civil Government*. Auckland: Floating Press.

Tomczyk, Józef. 1963. "Organizacja cywilno-wojskowa powstania styczniowego w Lubelskiem i na Podlasiu." *Rocznik Lubelski* 6:7–70.

Tompson, Stefan, and Patrick Ney. 2020. *Rozmowa o historii i przyszłości Polski*. Video. https://www.facebook.com/MorawieckiPL/videos/178117233445205/.

Topolski, Jerzy. 2008. *Jak się pisze i rozumie historię: tajemnice narracji historycznej*. Poznań: Wydawnictwo Poznańskie.

Trochimiak, Franciszek. 2018. Interview conducted by Ernest Szum in Trzebieszów on August 5.

Tuchman, Barbara W. 1996. *The Proud Tower: A Portrait of the World before the War, 1890–1914*. New York: Random House.

Tyszkiewicz, Jan. 1983. "Podlasie. Kształtowanie się nazwy i terytorium do końca XIX stulecia." *Prace Archiwalno-Konserwatorskie Na Terenie Województwa Siedleckiego* 3:3–21.

Universal Declaration. 1948. "Universal Declaration of Human Rights." December 10. https://www.un.org/en/universal-declaration-human-rights/.

Wasiluk, Marek. 2014. "Janosik z Podlasia." *Tygodnik Podlaski*, May 6.

Wehikuł czasu. 2013. "Niech zstąpi duch twój i odnowi oblicze ziemi, tej ziemi!." wPolityce.pl. June 2. Accessed on December 30, 2019. https://wpolityce.pl/polityka/158844-niech-zstapi-duch-twoj-i-odnowi-oblicze-ziemi-tej-ziemi-34-lata-temu-jan-pawel-ii-przybyl-po-raz-pierwszy-do-ojczyzny.

Weiser, Benjamin. 2004. *A Secret Life: The Polish Colonel, His Covert Mission, and the Price He Paid to Save His Country*. New York: PublicAffairs.

Wieliczka-Szarek, Joanna. 2013. *Żołnierze wyklęci: niezłomni bohaterowie*. Kraków: Wydawnictwo AA.

Wiktorowska, Bożena. 2019. "Były esbek wygrał z MSWiA." gazetaprawna.pl. July 4. https://serwisy.gazetaprawna.pl/emerytury-i-renty/artykuly/1420394,ustawa-dezubekizacyjna-byly-esbek-wygral-z-mswia.html.

Wiśniewski, Jerzy. 1977. "Osadnictwo Wschodniej Białostocczyzny. Geneza, rozwój oraz zróżnicowanie i przemiany etniczne." *Acta Baltico-Slavica* 11:7–80.

Włodarek, Jan, and Marek Ziółkowski, eds. 1990. *Metoda biograficzna w socjologii*. Warsaw–Poznań: PWN.

Wojtasik, Janusz. 1995. "Aspekty militarne powstania styczniowego (1863–1864)." In *Powstanie styczniowe 1863–1864: aspekty militarne i polityczne: materiały sympozjum*, edited by Janusz Wojtasik, 7–22. Warsaw: Bellona.

"World Bank Public Data." n.d. Accessed January 27, 2020. https://www.google.com/publicdata/explore?ds=d5bncppjof8f9_&hl=en&dl=en.

"World Economics." n.d. Accessed January 27, 2020. https://www.worldeconomics.com/default.aspx.

*Wydawnictwo materyałów do historyi powstania 1863–1864. t.1.* 1888. Lwów: Drukarnia Ludowa.

Zajączkowska, Joanna. 2012. "Akcja 'Szakal'. Polowanie na 'Janosika' z Podlasia." Onet Wiadomości. March 1. http://wiadomosci.onet.pl/na-tropie/akcja-szakal-polowanie-na-janosika-z-podlasia-artykul/c6337.

Zamoyski, Adam. 2009. *Poland: A History*. New York: HarperPerennial.

Zawada, Jolanta. 2011. "Cmentarz Parafialny w Radzyniu Podlaskim." *Radzyński Rocznik Humanistyczny* 9:135–58.

Zimbardo, Philip. 2007. *The Lucifer Effect: Understanding How Good People Turn Evil*. New York: Random House.

Złotowski, Maksymilian. 1913. "O bandytyzmie słów kilkoro." *Kuźnia* 11: 3–11.

# INDEX